The Logo
Decoded

If ever there were a way-shower for our times, it's Lora Starling. A corporate designer with a difference, Lora reveals in *The Logo Decoded* the *real* impact of the logo and how its invisible energies actually work on us – often in ways even their designers aren't aware of. From this perspective, she offers penetrating insights into the energies that are *really* operating in business, showing us the magic we're unwittingly wielding in our businesses.

Mary Hykel Hunt, author of 'Learning from the Future'.

I worked with Lora Starling in a major international brand development and which had the power to last a quarter of a century. I have since engaged, as a company CEO, in many large and small logo development and branding projects in different parts of the world, across industries as diverse as electricity, finance and the news media, keeping many of the lessons learnt from Lora. With *The Logo Decoded* we can benefit immediately from the huge insights that Lora has into logos and brands.

Lincoln Gould F:CEO The New Zealand Futures and Options Exchange, the Marketplace Co (electricity exchange) and New Zealand Press Association. CEO Booksellers NZ.

What does any logo make you feel? Lora Starling examines what a logo is and what impact it can have on a company, its market place, and its clients. Enlightening us to hidden powers and energies, communicating (or not) a corporation's identity and personality, this book tells how we all respond to logos, unknowingly and intuitively, and how they influence what we feel about a company and its products.

Richard Ward FRSA, Design Consultant, Designer Beatles '1' compilation album cover, Co-author of 'Fairground Art' and founder of the Fairground Heritage Trust.

The Logo Decoded

WHAT LOGOS CAN DO ~~FOR~~ *to* YOU

LORA STARLING

BALBOA.
PRESS

A DIVISION OF HAY HOUSE

Balboa Press books may be ordered through booksellers or by contacting:

Balboa Press
A Division of Hay House
1663 Liberty Drive
Bloomington, IN 47403
www.balboapress.com.au
1-(877) 407-4847

ISBN: 978-1-4525-0301-1 (sc)
ISBN: 978-1-4525-0302-8 (e)

Library of Congress Control Number: 2011919230

Printed in the United States of America

Balboa Press rev. date: 11/10/2011

For designers everywhere

Foreword

Most graphic designers I know love making marks, and one of the most challenging and rewarding aspects of this activity is the creation of an identifying mark for an organisation, whether it be a commercial company, an educational institution or a cultural establishment.

We used to have separate words for different types of marks. The three pointed star of Mercedes, or the apple on our computers and iPhones, or the Lloyds' horse would have been referred to as symbols, whereas the stylised letter-forms of IBM or Samsung would have been called logotypes. However, our language has evolved since then, and nowadays we refer to all of these marks as simply, a logo.

During the process of designing a logo, the focus will be on creating a powerful or beautiful, certainly memorable and recognisable mark. It must be distinctive, it must be appropriate and practical, and ideally, it should encapsulate the essence of the organisation. And that is about as far as the designer's consciousness goes.

This book challenges that complacency.

In a congratulatory letter to the first General Assembly and International Congress on Graphic Design in 1964, Prince Phillip wrote, 'Every day designers of all kinds are becoming responsible for a greater proportion of man's environment. Almost everything that we see and use that was not made by The Almighty has come from some designer's drawing board.

This is a very heavy responsibility and every effort by designers to improve standards, to encourage proper training and to develop a sense of social awareness is to be welcomed.

I hope everybody enjoys the first General Assembly and International Congress on Graphic Design and I hope its beneficial influence will spread all over the world`.

This book is a timely reminder of that responsibility.

The author, Lora Starling, has thoroughly researched her subject and offers a provocative insight into the true nature of logos and their power over us.

It is a call for a raised consciousness on the part of those who create logos, those who use logos and those who choose logos.

And above all, it is a fascinating and compelling read.

Mervyn Kurlansky
Co-founder Pentagram, Principal Mervyn Kurlansky Design

Contents

A powerful connection

'What is now proved was once only imagined.'

WILLIAM BLAKE

Are logos good for us?

Logotypes can affect us! We pick up all sorts of messages from logos, long before we see them, and certainly long before we use the product. In fact, the quality of the product itself can become almost irrelevant in eliciting the response favoured by brand experts as we are drawn to the brand promise embedded in the logo. Whether or not we like the design of a logo, when the branding experts get it right, we fall in love with it. A logo carries a powerful intention, directly to us from the company that commissions it, and we are affected by it. Whether or not we see it, wear it, or hear the name it displays spoken out loud, we can be influenced by the design itself.

Some of us appear more aware than others of the potential danger of entrusting our future happiness to this visible manifestation of commercialism.

A man makes prime-time television in England when he publicly burns his branded possessions. Elsewhere, a woman diligently cuts off all the logos on her children's clothes. Meanwhile, in America, parents are horrified to learn that their pre-school children are able to recognise brand logos before they can read and write. There is a school in Australia where children are banned from wearing any logos or commercially designed illustrations.

What do these people know that leads them to articulate the growing sense of unease that many of us are beginning to feel about logos? Whether we love them or hate them, brand logos defy our ambivalence.

When I first heard about these actions, I dismissed them as 'corporate-bashing'—discrediting large organisations and bringing claims of contentious business practices to light. However, as I looked further into the world of logos and symbols, I discovered a powerful medium that is capable of changing our minds.

A logotype, or logo, is a specially designed combination of elements around the name of a brand. It includes variations in type, symbols and colour to make it unique. What makes a logotype successful, however, is a different issue. Probably the most powerful way of communicating the brand ethos to the world, a successful logo has its own values beyond the simple identification of a brand. It carries the personality, values and spirit of the organisation or product to every corner of the company and to the outside world. The number of ways this can happen is limited only by our imagination. When we see the logo, we get a whole message. As the most apparent, permanent, stable and identifiable aspect of a business, a logo will only change when the company it represents signals a transformation akin to a death and rebirth.

Ancient esoteric symbols were designed to bypass our conscious processes, to connect deeply with us, and to affect us in specific ways. In a similar way, logotypes, which are imbued with their own intentions and values, strive to cross the same divide to the deeper reaches of our unconscious mind; a logo creates a powerful connection between the psyche of the company it identifies and our own psyche.

What if the logos we yearn to associate ourselves with, those that we carefully select to define our status—economic, social and even emotional—could truly affect our wellbeing? We may not even have to buy them, wear them or see the designs in order for this effect to succeed. Imbued with the created characteristics of the brand it represents, a logo delivers them directly to the front door of our psyche, where we gratefully receive them. But does this process enhance our lives? And, if so, for how long? Are there any personal, detrimental effects?

The journey that led me to the exploration of this logo effect began when I overheard a colleague discussing the possibility of energising water by using symbols. What I heard led me to a turning point in my beliefs.

Andrew Crane is a British artist, designer and dowser. He has the ability to form questions about our reality in a way that provokes and stimulates new ways of seeing the world. As usual, he had a small group listening attentively; I gleaned enough of the conversation to want to join the listeners. He began by saying that he believed it was possible to imbue a glass of water with healing characteristics by placing the glass over a specifically designed symbol. According to homeopathic principles this process creates a remedy that can then be sipped to alleviate symptoms. As you will see later, I have since discovered that this *is* possible—and this technique is used successfully by a renowned healer from India. But it was the description of an experiment that Andrew and fellow dowser Glenn Broughton had conducted that opened my eyes to a completely new, yet somehow obvious, way of understanding the power of symbols.

Andrew described how he was able to pinpoint a symbol that had previously and secretly been drawn in the air. A volunteer was asked to draw a shape, such as a circle or triangle, somewhere in the room, by using her finger, while Andrew remained outside. By using dowsing rods, he found the exact point in space where this symbol was 'hanging'. Glenn, another experienced dowser, was able to repeat this success independently. Andrew has repeated the experiment on numerous occasions. When I finally saw him perform it at a specialist art exhibition, he added to the intrigue by conducting a second version. Blindfolded, he walked towards a wall and his dowsing rods crossed about a third of a metre away. A symbol was subsequently placed on the same part of the wall (in this case it was a convenient 'No Smoking' sign) and the action was repeated. The rods crossed about a metre away from the wall!

As a corporate image designer, I was hooked. What if these simple symbols had an extra effect, an *energetic value* beyond their physical existence? That could mean that more complex corporate logos, invested with vast powers of intention and attention through design, branding, marketing and advertising processes, can reach out and touch us in ways beyond our imagination. Logos might possess their own *energy*, which would profoundly affect us when we merely walk near a poster displaying a brand logotype. While we are making a cup of tea during the commercials on TV, we would still 'get the message.'

Large corporations pull many of the strings in our world—from forming the mainstay of global economics through to creating our personal lifestyles—via the branding process. It seems timely and imperative that we learn more about this greater implication of the effects of corporate brand logotypes on our personal being.

I wanted to know how corporate symbols could affect me personally. I wanted to be able to make an informed choice about which of them, if any, to buy into.

The power of simple symbols to entrance and transform us has been recognised and used through the ages. Today this skill has been honed to a sophisticated process practised by designers who can articulate a corporate desire in a symbol (logo), which can be delivered effectively and quickly all around the world via complex branding techniques and technology. These symbols can transform our minds, the way we live our lives, and ultimately our world.

As a link between the three-dimensionally formed world we live in and the unformed world of our dreams and aspirations, as well as the connection between the corporate and human psyche, logos provide companies with an incredibly powerful tool to deliver brand messaging. We might not be totally aware of how a logo 'hits' us, but it may be more powerful than we know.

How do we decide whether a logo is good or bad for us? There might be good design and bad design, but even this judgement often remains in the eye of the beholder. Even designers themselves are often unable to agree on the best design standards.

We might choose to wear logos that we like, but where does this judgement come from? In order to raise our awareness to effective levels of decision-taking, we need to make choices that are informed from deeper levels. By learning to look beyond the surface of the design, we can begin to hear the underlying whispers.

By learning to enrol all of our thinking centres—our mind, gut feelings and heartfelt emotions—in our decision-taking, we can gain a clearer and more accurate view of that which depletes or fulfils us. We can learn to choose our logos wisely. Whether we wear them, eat or drink from containers displaying them, or commission a designer to create one for our business, we can learn to pay attention to the details as well as to the concept and the messages within. Everything, from the source of the design concept, to the components that make up the logo, right through to the delivery of the final design, shifts the effect of a logo and can add to the making and breaking of a brand, as well as the effect on us personally.

The logo is a powerful portal that links us firmly to the core of its brand. Understanding this link enable us to become truly informed about the choices we make on our purchases.

By becoming more conscious of our responses to logos, whether through intuition or gut feeling, or through a measuring technique such as muscle-testing or aura measurement, we can begin to connect with a deeper part of our self, and choose products that are right for our own wellbeing—not just for the companies that produce them.

The symbol effect

The theory of creating symbols to effect changes is not new. The logotypes we design and project into the world are treading a well-established path created by the ancient use of tattwas, mandalas and religious icons—symbols of something greater, created with deep intent to change, or maintain, the status quo.

We might carry a symbol such as a rabbit's foot or charm for good luck or a religious emblem for protection. Similarly, for those who wear the logo, there is the brand promise of good luck (desired values) and protection (by aligning and identifying themselves with their peer group). We display the Nike logo in the hope that we will run faster, or at least identify ourselves with the success of those who do.

When we begin to peel back the layers that make up some of our well-known logotypes, we begin to see how the complexity of the creative process forms one of the most powerful catalysts for change in our economic world today.

Our day-to-day response to our surroundings is affected in many ways. To be able to track the sequence of our neurons firing when we choose a particular product, and to stimulate this response over and over again, merely through a glimpse of the logo, is the ultimate dream of the brand experts. The technology for this exists.

One of the most powerful qualities of a symbol is that, once we have made the link between it and the attributed meaning, we instantly get the message when we see it without having to consciously work it out each time. When we see a certain logo, we will think 'thirst', 'lifestyle', or some other form of desire prompted by the design itself. It is the role of branding to forge and control this link. Brands help to form our memories, stimulate them at will, and can even ensure that we pass them down to our children.

Like the bell in Pavlov's experiments, the logo is the trigger. Pavlov's dogs eventually salivated at the simple ring of a bell, which had previously become associated with the serving of food. We are trained, through advertising and marketing, to anticipate an outcome and to produce a response. This response is powerful and instant. Once we are primed with the logo, our memory motivates us to buy. This is so effective that brand managers can save a fortune in ongoing advertising and marketing. 'In short, by increasing retention, you significantly reduce your marketing and sales cost while dramatically increasing overall profitability . . . Achieving that "irrational" connection with customers is the key to business success, and the answers lie within this fantastic puzzle box of our subconsciousness.'[1]

The power to inform

Our ancestors' survival depended on their reading symbols. By observing subtle messages in the outside, natural world, they would take decisions and live their lives accordingly.

We may not notice a hawk circling over us as we are about to go into a meeting, or a red cloud, or a leaky tap, or even be aware of being completely surrounded by square tiles when we have a shower—but if any of these things *did* happen to catch our attention, our ancestors would see it as a sign that an important message was being presented to us from the outside world and take action accordingly.

These potent signs of nature have been replaced with signs created by humans. The symbols we follow today are created by those wishing to enrol us in their personal dreams rather than have us be distracted by a deeper relationship with a natural world that is removed from the desire of economic gain. Our modern symbols have been imbued with a commercial voice, which shouts above the more subtle, but equally powerful, symbols in our surroundings. The branding experts have developed a highly sophisticated process that has turned ancient shamanic practices into a commercial art. We now look to brands for guidance in our own lives; logos stimulate us to take action and make choices in our lives.

Logos use a complex series of graphic codes that can bypass our conscious mind to stimulate a specific response. Beyond lengthy verbal explanation, language and cultural differences, we get a myriad complex brand messages in an instant. And we are motivated to act.

'The human psyche "reads" symbols; it is symbol literate or symbol sensitive. That is, the psyche recognizes symbols wherever they are and reacts to them at all times. Symbols are, as it were, messages pointing to a different and higher dimension, or consciousness.'[2]

The power to deliver

'Get your facts first, then you can distort them as you please.'
MARK TWAIN

Conveniently crossing language barriers and the rational mind, and capable of being slathered with meaning, logos provide effective tools that can deliver predetermined messages and information to us—whoever we are and wherever we live.

A logo can deliver messages instantly, with all sorts of subtle but effective nuances, which other means of communications simply cannot achieve.

This speed of delivery is vitally important today as we demand instant gratification and move swiftly on if we don't get it. According to the book *Digital Aboriginal*, by Mikela Tarlow and Philip Tarlow, we have become a nation of data-dodgers. Using the remote control, we can quickly flit from channel to channel and screen out television commercials. We can also choose to opt out of junk email and telephone marketing. This sets new challenges for the branding experts—to get their message across as quickly as possible before we move on. The value of the logotype thus increases dramatically. A quick glance will serve as an instant and effective reminder of a host of brand values that have been ingrained through advertising and marketing; we don't have to see the complete campaign all over again. We may not even have to be conscious of seeing the logo in order to get the effect.

The power to affect

Images affect us whether we are paying attention or not. The brain registers responses even when the person concerned insists that they have not seen the object or message.

One of the researchers, Dr Bahrami of University College London, states: 'We've looked at whether what we pay attention to and what we are aware of is one and the same thing because conventional psychology says they are. We found they were not. We show that there is a brain response in the primary visual cortex to subliminal images that attract our attention without us having the impression of having seen anything.' He added: 'The findings point to the sort of impact that subliminal advertising may have.'[3]

By not paying attention, we open our minds to the marketers. Fast-forwarding, for example on a television, as we search for an alternative programme, we are affected by the logos we fleetingly pass. In an experiment, 'researchers have found that fast-forwarding viewers actually pay more attention and can be influenced by brand images they view only for a fraction of a second.'[4]

If we enjoy creative advertisements, rather than those laden with facts and useful information, we are more likely to get the brand message. 'Viewers pay less attention to creative television advertisements' shows new research from the University of Bath, 'but may make themselves more vulnerable to the advertiser's message.'[5]

Because we have to pay less attention, we are not judging the hard facts and figures; we don't argue with the brand message, we enjoy the ad and trust it, and thus become more vulnerable to the advertiser's message. The value of a logo, with its ability to identify and prompt a host of messages, is paramount in these experiments.

This effect can extend beyond those intended by the marketers. Like pharmaceutical drugs that are designed to alleviate specific symptoms, logos can have unplanned side effects.

Simply gazing at a logo can affect our subsequent behaviour. There is substantial evidence that brands have automatic associations with specific goals. Consumer behaviour can be influenced by mental processes that occur outside conscious awareness.[6] Researchers examined how people behave after subliminal exposure to consumer brand logos. They chose to use Apple, since it was known to have carefully cultivated a strong and appealing brand personality based on the ideas of non-conformity, innovation and creativity. Consumer brand IBM was used as a comparison. Both brands are highly familiar to consumers, but each has a distinct personality. Whereas Apple's personality is seen to be innovative and creative, IBM is perceived as a traditional smart and responsible brand. Participants were exposed subliminally to images of either the Apple or IBM brand logos and then completed a standard creativity measure. Those primed with Apple logos performed more creatively than the control or IBM-primed participants. The researchers concluded: 'This provided the first clear evidence that subliminally priming a brand name or logo or both can influence consumers' actual behaviour.' In another experiment, people were exposed to the Disney or the E! Entertainment logos. Those who saw the Disney logo answered a series of questions more honestly. 'Every brand comes with its set of associations,' said study co-author Gavan Fitzsimmons, a professor of psychology and marketing at Duke University, USA. 'When we're exposed to logos, those associations fire automatically, activating our motivational systems and leading us to behave in ways that are consistent with the brand image.'[7]

The power to connect

When we recognize the symbolism behind everyday items through to abstract shapes, we are privy to a host of extra information at levels that are richer, more profound and informative than the face value of the object. Logotypes, imbued with their own intentions and values, strive to cross the same divide to reach the deeper realms of our unconscious mind; they aim to create a powerful connection between the brand and the consumer—one that they create and control.

Linked to an organisation or product, logos are designed and marketed to encourage familiarity and recognition, evoking a response beyond the physical design itself. The sight of a familiar symbol can, without doubt, lift our spirits when it touches our connection with past, fond memories and our future dreams and aspirations. Logos, with their embedded brand promises, have the power to change our moods; they can make us feel better, for a time, by aligning themselves to be our buddies even in moments of deep despair. And as with our best friends, we recognise these brands through their names and faces. Our memories are powerful motivators. This exposure effect, nicknamed the 'familiarity breeds liking effect' is well known to advertisers. People will express undue liking for things merely because they are familiar with them.[8]

Like the unending samsara of the cycle of birth, life, death and rebirth, branding continuously fills the voids that it itself creates in our lives, consciously imprinting the corporate message through exposure to the logo. This cycle extends into the past in order to secure the future.

The logo I saw on the soap powder pack in the laundry as my mother sang her way through the weekly washing could still be attracting me to the same brand. We seek out the familiar to anchor ourselves in the territory we reassuringly refer to as 'home', which, unbeknown to us, may well have been created through the media.

We can even inherit memories from our ancestors, from beyond the grave. Certain animals make huge journeys they have never made before, but follow the migration route of their ancestors; we, too, might be unconsciously motivated to act via inherited programming.

Epigenetics, the study of heritable changes in gene function, has discovered that our genes also carry memories. Since many symbols have been used for thousands of years, it might be possible that we have an inborn response to them.

A logo identifies the whole company, connecting every part of it as a 'whole'. It is the visible interface between the company and its staff, customers, investors and the public, and could affect its relationship with all of them.

Logos connect the past to the future through traditions and desires; transcending time and space, they connect us to the rest of the world as we share global products, and they identify our connection to our friends and colleagues. Moreover, they appear to have their own dynamics that might affect everything they touch—they are imbued with intentions to shape our future according to the ambitions defined by the brand controllers.

CHAPTER ONE

The logo effect

'A logo is the point of entry to the brand.'

MILTON GLASER

We are bombarded with logotypes daily and it is easy to become numbed by the media that deliver them to us with increasing regularity. There is a powerful intention behind this massive exposure; brand experts believe in its efficacy, or they would not continue with the relentless barrage of corporate stimulation. The logo delivers their message to us all.

Participants in an experiment[1] showed no preference for Coke or Pepsi when they did not know which was which. When they were shown the label, however, roughly three-quarters said they preferred Coke. 'There is a huge effect of the Coke label on brain activity related to the control of actions, the drudging up of memories, and things that involve self-image,' explains Read Montague, PhD, director of the Brown Human Neuroimaging Lab at Baylor College of Medicine (BCM) in Texas USA.

The BCM study, funded by the National Institute of Drug Abuse, was the first to analyse how cultural messages penetrate parts of the brain and influence personal preferences. By observing neural activity (all 67 participants submitted to brain scans), it was possible to predict with a degree of accuracy which people preferred Coke or Pepsi, before they even took a sip. It seemed that they made their choice and their brains experienced a Coke response purely by looking at the label!

'We live in a sea of cultural messages. Everybody has heard of Coke and Pepsi, they have messages, and, in the case of Coke, those messages have insinuated themselves in our nervous systems,' said Montague, the principal investigator of the study. 'There is a response in the brain which leads to a behavioural effect—in this case, personal preference—regarding these beverages . . . We were stunned by how easy this was. I could tell what they were going to do by looking at their brain scans.'

This ability to track the sequence of our neurons firing is a gift for brand researchers. They can read, at a glance, how we respond. Bypassing complicated analyses of research findings, they get to the truth of our response—we cannot lie when parts of our brain fire up when we feel pleased, perhaps by the glimpse of a product or a logo, before our reaction is hijacked and tempered by our rational mind.

Companies want us to fall in love with their logos as quickly as possible, so we will want more. But what makes us fall in love with a logotype, enough to display it? We rarely fall in love with all of a person; usually it is a bit of them that resonates with a bit of us, enough to make us want to know them better.

With a logo, we may love the colour or the name, or a part of the name; we may not know why in our conscious mind. We may love it because it represents somewhere we love or something we desire to possess, or even because actions of our parents or grandparents have ingrained some link in our memory of good times.

The same symbol can evoke different responses in people due to personal preferences, and we all see the world differently. Our memories, sex, nationality, experiences, profession, desires and personal preferences, to name just a few factors, may affect our response to a logo design. But to secure their slice of the marketplace, companies need a lot of us to think in *their* ways to *their* commercial benefit. They spend millions trying to ensure that we all see the same thing, when we are exposed to their symbol, by controlling this response through advertising and marketing. Colours, shapes, type style, words, the shapes of the spaces between the elements, and the chosen symbols—from triangles and circles to horses and lions—will all reach out to grab our attention. This response can be conscious (I like it, I don't like it, I understand it, I don't understand it) or subconscious—in which case we may love it, or hate it, and we might never know why.

If the branding experts have got it right, the logo will resonate with us at levels beyond our subjective awareness; we will be attracted to at least one part and grow to love the whole. The design process has been honed to the stage where we might even buy it because the brand image resonates with us, even if the product is less than ideal.

The design details and the shapes in the logo themselves can contain archetypal imagery, which stimulates an even deeper response in our psyche. Swiss designer and author Adrian Frutiger says: 'It may even be that certain archetypal forms are inherited, and therefore present from the beginning, even in the mind of an unborn child.'[2]

Blame the ancestors

Our DNA carries memories; the heritage of our ancestors resides in every cell in our bodies. Science is able to present some sound evidence of how we can inherit responses, which can affect our views and perceptions of things at levels that our conscious brain cannot begin to comprehend logically.[3]

Our distant ancestors could be sparking our responses to symbols from beyond the grave. Our more immediate ancestors could influence our feelings towards different logos. Experiments with newborn goslings have illustrated that they recognise the shape of a predator from birth, long before they have experienced its effect. A cross shape with one arm longer than the others, when passed over the nest, was seen to have two effects: if the shorter arm led the movement, the goslings became distressed, as the shape resembled the silhouette of a bird of prey with a short neck and long tail; if the direction was reversed, they began chirping for food, as it appeared like the shape of their mother, with a long neck and short tail.[4]

The Christian cross, in the usual stance with the short end upwards, is referred to as the Latin cross and is a symbol of Christianity; in its reversed form, it has been used as an emblem of Satanism and a symbol of humility, representing St Peter's refusal to be crucified in the manner of Christ. We could, like newborn chicks, respond differently to these identical but differently positioned crosses.

Ancient abstract and realistic symbols appear in many logotypes. Our response to these can be triggered from deeper resources within us than the more cosmetic stimuli intended by the brand experts and designers.

Scientists have observed that our genes can be affected by events around us—and we can pass on these memories to our offspring. The discovery of epigenetics—hidden influences upon the genes—could affect every aspect of our lives. At the heart of this new field is a simple but contentious idea: 'that genes have a "memory". That the lives of your grandparents—the air they breathed, the food they ate, even the things they saw—can directly affect you, decades later, despite your never experiencing these things yourself. And that what you do in your lifetime could in turn affect your grandchildren.'[5]

Unlike the conventional view that our DNA is fixed from birth, epigenetics suggests that experiences in our lives can switch genes on or off. This not only affects our own DNA, but means we can pass on these changes to our children. This means that a cellular 'memory' of an event could be passed down through generations.

One of the first noted pieces of evidence for this theory came from a small town in Sweden where it was observed that a famine, experienced by grandparents, affected the life expectancy of the grandchildren. This effect has been noted more recently: 'After the tragic events of September 11th 2001, Rachel Yehuda, a psychologist at the Mount Sinai School of Medicine in New York, studied the effects of stress on a group of women who were inside or near the World Trade Center and were pregnant at the time. Produced in conjunction with Jonathan Seckl, an Edinburgh doctor, her results suggest that stress effects can pass down generations.'[6]

Biologist and author Rupert Sheldrake believes that heredity depends not only on DNA but also can be based on morphic fields, evolving fields of collective memories. Unlike genes, these fields are inherited non-materially by resonance with our ancestors as well as from others. These fields have a cumulative memory based on what has happened in the past.[7]

In 1920, psychologist William McDougall carried out experiments with laboratory rats at Harvard University. Rats placed in a chamber were presented with two exits, one identified with bright lighting, which gave a non-fatal shock. The rats quickly learned to use the alternative exit, but successive generations managed to consistently choose the correct exit in less time.

If we imagine that the doors were replaced with logos and the rats with our ancestors, it is possible that our mothers and grandmothers consistently purchased Kellogg's cornflakes, Bisto gravy or Bird's custard because of their warm association with family values. By the same logic, we could still

Luxurious new HOOVERMATIC which washes, rinses and spin-dries all in 8 minutes—a full family wash clean and damp-dry in less than half an hour! New Persil is ideal for this magnificent new washer.

AND <u>NEW</u> PERSIL WASHES EVEN WHITER!

New Persil's rich long-life lather means even greater deep-cleansing—the secret of Persil whiteness. Try it and see the increased whiteness in your clothes and linen. You'll be amazed! *New* Persil washes *even* whiter—and that means the cleanest wash of all.

Our memories can be passed down through generations via our DNA. What you do in your lifetime could affect your grandchildren.

be making the same purchasing decisions. According to Rupert Sheldrake, they would not even need to be our own mother's or grandmother's, or any relation at all. A morphic field can be established when enough people behave in a particular way.

Our most successful brands are in the process of creating our memories for us, of making us long for the times in our (or others') lives that were filled with satisfied desires. Whether it is our feelings about our first day at school or the taste of a hamburger, these sensations can, according to the above principles, be affected and collected via the unconscious from the morphic field. Tried and tested brands give us a sense of security, their longevity displaying proof of their ability to satisfy us through our lives. They create the offer and we co-create its reinforcement.

I heard a story about a missionary who converted a tribe to Christianity. As part of the procedure, he set his alarm clock every day so that he would wake for early-morning prayers with the tribe. When the missionary finally died, the tribe continued the process, believing that the real 'boss' was the familiar alarm clock; after all, it appeared to control the missionary's schedule by 'telling' him it was time to pray. For them, the clock was the symbol of God. The non-living symbol of organisation was more important than the man who preached the message.

While this may sound amusing or even ridiculous to our Western-educated minds, we too allow our strings to be pulled by a logo, a non-living entity, when we happily buy an identified product that reassures us of a promise of fulfilment.

The value of ingraining brands into our psyche at an early age is irresistible for businesses. Children represent a $20-billion market, and they see an estimated 40,000 ads a year. The US Campaign for a Commercial-Free Childhood reports that marketers are spending at least $15 billion a year to reach children under 12 and wants the Federal Trade Commission to regulate children's advertising. To find out just how brand-conscious young children are, WCCO-TV, a US TV station, visited three-, four- and five-year-olds at a children's centre and showed 12 flash cards to the children. There was a different corporate logo on each card. The three-year-olds saw the Target bulls-eye, and started screaming: 'Target! Target!' Researchers noted: 'An even wilder celebration ensued when we showed the kids the picture of the McDonald's golden arches. The three-year-olds kicked, laughed, and screamed about McDonald's. They recognized the "M".' Although they did not know what the Nike swoosh stood for, they did know it related to shoes—with one three-year-old stating: 'They help you do sports really good. Like soccer.' The five-year-old group recognised every logo showed to them; even though they couldn't read the names, they knew the Starbucks coffee logo, KFC, Pizza Hut and Pepsi.[8]

The familiar reassures us and I cannot help feeling that if I were running out of petrol in the desert, and came to a service station identified by a familiar logo, I would feel more uplifted and reassured than I would if a foreign-looking one presented itself. My husband still seeks out the sweets of his childhood. Those sweets are nothing special, yet our children now associate these sweets with their own childhoods and continue to buy them.

The logo attraction

We may grow out of listening to what our parents tell us about what to wear or how to behave, but we willingly succumb to the advice of a stranger offering a set of values identified with a logotype. But just how much nurturing and feel-good factors can a logo give us? How can a mere symbol irresistibly tempt us to purchase stuff we don't need and may not even be able to afford?

Logos are designed to make us feel good when we buy the product. The sight, or vicinity, of a familiar logo can affect our mood and make us feel happy.

I have seen two friends, each at times chronically short of money, fall into the retail brand therapy trap. The husband of the first even cut up her credit cards; this was probably a wise move, since I remembered going to her house to console her about her lack of funds, only to witness the addition of a new, very expensive, 'must-have' rug, from a highly fashionable, well-branded store. She had bought it to cheer herself up.

The second friend often claims she often does not have enough money to feed herself and her two children. Yet, when given a lump of money by her father to help alleviate this situation, she spent it on (another) latest branded mobile phone.

Neither of these women ever bought an 'average', unbranded product because they *needed* it. For a short time, both of them were happy! They got their hit—but it was short-lived.

Whether we are rich or poor, happy or sad, brands will reach out to meet us. Logos can be designed to meet with us in our darkest, most vulnerable, moments—and there are plenty of those to be found in today's tumultuous world, which homes a vast range of potential brand targets, from hormonal teenagers to impoverished mortgage-payers.

Death-related imagery, such as the skull and crossbones, is all the rage in fashion on sale in mainstream retailers including Walmart. The value of this resonance with our inner state of mind is apparent in the music industry. Music has proven to be successful in treating depression; like a brand hit, it can lift our spirits. Logically, one would imagine that cheery tunes would help pull someone into a more positive frame of mind, and for someone suffering from minor blues this can hold true. However, for major clinical depression, the most effective music was found to be that which resonated with the mood of the listener: sombre, melancholy, classical pieces. A blogger agreed with these findings stating 'Dark, sombre music has its place—I went through a stage where it was all I listened to 'cos I could relate to it.'[9]

We need only to look at the names of some of our current brands to see how they might resonate with our darker sides. FCUK, Criminal, Poison Angel, Dead Frog and Fat Face are at the least vaguely derogatory. Those responsible for these brands may have taken heed of the success of the melancholy music, to name brands that can not only meet with our deepest moods but also can align themselves to become our sympathetic friends.

Catching our attention in the right way

Architects, interior designers and graphic designers all work to ensure that items are positioned to catch our eye and appeal to us in a desired manner. Those in marketing and research are aware of the different impact on us of goods that are strategically placed to secure our attention in a particular way.

Our eye positions stimulate different responses in our brain. When praying, people look up to access God; if they want to be unobtrusive, they will lower their eyes as if lowering their presence. We respond differently when we change our eye position. It follows that the positioning of a logotype in a reception area could affect how we feel about being in the company as we walk through the front door.

Robert Dilts, co-founder of NLP (Neuro-Linguistic Programming), conducted a study, attempting to correlate eye movements to particular cognitive and neurophysiological processes. In the practice of NLP, the practitioner assesses information from clients by observing the direction of their eyes to give clues as to where they access information. For example, if a person answers a question while looking up and to the left, they are remembering imagery; up and to the right they are constructing the imagery; directly to the left and right, they are remembering sounds and words (right is constructed, left is remembered); down and left accesses their internal dialogue, while eyes down and right is where we look when accessing imagined feelings.[10]

Using this as a guide, the direction that we look towards to observe a logo could in theory affect our perception of that logo. As we recall it, it could also tell us what we believe about it.

Tattoos, water and emotions

Symbols have been used to affect our wellbeing for many years. The following report prompted me to theorise just how long ago they might have been used in this way.

At the end of the 20th century, the mummified remains of a man who had died in the Alps 5,300 years before were discovered. While the find was extraordinary in its own right, one of the most curious and exciting observations was the presence of tattooed symbols on the acupuncture points. Scientists first believed that the marks, made with a mix of coal dust and water, were purely ornamental because they were associated with symbols of animals, humans or ceremonies. However, this theory was dismissed as they were on the back of the man's legs; they were subsequently attributed a medical role because they were on acupuncture points.[11]

But what if the symbols themselves, placed over sensitive meridian points, caused energy differences that redressed imbalances in the body? The iceman was found to be suffering from a medical complaint, arthrosis, and it is not beyond belief that placing specific permanent symbols over the acupuncture points might supply ongoing relief, without the necessity of constantly piercing the skin as is practised in acupuncture today.

The effect on us of tattoos, or writing, on our skin is articulated powerfully in the film *What the Bleep Do We Know?* Made in 2004, this film, about the radical knowledge that modern science has uncovered, includes a scene where a woman wipes off detrimental words she had written on her skin, and replaces them with the word 'love'. The objective was to articulate the effect on our wellbeing of drawing on our skin.

This point is inspired by Dr Masaru Emoto's work. An internationally renowned Japanese scientist, Emoto has discovered that molecules of water are affected by words, pictures and music, as well as our thoughts and feelings. In his book, *The Hidden Messages in Water,* Dr Emoto demonstrates how emotions such as love and gratitude affect the molecules of water. A bottle of water exposed to loving emotions produced beautiful organised crystalline structures like snowflakes. An identical bottle, subjected to aggressive emotions such as hate and anger, produced a jangled, uncoordinated, messy-looking molecular pattern. Simply writing different words describing the emotions, such as 'wisdom' and 'Om', or 'hate' produced the same results.

Since the majority of our bodies are made of water, it is worth giving detailed consideration to the subject matter of any tattoo, especially in this increasingly popular process sanctified by celebrities and emulated by fashion followers. Girlfriends' and children's names, eagles, jagged abstract shapes and words such as 'hate' and 'love' could, according to the principles above, have an effect that extends well beyond the display of an impressive design. The choice or size, position, colour, design detail and intention behind the design will all combine to fine-tune this effect. Apart from displaying our design preferences to the outside world, we may well be imposing unknown dynamics onto our internal world as well. And the blood flowing under the tattoo will take the message to every other cell in

A word, an emotion or an intention in the design of a label can affect the contents in the container.

the body; cells have memory that can be passed on to our offspring. Our desire to decorate our skin could affect future generations.

A recent *Sunday Times Magazine* listed the subject matter of celebrities' tattoos. When we look at the meaning behind some of these symbols, it is easy to wonder about the subtle effects on the wearers. According to the article, Sienna Miller, Britney Spears and Victoria Beckham have stars; Drew Barrymore, Angelina Jolie and Nicole Richie have crosses; and Jennifer Aniston, Kate Moss and Nicky Hilton have hearts. Angelina Jolie also has a tattooed incantation in Khmer that translates as: 'May your enemies run far away from you/If you acquire riches may they remain yours always/Your beauty will be that of Apsara/Wherever you may go, many will attend, serve and protect you, surrounding you on all sides.'[12]

The Khmer still follow a tradition of tattooing for protection that stretches back to the first century. Specially selected designs, applied to relevant parts of the body, continue to be ritualistically applied by Buddhist monks. Thousands of designs exist, each intended to produce a specific outcome. Designed to ward off evil or harm, there are also specially designed tattoos that are widely believed to make the wearer bullet-proof.[13]

A programme in 2010 to tackle speeding in the USA portrayed a police officer who admitted to having an unacceptable number of crashes early in his career. He solved the problem, which he attributes to the application of a tattoo, of a crash dummy for protection, on his arm.[14]

A logo near our skin might have a similar effect. By changing the crystalline structure of the liquid blood and plasma flowing beneath the design, the effect could be carried to every cell in our body and connect with our DNA. If we imbue a product labelled with a logo, the design and the word will potentise the liquid within in the way that Emoto's words and intentions affected the water in his experiments. What are the changes a logo makes to the ingredients? How can we measure them? We need to know, because we will be affected, one way or another.

The influence of branded promotions such as mugs and glasses displaying the logo might extend beyond visual aesthetics. During a recent meeting, I was offered water from a beautiful bottle branded with the corporate logo at the company's main office. Perhaps it is no coincidence that special logo-engraved glasses are often reserved for those at senior or board level, where all the important decisions are made regarding the progress of the company. This subtle form of branding might be extremely effective according to Emoto's findings.

If Kellogg's gets its way, we could soon be imbibing a potent brew of milk. The company has developed a technique of imprinting its logo onto each flake of cereal. Helen Lyons, leader of food technologies at Kellogg's, said that 'We want to be under absolutely no illusion that Kellogg's does not make cereal for anyone else. We're constantly looking at new ways to reaffirm this; giving our golden flakes of corn an official stamp of approval could be the answer.'[15]

The business intention, the emotions and the brand values embedded in the logo could affect the product and ultimately the consumer. Do we really want to eat a hamburger labelled and promoted as an 'Angry Whopper' with 'sizzling angry onions' and an 'angry sauce'?[16]

Symbols affecting our health

If logos can make us feel good, can they benefit our wellbeing, even heal us? The word *healing*, applied to corporate logotypes, is probably not a description that sits happily in the cut-throat business of today's commercial world. Nevertheless, companies do want us to feel better, happier, satisfied and even healthier when we use their products.

The brand promise is paramount in our purchasing choice and it is recognised and authenticated via the logotype. We feel good when we make a choice identified by a desirable logo; we might even hypothesise that we self-diagnose and search out those according to our needs at any one time.

This theory gains credibility as we consider the components that make up a logo. Colour, words, letterforms, typography and symbols all have the ability to affect us at profound levels; the inclusion and arrangement of these elements can often be wittingly or unwittingly combined to form a logo that has an effect that is much greater than the sum of its parts—over and above the more commercial meaning bestowed on it through branding.

Several healing practices use symbols as the basis of their process. Reiki is one such practice that uses the power of special symbols to enable and accelerate the healing process. Details of the designs are kept secret and passed on, via an elaborate, ritualistic 'attunement' procedure, to future practitioners. According to the principles of Reiki, these symbols enable those with the 'attunements' (knowledge of and permission to use them) to tap into the universal energy that surrounds us all, and to magnify our natural healing process.

Reiki is usually performed using a hands-on, or slightly off, approach, with the practitioner and the patient together. It can, however, also be used for healing from a distance and there are specific symbols for this. The range and style of symbols is specially controlled, with the same attention to detail as a brand logo. Some practitioners place great emphasis on maintaining the accuracy of these when visualising them. Many people subscribe to the power of Reiki healing and can attest to its efficacy. Even animals appear to respond well to this system of healing; I recently heard of a practitioner who is regularly called over to Spain to practise Reiki on horses. They are unlikely to be experiencing a placebo effect.

Personally, I find it both curious and fascinating how Reiki, and the belief in the power of the symbols used in its practice, has taken off. Thousands utilise it in their healing practices and it has turned into a worldwide phenomenon. The symbols used in Reiki don't immediately look magical, or beautifully designed, yet many people spend large sums of money to use them. Like a corporate franchise, budding practitioners have to be given the authority to use the selected symbols with their inherent promises.

Whether or not we believe in the power of symbols to heal, or to change the way we feel, if enough people believe in them (like those who believe in Reiki) then it becomes a self-fulfilling prophecy. If it comes from a deeper purpose, then it will carry a deeper purpose. It follows that, if we believe in the logo, then that too becomes a powerful motivator to change our lives.

Ulli Springett, MA, psychotherapist and author of *Symbol Therapy*, has found that symbols can heal people. Working with this method in her counselling practice, she has found that clients improved after only a few sessions—with many improvements being dramatic, even 'miraculous'.

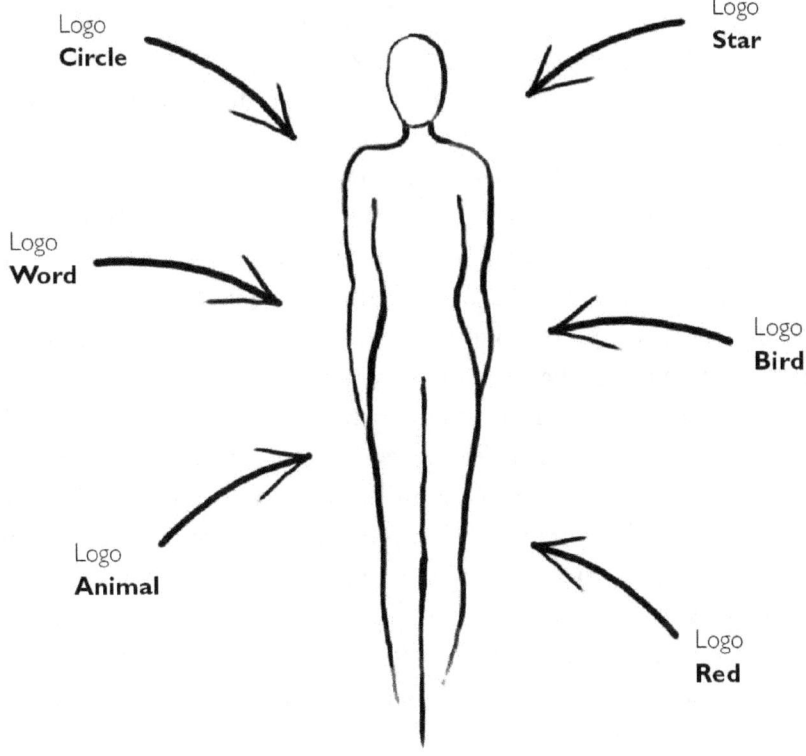

Logo
Circle

Logo
Star

Logo
Word

Logo
Bird

Logo
Animal

Logo
Red

Every element in a logo can have an effect on us.

Many clients with chronic problems, including depression, panic attacks, eating disorders and relationship difficulties, as well as chronic pain and fatigue, were free of symptoms within weeks.

The core of her practice is to work with a specific symbol for a particular effect or purpose. Ulli stated that the symbols used need to be beautiful and be a bright colour. Anything ugly, unpleasant or with a dull colour never produced good results. Working with the symbol for two minutes, twice a day, for two weeks could help alleviate the original disease or distress.

Ulli stated that: 'My own understanding of symbols is based on Tibetan Buddhism, which uses symbols in many ways. My Buddhist teacher explained that a statue or a picture of a Buddha, for example, is not separate from a 'real' Buddha; it is imbued with all its divine qualities. For me, that was a very powerful teaching that made me appreciate the power of the many symbols that surrounds us more deeply.'[17]

Frank Eickermann practises and teaches a style of Feng Shui, which he claims owes its origins to ancient systems of geomancy. With this system, it is not necessary to work physically with the spaces in a building by knocking down doors or moving furniture; it works with the energy within spaces. By sensing where blockages lie, and where strong points exist, the system works to harmonise the energy in the least intrusive way. The most fascinating detail of this process is that the practitioner works with symbols to effect desired changes. The only tools required are a red and a black pen, paper on which to draw the symbols, and a box of matches to set fire to the chosen symbols in the appropriate space. The match is like an ignition key that energises the symbols. Clients notice the difference in the spaces treated and their furniture remains in their preferred position.[18]

Our beautifully designed and charged brand logos similarly hold the potential to create change. Rather than releasing their energy through fire, the spark that kindles their power comes from the exposure through marketing, which carries the intention to the rest of the world.

Voodoo traditionally uses a symbol of the person to effect changes in them, for example by sticking pins into an effigy or burning it. While the effectiveness of this may be regarded as questionable by today's scientific convictions, there is evidence that this type of intention, using a physical representation of the person, can work. Dean Radin, researcher at the

Institute of Noetic Sciences, USA, tested the effectiveness of this practice by asking subjects to create a small effigy of themselves. These effigies, along with information on what made the subjects feel nurtured and comfortable, were used by a 'healer'. Direct, measurable effects on the subjects were noted, including a relaxation response as well as an increase in their autonomic nervous system. The latter increase was found to be a direct effect of the healers rubbing the shoulders and stroking the hair and face *of the effigies*. It was having the effect of a 'remote massage' on the subjects.[19]

A successful psychic and astrologer in Melbourne, Australia, employed a range of symbols to effect change. He visualised a vertical line for meditation implying 'oneness'; a five-pointed star to open spaces for physical effect, such as releasing bowel problems and other muscular tightness in the body and mentally to open psychic or thinking spaces; and two dots side by side to represent peace, represented by balance and harmony as seen on the yin and yang symbol. His intention behind these helped create their success. As in Reiki, these symbols can be visualised, drawn, projected towards people or into a space, or expressed in any way that seems appropriate to the trained user.

Radionics, originally developed in San Francisco by Dr Albert Abrams (1863-1924), is a method of healing that, with the help of specialised instruments, is effective with or without physical contact with the patient. Abrams believed that everything that exists has a unique vibrational signature. This signature is represented in Radionics by a system of codes, each of which is known as a Rate. These Rates are used to both test and treat disease, using energy patterns to correct the imbalances found by the practitioner. These patterns include symbols, as well as homeopathic remedies, flower remedies and colours. The patient can be with the practitioner, connected to a machine, or be many miles away.

Selected symbols can be used homeopathically. Even today, the Berber medicine man writes a potion—rather like a prescription—in a bowl and fills it with water to create the right medicine.

At the Sai Sanjeevini Foundation in India,[20] a range of related symbols has been developed, each of which is attributed with the ability to affect a specific body part or ailment. There are 198 symbols, or Sanjeevis, as they are called, each looking similar to the next but with subtle differences.

Some 54 of these symbols relate to body parts, and 144 more to diseases. According to this practice, subtle (spiritual) vibrations of healing forces have been 'harnessed' on the cards to heal specific health problems. These cards are used by placing a medium, such as water or lactose pills, onto the symbol for 15 seconds and then giving the subsequently potentised 'medicine' to the patient as a remedy. This process can even work when the patient is not physically present, by using a specific card to broadcast the remedy. The idea of using corporate symbols to potentise an intermediary element that can then be used to effect change certainly has far-reaching and moral implications!

Denise Linn, author of *Sacred Space*, says that once, after going for a walk, she returned and noticed that the energy of her home felt charged in a very positive way. On investigating further, she discovered that a guest staying with her had been going through the house, drawing the sign of infinity in the air with her hands. Denise Linn said: 'The difference in the energy of the whole house was palpable.'

These are some of the practices that use some form of symbols to change energy. The success of these is referred to as an energetic, or vibrational, effect. The effort that goes into the detailing and intention behind these symbols for healing is directly comparable to that which goes into a logo, with its own powerful objective, to make us feel better.

Luck and protection

We have used symbols to protect us through the ages. Sometimes we wear them; sometimes we carry them in our cars. Athletes, travellers and students alike will use good luck symbols such as a favoured teddy bear, medallion, rabbit's foot or four-leafed clover. Religions are full of symbols, from the Christian cross to the Hindu god Ganesh. Attributed with powers, from absolution to protection, we keep them close in the hope that a little will rub off on us.

A renowned psychic wallpapered a room with images of angels, and then covered it with plain wallpaper, so that the energy of the angels existed in the space of the room. A celebrity covered his expensive car with protection symbols, before spraying it over again with his chosen colour.

In both of these cases, the symbols incorporated were not visible to the human eye.

Kick Ass Miracles[21] broadcast on Dave TV in 2009, sets out to explore the truths behind this type of 'magic'. In one of its programmes, it showed amulets, specially designed for protection, being placed into brown envelopes and attached to targets. An expert marksman stood within a few feet of each and fired. Despite the proximity, he missed the envelopes and then, before he could try again, the gun jammed.

Companies also wish their symbols to bring them luck, a healthy profit and balance sheet, as well as protection from aggressive competitors and undesired market forces. Corporate symbols—the logotypes—are among the greatest influencers of company health. When we wear the logo, we buy into the promise of a better future. But we might be buying into more than we choose.

CHAPTER TWO

The essence of the corporate soul

'Every tool carries with it the spirit by which it has been created.'

WERNER KARL HEISENBERG

A logotype embodies the character of the business it represents and gives it individuality. But it expresses and delivers a deeper part of the brand it identifies.

Naomi Klein, author of *No Logo*, states: 'We are invited to think of the brand as the core meaning of the organisation.' A successful logo forges this core and connects it to the rest of the world. It touches us in many ways; some are obvious, others enable the imprint of the logo to seep into our personal space and create an unconscious motivation.

Connecting at new levels

Reaching through us to touch our emotions, logos connect with us at many levels. Encouraging us to live our lives so that we benefit the corporate balance sheet, brands align their standards to meet with ours or manipulate our standards to suit theirs. The dialogue they create to enable this beneficial connection is manufactured via branding techniques: marketing, design, public relations and advertising. We recognise businesses and their brands through exposure to their logos. Attributed with human characteristics and desirable personalities, we see them as our friends, someone whom we can lean on in both good and bad times.

As stated in *No Logo*: 'After the introduction of identities, manifested into logos and promoted through advertising in the 1880s, it was obvious that the corporate personality had arrived.' Renowned corporate identity designer Wally Olins often refers to this 'corporate personality', stating that the logotype, symbolising everything the company stands for, is at the core of this.

As they take on this corporeal aspect, we can define our connections to the mind, body and spirit of brand entities and explore the effect of these on us.

Connecting with the body of a business

Unless we work for a company or own some of its shares, our physical connection will be made through the products we buy and use. It might start with meeting sales staff as we enter a high-street bank, or pick a packet of cereal off a supermarket shelf. When we choose our mobile phone, drive our car, display our branded clothes or spray ourselves with a well-known body mist, we make numerous connections with the brand that extend from the initial concept, through research, design and marketing. Without these physical connections and resulting purchases, the brand simply would not exist; however, physical motivation alone is not enough to secure a future for a brand. We are motivated by forces that extend beyond those that prompt our survival or our physical comfort.

Connecting with the mind of a business

Our feelings towards a company are affected by its advertising, publicity and marketing. Those who are responsible for the flow and content of this information aim to influence our emotions to their benefit. Whether it is a complete advertising campaign to promote the irresistibility of a product, or press coverage of a dramatic share price movement, our impressions and attitudes about a company will be shaped by the content, appearance and delivery of the information included.

We know that brands have personalities; companies spend millions on making them our trusted friends. Companies specifically develop unique attributes to make them stand out from the competition and to give them characteristics that we, the consumer, desire.

A spokesperson for Newcastle Brown ale stated in a television interview in January 2006: 'Our brands can talk like a friend or older brother rather than a government-style health warning.'

We are aware of the differing personalities of brands—the gregarious Virgin selling a range of items from bridalwear to flights; the specialists such as Coca-Cola and Starbucks; the parents such as Proctor and Gamble or Diageo. Whatever they are *selling*, we are buying more than a product. We invite them into our lives in the hope that they will nurture our emotions, a key differentiating factor in the success of competitive brands. The personality of people is reflected in the personality of brands. We search out and interact with our 'new best friends'; those who really understand us. By arousing specific feelings in us, brands can develop an emotional relationship with customers that can give people meaning in their lives.

Most of us want happiness—and brands aim to deliver this. We talk about people being depressed, and we refer to a 'Depression' when the economic world flounders. Money, brands, emotions—all are inextricably linked for mutual gain.

Brands are also taking a more authoritarian approach, creating our needs and becoming the caretakers of our lives through our emotions and ambitions. By enrolling the involvement of celebrities (from pop stars to actors) and specialists (including doctors, scientists and former police chiefs) and creating elaborate marketing campaigns supported with 'scientifically proven' facts and figures, new brands truths are created. We respond to this authority. Shocking proof of our ability to respond unquestioningly to a perceived higher authority lies in the experiment conducted by Stanley Milgram, an American social psychologist, who in the 1960s studied the relationship between obedience and authority. A (perceived) expert asked a group of students to administer potentially fatal shocks in order to teach another group how to answer questions correctly. The scientific world (and the world at large) was alarmed to discover that the participants administrating the shocks exceeded the level that they believed would cause extreme harm (even death) when encouraged by an 'expert.'[1] Our willingness to believe information imparted by an authoritative, respected source might have appalling consequences, but we feel we are absolved from taking responsibility.

The ultimate brainpower of a brand resides in the board members, those who ensure the survival of the business by strategic decision-taking. We take note of their characters when choosing to invest in shares, or, for example, if the brand experiences a crisis.

Connecting with the spirit of a business

We probably connect with the spirit of a company in many ways, but have not developed a formal process to recognise them. The spirit of a company is by nature more intangible than the body and the mind. It is a more elusive quality that reaches beyond the more superficial promises of fulfilment, satisfaction and the like. This more intangible 'energy' of the business is all around, all-pervading, and lies in subtler levels. When we look beyond the physical, and ignore the chatter of the mental, there is something else there.

When we connect at this level, powerful motivators such as gut feeling and intuition come into play. This requires the use of senses that we often distrust—and that few of us are formally trained to use. To truly connect with the pure energy of a company, we may need to look to tribal wisdom and techniques long forgotten in our Western world with its preoccupation with the physical.

Tribal peoples, including the Sentinelese, live in the remote Andaman Islands in the Indian Ocean. They have largely been isolated from the rest of the world for an estimated 30,000 to 60,000 years, and it was widely believed that they had been wiped out by the Asian tsunami in 2004. But they had in fact left for the highlands prior to the event. They are likely to have preserved the kind of sensitivity to disturbances in the climate that animals still have. Ervin László, Hungarian philosopher and theorist, states that we have lost our connection to this 'celestial receiver', but that laboratory experiments show that we have not lost the receiver itself. We can pick up on information before it reaches the physical world; so, too, we could tune into the underlying emotions stirred by the brand marketers and be instinctively guided towards the identifying logo.[2]

We are aware when we physically interact with a brand through its products or shares, for example. We sense changes in our feelings when we are confronted with a choice between brands. Although we might be less aware of our relationship to the spirit or energy of a brand, which is less tangible, it is a comparably effective connection. Unlike physical and mental aspects of a brand, this energetic value has no boundaries and can be manipulated effectively to suit the brand's objectives.

An energetic imprint of the corporate soul

While a business or brand may not have the sort of soul that is attributed to humans, it does present an essence, a spirit, or a measurable energy value, which reaches out to connect with us at levels beyond the physical. In order to discover this more subtle aspect, we need to look to that which we will consistently recognise through the lifetime of a brand. More than that, it needs to inspire us beyond the mundane. This corporate soul would not logically reside in the ever-changing board members, the manufacturing or office bases that might relocate, the fluctuating shares, or the frequently updated ingredients and packaging. Its energy pervades, links and affects all of these, but it is not how we recognise this extra dimension. It must reside in the long-term familiar; as long as we recognise the logo, we have a deep sense that we are dealing with the same, memorable brand. The logotype is the most apparent, permanent, stable and identifiable aspect of a business. If a brand changes its logo, we see a different brand. A company that changes its logo usually only does so when it is signalling a transformation, akin to a death and rebirth, into a perceptibly new business.

Designers often recognise this as they connect with the organisation during the design process. Many have the ability to tap into this higher sense of the spirit they hope to articulate in a piece of design.

English designer Steven Medhurst creates extraordinary pieces of jewellery. He says that when he is commissioned to design a specific piece, it is as if he takes the energy of the client and assimilates it into the design.

Often, the person will say that the necklace, or brooch, was not what they expected—but that it feels perfect for them.

It is similar for the designer of company logotypes: we tune into and encapsulate the essence of the company; then we create a design combining individually powerful elements: symbols, colours and a name, so that it can be displayed and shared with the world.

Christian Kyriacou, architect and Feng Shui consultant, succinctly articulates the power and importance of a design in this way: 'The energy of symbolism and colour reflects the vibrational symphony of the universe. Get the shapes, colours and forms in tune with each other and with natural law, then the logo will carry power and connection to the human spirit.'[3]

The logotype is much more than a combination of design elements. In an article on rebranding,[4] Brian Eley, design group Lambie-Nairn's then creative director said: 'You can't put a value on branding. Controllers know they aren't just paying for a logo—it's a holistic approach.'

Creativity is the language of our soul; we yearn for the creative. Words, colours and pictures are elements over which we have control. We can create our own limitations and boundaries. When we work with these through our imagination—whether it is to construct a painting, advertisement, logo, book or poem—we can deliver powerful messages that evoke potent responses, effective well beyond the elements used to create the final result. The following piece by William Blake illustrates the power of words:

To see a World in a grain of sand
And a Heaven in a Wild Flower
Hold Infinity in the palm of your hand
And Eternity in an hour

This poem did not spring from any 'logical' mind. The poet uses his palette of 26 letters to fire our imagination as the artist uses his canvas, paints, brushes and easel. Meanwhile, the designer dips into his own specialist tools of printing colours, computers and specialist software to combine simple elements into a logo that, with the support of branding, can motivate our senses and move us to respond powerfully.

Our thoughts and emotions provide the driving force that calls us to pay attention to brands. When we see a logo that provokes our imagination and tugs at the emotions of millions, it is easy to realise how an abstract form can stimulate a global response to the benefit of the organisation it represents.

Logos are the ultimate manifestation of the corporate dream in the material world, and they play a major part in creating it. The ability to create a future through symbolism is not new.

The power of symbols

'Every status has its symbol.'

ADVERTISING SLOGAN, *THE ART OF LOOKING SIDEWAYS*

The power of symbols to entrance and transform us has been recognised and used through the ages. The art of symbolism has been known to humankind for at least 30,000 years and formed a vital part of communications for our ancestors. During the Upper Palæolithic period, in the regions that are now France and Spain, people began to make objects that had no practical use, such as jewellery and ornaments, and decorated them and the walls of their caves with patterns thought to have specific symbolic meaning. Some of these are so prolific that one, the Lascaux Grotto, is sometimes referred to as the 'Sistine Chapel of Palæolithic Art'.[5]

These symbols fall into two categories: *realistic* (including animals), and *abstract* (including dots and spirals). Some historians believe they are all symbols of abstract ideas associated with the rituals of hunting, fertility or social ceremonies. Anthropologists believe that this rich tradition of pictographic marks, also found on other continents, were of great significance to prehistoric peoples. Whether they are designed to encourage the spirits of wellbeing, or used as an early form of financial security, it seems apparent that they are more than decorative paintings chosen to sit over the hearth to enhance the sitting room of the cave and impress the neighbours! The design and ritualistic application of these marks mirrors the objectives of our current branding process by attempting to secure a desirable, predetermined future using symbols as a device. According to Renfrew and Morley, in their book *Becoming Human: Innovation in Prehistoric Material and Spiritual Culture*, Palæolithic imagery has the potential not only to elicit feelings, but also to produce further knowledge. It can mobilise meanings. 'Those who engage with the images (images in the widest possible sense) not only begin to "see the world" differently, but learn how to create a new world.'[6]

Like our commercial logos, these symbols were designed and drawn with intent for a desired outcome. 'Since early antiquity, people have orientated themselves by natural signs: sailors navigated by constellations, the Magi followed a star. When these proved insufficient, we invented others, some of which are culturally specific. Invented signs were added to the natural ones.'[7]

It is only in the past few hundred years, since the invention of mass printing, that the bulk of the Western world has been able to read and write. Before then, these skills were the privilege of a minority; most people were thought to communicate by using pictures, signs, symbols and signals, which were either clearly understandable or had a more hidden, encoded meaning.

Today, the fields of heraldry, chemistry, cartography, astronomy, biology, traffic control, mathematics and music—to mention a few—all depend on symbolism for communication. Logotypes, used to communicate potentially elusive brand values, may not be so literal or definable, but they are equally as effective in informing us.

This ability of symbols to conveniently transcend language and social barriers makes logos excellent tools to deliver the branding message to countries with different languages or where there is a degree of illiteracy.

Creating symbols for change

Historically, symbols were attributed with powers to affect us on many levels. They were seen as sacred devices with energy of their own that could even affect, or indicate, our future.

Today, we have our own forms of 'symbol practitioners' who are able to change the mood in a room (Reiki practitioners); to alter the molecular structure of water (Masaru Emoto); and heal those in need, wherever they are in the world, via a machine (radionics practitioners).

But our most powerful symbol practitioners are the designers who can express the essence of the corporate soul in a logo in such a way that we get the message and become attracted to the brand it identifies. Ideally, we will want to visibly link ourselves with the brand by displaying the logo on our proudly purchased, branded possessions. These logo symbols can transform our minds, the way we live our lives, and ultimately our world. Through this process they secure a positive future for their owners.

Clark and Crossland[8], authors of *The Leader's Voice,* believe in the importance of the brand symbol; they suggest that many business leaders fail to use symbols to communicate ideas, believing that marketing alone will do the trick. They remind us that the human brain uses facts, emotions *and* symbols to create complete thoughts; it is important for leaders to communicate on all three channels if the audience is to pick up on a complete message. After listing a range of symbols including logos, words, designs, myths and rituals, they ask whether the readers' business symbols are allies or enemies: 'Are they defined *by* you or *for* you?' They state that symbols are the 'shortcuts to the great truths that guide our lives'.

Denise Linn, world-acclaimed expert in Feng Shui, believes: 'Symbols have been essential for understanding and relating to the world since the beginning of the human species.'[9] José Argüelles, author, artist and educator, says: 'The world is a weave of symbols, and it is through symbols that we weave our understanding of the world. When we understand that symbols are actually resonant structures, vibratory form-fields, and that we ourselves are resonant to our very core, then we can see that symbols are completely vital to our functioning as whole beings.'[10] And author Malidome Patrice Somé states: 'We may refer to symbols and our reactions to them in more comfortable terms such as instinct or intuition, but beneath this is the recognition that a separate entity in us experiences reality in ways different from the way the conscious self perceives the world.'[11]

But unlike the symbols that were presented from the world of nature, where our ancestors had to be vigilant and observant to get the message, in our modern world we are bombarded with logos by impatient organisations that cannot afford to rely on our innate senses of observation. The designers of today have replaced the shamans of old utilising the power of technology instead of the natural world.

Effective messages

A vast array of emotive responses is triggered at the glimpse of a logo. Whether or not we are hungry or thirsty, in need of financial credit, or wish we owned a home in Spain, the appropriate logo will inspire the thought in our minds. Unlike words, which need to be read or heard to be understood, symbols can transcend time and space. Edgar Mitchell, Apollo astronaut and the sixth man to land on the Moon, successfully transmitted telepathic messages during his trip into space. Four participants, in different parts of the world, attempted to identify the order of symbols on cards that he focused on. Mitchell's colleagues on Earth successfully picked up the order despite the fact that he was a quarter of a million miles away. Mitchell stated that the results were 'far exceeding anything expected.'[12]

This speed is important when we realise that, according to the brand company Interbrand, 85 per cent of all consumer purchases are made on impulse.[13] That means most customers make up their minds at the shelf, and the logo needs to deliver the brand message quickly and effectively.

The instant response we have to a symbol is illustrated in an experiment proving that people can learn to react, like Pavlov's dogs, to an unrelated abstract prompt. 'Volunteers have been taught to associate abstract computer images with ice cream in an experiment that shows humans can have a similar response to Pavlov's dog.'[14] Once we have been trained to make the link between the logo and the product, like Pavlov's dogs, which salivated at the sound of bell previously associated with food, we respond to the abstract. We see the symbol and we begin to 'salivate' in anticipation and, unlike the dogs, we are able to satisfy that response through our purchasing ability.

Companies have trained us well. A glimpse of a logo can spark a whole programme that has been predetermined by the brand marketers. Changing and controlling our thoughts and beliefs about a particular product or service, via a symbol, can effectively benefit the business it represents.

Logos changing perception

According to Georges Jean in his book *Signs, Symbols and Ciphers*: 'The word *symbol* derives from the ancient Greek *symbolon*, a token composed of two halves, used to verify identity by matching one part to the other.'

A symbol is commonly known as 'that which stands for or suggests something else'; thus, almost anything can be regarded as a symbol. It is the 'something else' that is important in triggering a specific response. A light bulb could communicate the concept of light or a bright idea; a shell could remind us of a day at the beach or the fact that we need petrol; a circle could represent a zero, a sun or a book publisher (O Books).

A logotype is a unique type of symbol specifically created to produce a benefit to the business it identifies. It a complex piece of art, which is a uniquely cognitive ability, identified in a simple icon, created by a (commercial) artist. This link between a symbol and art is apparent in the following definitive features of art:

- it influences the minds of an audience
- it occurs in the context of a distributed social network
- it is constructivist in nature; that is, aimed at the deliberate refinement and elaboration of some aspect of the worldview of the artist
- it engages in self-reflection, individually and socially
- the forms and media of art are technology-driven
- neither the role of the artist, nor the local social definition of art, are fixed and may change as a function of the state of the social-cognitive network in which the artist works
- art, unlike conventional physical engineering, is always aimed at a cognitive outcome; that is, at influencing the mind of an audience (even if the audience were to be the mind of the artist).[15]

Since the beginning of the commercial world, logo designers have drawn on an infinite number of visual resources combining animals, plants, words, type, colours and shapes to create a sort of filter between the company product and us.

Applied to packaging, marketing materials, products—as many of the company's manifestations as possible—the logo translates the information that the brand wants us to know, sieving out the undesired, stimulating the desired, and appealing to our senses.

Symbols are highly successful tools of transformation. Jung states in *On Psychic Energy*: 'The psychological mechanism which transforms energy is the symbol.'[16] 'Symbolism is the science of the relations which unite the created world with God, the material world with the supernatural; the science of the harmonies existing between the diverse parts of the universe (correspondences and analogies).'[17] And René Guénon author of *Symbols of Sacred Science* believes: 'The true basis of symbolism is, as we have said, the correspondence linking together all orders of reality, binding them one to the other, and consequently extending from the natural order as a whole to the supernatural order.'[18]

Buddha believed that attempts to capture spiritual truth in written form were bound to fail. Ultimate reality could only be grasped through the power of symbols; words merely offered pointers towards truth. In one of his most famous sermons at Vulture Peak Mountain, in front of thousands of people, the Buddha sat in silence and simply held up a flower.[19]

DK Holland, editor of *Design Annual*, says: 'People always talk about the impact that visuals make on the human mind, but when you get right down to it, there is a real failure to take into account the depth and breadth of meaning that symbols have on the human psyche.'[20] Wally Olins, in his book *Corporate Identity*, says 'The power of the symbol should never be underestimated . . . Symbols have the same power as music to play upon the emotions, memories and sensitivies. Symbols can evoke fear or horror, as in, say, the Nazi symbol; they can also, and with equal immediacy, evoke pleasure, a smile—Mickey Mouse in the entertainment world, or the Michelin man, Mr Bibendum, in the business world provoke pleasurable ideas.' He goes on to say: 'Design consultants involved in building identities for organizations usually, and very properly put the symbol at the heart of the creative process. If you get it right, the symbol can in a magical way summarize the idea of an entire corporation.'

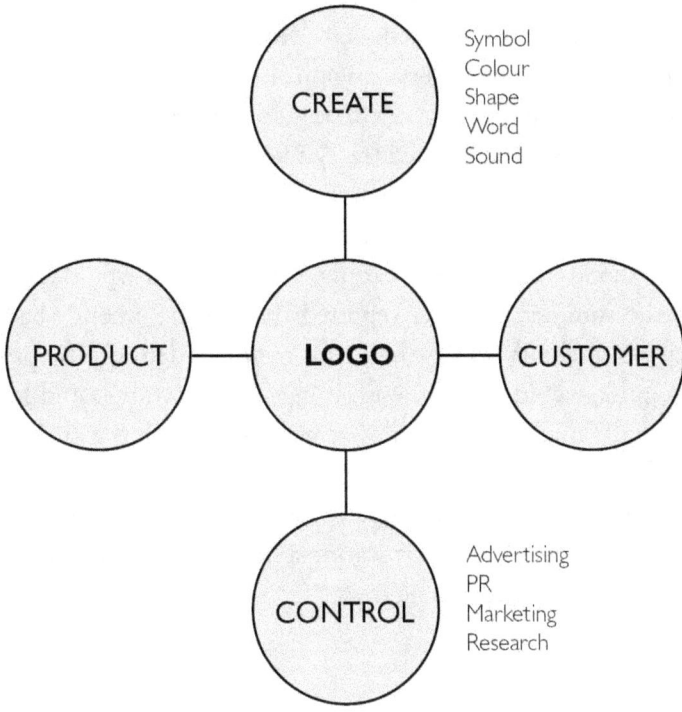

CREATE

Symbol
Colour
Shape
Word
Sound

PRODUCT

LOGO

CUSTOMER

CONTROL

Advertising
PR
Marketing
Research

Created out of carefully selected elements and controlled through branding processes, the logo is pivotal in delivering selected information about the product it identifies.

A type of symbol known as a talisman is defined by the *Shorter Oxford English Dictionary* as 'any object held to be endowed with magic virtue' and can be used to protect, manifest and heal depending on the intention behind it.

Once-famous British television presenter Noel Edmonds made a surprise comeback in 2006. During his new, successful series, specially drawn symbols were displayed on his hand, which led to intense speculation in the press. One headline read: 'OK Noel, what's the deal over those drawings on your hand?'[21] Reporting on the success of his comeback, the article stated that it is ' . . . proving to be more captivating than was perhaps originally intended.' It described the symbols, inked on Noel's right hand near his little finger, as a little black star, a black arrow followed by a faint circle and further on a cloud with little drops of rain. Noel's spokesperson refused to disclose their true meaning, stating that it would all be made clear in the summer. Another reported that Noel Edmonds had signed a lucrative deal about his new belief in 'cosmic ordering'. The presenter's self-help guide would reveal the meanings of the symbols and he stated: 'It's not totally mad. You'll think I've gone away with the fairies, but it's fantastic.'[22]

Noel had put his faith in a book called the *Cosmic Ordering Service*, by German guru Barbël Mohr, advocating a new-age faith, and he had since seen a string of his wishes come true.

Logos and our beliefs

These sorts of connections and beliefs around symbols touch us deeply and effectively; they come from the voices of our ancestors. Since the beginning of the human species, we have designed and used symbols to give meaning to our world and to harness the inexplicable forces around us to our benefit. Our new symbols, brand logos, may not be so blatantly esoteric, or religious, or deeply meaningful, but they are no less powerful and, with the backing of technology to support and deliver their message, their effect is relentless and unrestrained. They weave a global promise of a better world that is so successful we continue to believe it despite seemingly irrefutable evidence that the converse is true as precious resources are used up in the pursuit of profit. The effect on us of the marketing process and resulting brands, identified with logos, defies logic. It extends beyond our minds into the deeper recesses of our being and taps into dynamics that go beyond our mind and into the realms of spirit.

CHAPTER THREE

Our aura meets the 'Loglo'

'When we work for, buy from or otherwise deal with a
company, we become associated with that company and
assimilate a little of its identity.'

PER MOLLERUP, *MARKS OF EXCELLENCE*

How can a logo design affect us physically?

USA research scientist Dr Valerie Hunt[1] has studied the human aura for more than 30 years. In her book, *Infinite Mind: The Science of Human Vibrations*, she concludes that: 'As a result of my work, I can no longer consider the body as organic systems or tissues. The healthy body is a flowing, interactive electrodynamic energy field.' This field interacts with, and is affected by, everything around us. Denise Linn, author of *Sacred Space*, believes that symbols have a life force of their own that interacts with our own energy field.

The human energy field

The aura is the name of the field of energy that surrounds and permeates our physical body. Indian tradition, more than 5,000 years old, specifies that there are seven layers of the aura, each linked to a chakra (a 'wheel' of energy) that exists within each of us. There are seven main chakras, from the top of our head to the base of our spine. Each of these is associated with a major nerve plexus and endocrine gland. Each chakra has a connection with a particular colour, which it both radiates and absorbs. The Chinese tradition, from the third millennium outlines an invisible meridian system that runs through the body and states that energy enters the body at specific positions known as acupuncture points. Both traditions refer to

37

the energy of this as *prana* and *ch'i* respectively. Many other traditions have an awareness of this force and, more recently, advanced scientific equipment has been able to validate the presence and condition of our energy bodies.

Alberto Villoldo, in his book *Shaman Healer Sage*, states: 'We all possess a luminous energy field that surrounds our physical body and informs our body in the same way that the energy fields of a magnet organise iron filings on a piece of glass.'

James Van Praagh, in his book *Heaven and Earth*, says: 'Think of the aura as a brilliant glass shell surrounding your body. From the moment of your conception to the end of your physical incarnation, your aura accumulates every thought, word, feeling and deed of your life. Like rain, dirt and dust coating a glass surface, your aura is covered with debris from years of life experiences.'

Barbara Brennan, in her book *Hands of Light*, describes how she was able to see these energies as a child. As an adult, she gained a job at NASA, where she researched the interaction between the human energy field and the universal energy field. With their highly developed scientific equipment, NASA scientists were even able to detect and validate the different energy centres within the human body that had previously only been known to ancient Eastern religions.

Barbara fine-tuned her childhood skill to become one of the foremost teachers in the world on the subject of human energy fields. Using her developed 'Higher Sense Perception'[2], she is able to see a person's energy and how it is intimately associated with that person's health and wellbeing. She is able to use this ability to diagnose both physical and psychological problems and reveal how most diseases initially exist in our energy fields and are then, through time and living habits, transmitted to our bodies where they can develop into a serious illness.

As an experiment, psychics were asked to ascertain the energy fields of apparently healthy people. Those with abnormalities were subsequently tested using modern scientific diagnostic equipment, and were found to have hitherto-undiagnosed disease in the defined area. Brennan noted that in one such case, a woman with a 'black spot' in her energy field was found to have an undetected cancerous growth in that area. 'The black spot correlated in size, shape and location with results taken from a CAT scan later.'[3]

7 CROWN CHAKRA
White. Our connection to spirit
6 THIRD EYE CHAKRA
Indigo. Intuition
5 THROAT CHAKRA
Blue. Self expression & communication
4 HEART CHAKRA
Green. Love & Compassion
3 SOLAR PLEXUS CHAKRA
Yellow. Personal power
2 SACRAL CHAKRA
Orange. Creativity & confidence
1 BASE CHAKRA
Red. Raw energy. sexuality & security

We each possess seven main energy centres, known as our chakras that receive and transmit energy.

This skill can probably be learned through experience. Neurologist and psychiatrist Shafica Karagulla[4] encountered several people who could accurately diagnose from auras and set out to see if any of the usually conservative medical profession could do the same; she found that many could. Most of them keep this ability a secret for fear of being derided by their colleagues.

Dr Valerie Hunt discovered that electromyography, normally used to measure the electrical activity in muscles, can also detect the human energy field; she has developed a high-frequency instrument that records the bioelectrical energy that emanates from the body's surface and proved that energy radiating from the body's atoms gives frequencies 1,000 times faster than any other known electrical activity of the body. She noted that when an aura reader noted a particular colour in a person's energy field, the electromyography would record this frequency as the same as the colour attributed to the specific area of the field by ancient traditions. For example, she could tell if the colour was green, matching the pattern on an oscilloscope (a machine that converts electrical waves into a visual pattern on a screen).

The overall colour of the aura can also say something about the condition of the person it surrounds. Red and pink can represent anger and compassion respectively; green can indicate the ability to heal; blue can show intuition and clairvoyant tendencies; and purple has spiritual indications.

We create our own colours, which in turn are affected by, and affect, the colours that surround us. We even describe our emotional state using phrases such as 'feeling blue', 'in the pink', 'green with envy', and so on. Colour is so good at affecting and describing us that it is used as an analytical tool as well. One system, used by Jung, defined us in terms of predominant function: thought, feeling, intuition and sensation; each of these was attributed a colour. Blue is linked with thinking and rational analysis. 'Blue' people have questioning minds skilled in seeing cause and effect, connecting ideas and judging things logically. They are good at adapting to new circumstances and include scientists and philosophers. 'Red' people are defined as 'feeling' people, although Jung meant 'feeling' to refer to a rational function such as putting things in order of value. 'Feeling' people will judge things as they see them, how 'pleasant' they are, or 'good' or 'bad'. They have a strong sense of traditional values. 'Yellow' people work on their hunches. Through their intuition, they tend to be more aware of and inspired by new and different possibilities and are often very creative. Finally, 'green' people rely on their sensations and perceptions for information about the outside world: how it looks, smells, feels and so on. Tending to be lacking in imagination, even a little boring, they are usually easy-going.

Our colours tell the world a lot about what is going on within us and they will change according to how we feel at any time.

What affects the human energy field?

'Our fields are organised by our emotions.'
DR VALERIE HUNT

We are affected on some level by everything that surrounds us, whether or not we are conscious of it. For example, most of us have been aware of how some people or places drain us of energy, and of how others tend to make us feel good.

My mother used to share a story about a trick that she and her friends would play on unsuspecting colleagues in the mill where she worked in Scotland. A perfectly healthy-looking person would be reduced to feeling physically ill after a group of co-conspirators asked after her wellbeing while intimating that she looked unwell. Usually the victim would go home—but more than this, she would actually begin to look ill, and her persona would change.

Perhaps this is most apparent in our sports heroes. They can be elevated almost to the point of worship, where it seems they can do nothing wrong—until they are responsible for losing a match or acting in some way detrimental to our understanding of them. At that point, they seem to turn overnight from shining stars into skulking outcasts.

This also happens regularly in the business or political world, when a person falls out of favour. When the success of executives, once the darlings of the City, is found to be the result of illegal manoeuvres we can almost see them shrink and look old. They may even become physically ill, as in the cases of Ernest Saunders of Guinness and Christopher Skase in Australia when they were discovered to be responsible for unlawful business practices. Down the line in business, we can see it when a colleague is made redundant or publicly criticised—even when the fault may lie elsewhere. We even refer to them looking grey or downhearted.

We can affect, and be affected by, our surroundings, including others around us. Lynne McTaggart, in her book *The Intention Experiment*, cites extensive research on how our good thoughts about a person can make them feel better. In *Synchro Destiny*, Deepak Chopra says: 'With every encounter, we exchange information and energy and we come away changed just a little bit.' On a much larger scale, a global event such as the 9/11 attacks can have a measurable effect that reverberates around the world.[5]

Brands reach out to us constantly, prodding us for attention via the media. Their thoughts and wishes for us will depend on the product they are promoting. If it is a dietary product, they might visualise us fat or ill; a financial product might entice them to see us as poor and in line for a loan, or rich so they can secure our funds for their wellbeing. Ultimately, any image of the consumer must, by logic, be one that is lacking so that that they can fill the space. Where there is no space, the marketers have the ability to create one, and we will soon find ourselves dissatisfied. These sorts of feelings, which surround us daily, have the potential to affect the auras and potential wellbeing of consumers. Brands are more interested in building up their own energy than ours.

We are drawn to people and places with large auras; this very act of admiration, even worship, further builds up their energy field. We want to be near them, to be a part of them and accept whatever they are offering, from healing to fame. This explains why celebrities are used so successfully to promote brands. We can identify with a part of them by displaying the logo.

While we can argue that only living objects have a measurable aura or energy body, which can be recorded using Kirlian photography, a process that registers energy fields, we have noted that symbols also have their own energy space—and in the world of quantum physics, everything is energy. While logotypes may not have a traditionally conceptualised living energy field surrounding them, it would seem that they might be able to influence, even to transform, the energy around them. After all, this is what they are designed to do, and corporations invest heavily in branding to ensure they achieve this objective.

When we encounter a logo we can be affected.

How can we take care of our field of energy?

Some people are more aware of their energy state and that of the area around them, and are able to translate the information coming in through their personal field; most of us just feel affected by it with little idea of why. By becoming more aware of this effect, we can learn to act accordingly for our own wellbeing, as well as the health of those around us and even of our world as a whole. We can become more discerning about our surroundings, including our choice of friends, food and clothes, and we can learn to make a conscious decision on what brands to invite into our lives for our benefit and which logos to associate with.

As documented in Barbara Brennan's book *Hands of Light*, and scientifically established by Dr Valerie Hunt, the condition of our own energy field directly affects the health of our physical body. By caring for the former, we can avoid physical symptoms in the latter.

Some complementary therapies, such as homeopathy, hands-on healing and flower remedies, aim to treat the energy body to affect the physical body. Patients being treated homeopathically, for example, can be profoundly affected by a carefully prescribed dose of a remedy that is so diluted there is absolutely no physical evidence of the original source of the prescription. Queen Elizabeth II is reputed to use this treatment and, apart from the fact that it seems to be working extremely well—she is rarely ill—we would also have to consider that her aura seems strong. Crowds gather to see her and people are deeply moved in her presence. The singer Beverley Knight was struck by the Queen's 'remarkable aura.'[6]

Our auras are bombarded from outside sources and our lives are affected beyond our deliberate control. Companies, of course, tap into this by making enormous efforts, through marketing and publicity, to ensure that we feel good when we wear their brand of clothes or use their branded

A logo radiates an energy that extends beyond the design itself.

products or services. Brands and their identifying logos have their own energy values that connect with us at subtle levels. The value of these can also make the difference to whether we buy or not.

By learning more about the energies around us, we will be in a better position to make informed choices about how we run our lives—as well as what logos to buy into, and where to wear them—because these things can deeply affect us.

The energy field of logos

Naomi Klein, in her book *No Logo*, says: 'Logos that have been burned into our brains by the finest image campaigns money can buy, and lifted a little closer to the sun by their sponsorship of much-loved cultural events, are perpetually bathed in a glow.' Klein refers to this glow as the 'loglo' and goes on to say that it is so bright that even 'activists' are able to 'bathe in its light.'

While the actual word or symbol has little physical value (we can't eat it, or wear it or drive it on its own), a successful logo becomes, through branding, synonymous with the product—to the point where it can become equally or even more important. This is particularly obvious in the fashion industry, where we blatantly wear the brands so that the logotype becomes more desirable than the product.

In a discussion about this aspect, a friend commented that her husband refers to his favourite T-shirt as his 'French Connection' without any allusion to the item itself. If, however, she were to remove the logo, she felt strongly that the T-shirt (still as comfortable and colourful as before) would, without doubt, cease to be his favourite.

The power of a logo is undeniable. Successful brands are bought on the promise of the logo, a promise of some sort of fulfilment in our lives. For example, without the identifying logo—one of our main criteria for choice—a T-shirt becomes just one more among similar competing shirts. While much of this logo effect is created and supported through advertising, the design itself carries its own unique imprint and ability to influence.

Symbols are huge portals to our subconscious. They have been for thousands of years. In today's commercial world, we are combining elements that are individually powerful into a single design that can deliver a mind-blowing and seductively irresistible message to potential consumers, in an instant.

Ex brand-addict Neil Boorman decided to break this bond with his branded products by publicly burning them. He shares how he would tap into the different brands depending on his requirements: 'I normally wear Lacoste during the daytime, especially if I am feeling youthful or frivolous. The Gucci is more of a grown-up shirt, good for an informal meeting or drinks in a smart-ish pub.'[7]

There is an aura around successful brands, underpinned by a series of marketable values, which resonates with something inside us. By associating ourselves with the name, we associate ourselves with the values.

The French academic Bernard Cova argued that modern consumers have become less interested in the objects of consumption than in the social links and identities associated with those objects.[8] According to Cova, the strains of globalisation have reawakened tribal instincts in all of us, leading us to form tribal communities around selected consumer brands. Our beloved logos, for which we pay a hefty premium, are created and endorsed by the most powerful people in the world. When we buy the logo, we are helping create the dream of a few. In war we follow the flag of our country, wear the uniform to identify our individual selves with powerful military tribal communities and gain symbolic medals to display our success. The battlefield might have changed in times of peace, but we still follow and proudly display symbols to win the commercial war.

Just as humans are more than their bodies—blood, flesh, nerves and bones—so it is true that symbols and logotypes are more than their physical manifestation—curves, lines, forms, ink and paper. This is where the true relevance of Andrew Crane's dowsing experiment to assess the detectable space around a symbol lies (see Introduction). Andrew has long been fascinated by symbols and their effect on us, whether controlled by the media or from other sources. His experiments on detecting the energy of symbols beyond their physical manifestation support the hypothesis that we do not have to see or touch a logotype in order for it to interact with and affect our own energy field. He goes as far as to state that the energy from a logotype or symbol can come simply from the intent of the designer or producer of the symbol. Many logos are created by some of the most powerful people on the planet and they are delivered with an equally powerful intention. We can feel this; we want some of it. Thoughts and intentions have a material value that the logo delivers.

In the world of quantum energy, currently becoming more accepted in our mainstream scientific world, logos, along with everything else, are part of the energy field as a whole and can hold a unique imprint that can affect other parts of the field. Lynne McTaggart's book *The Field*, quotes: 'Every object absorbs and re-radiates the Zero-point Field.' She describes this field as 'an ocean of microscopic vibrations in the space within things', a 'shadow of the universe for all time' and 'the beginning and the end of everything in the universe.'[9]

With the commercialised skill of branding, combined with the technology to create and display visual communication, we have, for the first time in history, the means to design sophisticated symbols, charged with emotional values via branding and the means to transmit them globally in an instant. We are working with pure energy and an incredibly efficient delivery method—the logo.

What contributes to the energy field of a brand logotype?

At perhaps the simplest level, each component of a logo—shapes, colour, typefaces, layout size and the design itself—has its own characteristics that affect the whole. Words (both written and spoken), symbols and colour are individually powerful elements, which have all been used, since ancient times, to motivate change. Each contains its own quantifiable influence. But when each of these is carefully selected, primed and detailed, and is eventually combined into one logotype, we have the means to deliver a powerful message that can change the way we see the brand. A good logo can play a primary part in securing the success of a business. Logos are a commercial art form that reaches out to our deepest senses to connect

words

colours   *symbols*

INTENTION

logo

A logo is formed from a specially selected combination of powerful elements chosen with an intention to deliver specific brand values.

us with the brand dream. Like traditional art, logos have the ability to move us, and that movement is carefully calculated in the brands' favour.

The quality and success of a corporate logo is due to more than simple design skills. Quantum physics theory states that our world is manifested via our thoughts and even the state of mind of an observer can affect an outcome—there are cases where the results of scientific experiments have been swayed by the emotions of the person feeding the laboratory rats. The state of mind of the client, the designer, and everyone who has a vested interest in the outcome of the design, has the potential to affect the final outcome. We have the most powerful people in the world briefing an intention into a symbol. Huge design groups with sophisticated technology create and imbue the design with that intended brief, and marketing techniques ensure that we are exposed to the logo so we learn to love it. These processes combine to create an irresistibly tempting field of energy around the logo and, as its familiarity seeps into our psyche, we continue to buy it. This in turn further builds up the energy around the logo.

A logo might be created by a famous designer or hatched from a scribble on the back of an envelope. It might be printed in blue or red, carry imagery, or display a name that reflects abstract or realistic values. Every part of the design and implementation process will contribute to the energy of the final logo. Whether applied to a soft drink, sewn into our clothes, or beamed towards us from a television screen, we will get the corporate message in one way or another, whether we want to or not.

More than we bargained for

Most of us are not inclined to cut out our clothing labels or burn our branded possessions. But if we knew a little more about the effect a logo can have on our personal psyche, we might become more cautious about what we ingest or wear close to our body.

If we accept Japanese scientist Masaru Emoto's evidence that emotions affect the crystalline structure of water, it follows that since humans and the Earth are composed mostly of water, we too can affect one another with our thoughts and feelings. What we, as individuals, are able to perceive and feel about the world can be transmitted to others. Our emotions can literally create our world. As the fundamental success of a brand depends on its ability to control our emotions, businesses are tapping into this powerful resource. With the support of advertising and marketing we are encouraged to love a brand and fear the consequences of choosing another.

Emoto's findings certainly provoke further questioning about the effects on a product of its label design, incorporating graphics, symbols and text, as well as the subsequent effect on any person consuming the product. If a single word can change the crystalline structure of water, commercial drinks could be carrying hidden messages imbued from the logo. At a cellular level we are absorbing the powerful intentions for the success of a brand. There may be little doubt that cigarette smoke is bad for your health—but imprinting huge letters stating 'smoking kills' on the front of a pack may do more harm than good. Actress Sienna Miller appears to have grasped this principle when she was quoted as saying; 'I love cigarettes. Love them. I think the more positive approach you have to smoking, the less harmful it is.'[10]

A teacher friend described a direct experience of this intention effect. She recounted an experiment she performed for her class. Two identical plants were simultaneously watered from the same source, the only difference being that one watering can was imprinted with love, the other with hate. The plant watered with the former grew abundantly, blossoming into a large, leafy, healthy plant; the other hardly performed at all. Using Emoto's techniques, I feel sure we would see some interesting effects on the structure of water using imprints of our favourite logos on the container. Many labelled foodstuffs, as well as our bodies, contain water.

I personally witnessed the ability of an intention to change energy while attending the Intention Experiment Conference in London in March 2007. One of the speakers, Konstantin Korotkov PhD,[11] placed electrodes into a glass of water, from which he had been sipping, and recorded the energy levels using his specially developed state-of-the-art equipment. We were then asked to send an intention to the water. The energy levels measurably rose. Korotkov posed the question that perhaps this was what was meant in the Bible when Jesus turned the water into wine. With positive emotions imprinted in the water, it would theoretically be possible to get a feeling of being drunk with pleasure. In the same vein, he went on to say that we should never eat food that has been prepared by an angry person. The quality of the energy that is put into the making of products is directly related to the quality of the energy that comes out. Writer and restaurant critic AA Gill appears to recognise this effect. Writing of canapés in his article headed 'A Little Bit of Hell', he stated: 'Just think how much hard work goes into that one little mouthful, then think whose hands have made such light work of it. Do you believe they're happy, well-paid hands?'[12] Similarly, a local convenience meal factory produces quite delicious-tasting ready meals—but I know several people who have worked there describing a working environment that is filled with bitchiness and resentment. I would rather avoid food that could fail to nourish my wellbeing at deeper, sustainable, core levels where it really matters.

Our purchases can affect our health and environment. When we wear or use goods that are made in the developing world and may have cost the life of a child or the health of a peasant worker, or choose products that damage the environment, we could, according to Emoto's conclusions, be affected by the emotions of the person making the goods or by the attitude of the management. The quality of the final product on our shelf could be affected by all those responsible for the source and content of the raw ingredients, through to the processing, packaging, stacking and distribution. Finally, the application of the marketing and design can further tip the energy effect. We absorb all those qualities.

Few mass-produced products will have been made by those who really love their work, but at least one company appears to understand this energy theory, and acts on it. Compania della Buono Terra, a specialist luxury food company in Italy, pays great attention to the energy of their product at every stage of its manufacturing process. Measured using Kirlian photography, their food, sold in shops such as Fortnum and Mason in London as well as some of the largest stores in Italy, Japan, Scotland and Germany, is shown to have revitalised the energy that normally begins to diminish from harvesting time and generally continues to do so through normal food-processing facilities.[13]

One design group also appears to have recognised and tapped into knowledge of energy and used it as a resource. The Advertising Energy Group[14] in Melbourne, Australia, states on its website: 'We always add value by adding our energy. This energy can be felt and visibly seen throughout every level of our company from what we do, to how we do things.' Director Craig McConnell stated that they like to employ people with an effervescent quality and that it is the company's intention to deliver an experience rather than an empty design.

I dislike shopping for clothes, but once found a delightful independent shop tucked out of the way near Brompton Cemetery in London. I liked it because it was tiny and filled with clothes designed and produced by qualified, struggling, unknown young designers. I thought the clothes were fabulous. The enthusiasm, passion and care that came from their work led me to buy clothes that I knew I was going to feel good in energetically. Sadly, this shop has since closed, unable to compete with the larger stores.

As designers, we are creating powerful little packages of energy that affect everything they come into contact with, including the space surrounding them. A logo on a jar can therefore affect the contents, along with the printer who printed the label, the driver of the delivery vehicle and the person who stacks it on the shelf. Those who eat the jam inside have no idea of these unidentified, added 'ingredients'. How can we become more informed?

Unless we are particularly sensitive, we will not be aware of the underlying energies that could affect our purchasing choices. Knowledge of the physical origin of products can go some way to informing us of possible inherent effects. Given a fairly boring-looking lump of rock, for example, the average person would probably not make much of it. If it were subsequently identified as a part of the Berlin wall, however, or a piece of Martian rock, we would all understand the difference. When we learn that a prestigious car manufacturer is making bathroom accessories from wrecked cars, a smart toilet-roll holder takes on a new appeal. In each of these cases, the energy field emanating from these objects would probably be different from that of an average lump of rock or toilet-roll holder. The role of branding is to initiate, or increase, this 'more than . . . ', whether it is based on a physical or mental reality.

In today's hype, it can feel so much easier to buy into the irresistibly tempting brand promise. But if we are brave enough to drop out of the spin, we may see beyond the mist of the clouds in the dream world of marketing and into a world that offers us real choice.

Logos on our heart
area cover and affect
our centre of love and
compassion

Logos are often displayed across our chests.

Different body part, different effect

'It's fun seeing my label on someone's behind—I like that.'
CALVIN KLEIN

As we learn more about our own energy field and its intimate, inseparable, inter-relationship with the world of energy that surrounds and permeates us, we can begin to understand how we can experience a direct effect of the logotype on us when we wear it. The effect of a logo on our body will be influenced by its position, its size, colour and content.

Every part of our body has its own energy value—our arm, head or heart, for example—and a logo placed over this part is capable of shifting the energy. Each chakra absorbs and radiates a specific energy that affects us in different ways. Some believe this affect to be so powerful that, at a Rudolf Steiner school I visited, the children are banned from wearing any clothing with symbols. This included designer labels as well as other devices such as butterflies, angels, Tinkerbell and Mickey Mouse. I could not help feeling that, once we become aware of these subtle but powerful effects on our body, as Rudolf Steiner certainly was, we will become more careful about the colours and decorations we place on ourselves.

Employees who walk under the corporate fascia on the way into work, or brush the soles of their shoes against the company logo woven into the carpet at head office, may be unwittingly bathed in the 'loglo', the aura of the logo described by Naomi Klein. Reflexology (a complementary therapy that works on the feet to help heal the whole person) can affect our health; with this knowledge we can understand that subtle levels of energy from the logotype could impact us through the soles of our feet.

Do we really want Calvin Klein wrapped around the area of our body attributed to physical manifestation, or Nike, and all it stands for, across our heart, the area of compassion and healing?

The sacral chakra governs
our self confidence and
creativity

'It's fun seeing my label on someone's behind – I like that.'
Calvin Klein

Logos seep into our psyche

Journalist Hilary Curtis, states about the rebranding of the terrestrial TV stations that the new logos '. . . should, if the branding gurus have done their job, have seeped into the nation's psyche, reinforcing viewers' loyalty.'[15]

Depending on the value and extent of the energy around a logotype, it could be affecting us from some distance, even as we walk past or watch an advertisement, or when we wear branded clothing or eat branded products. The impact of this effect is also dependent, for example, on the strength and susceptibility of our own field and the energy and strength of the logo including its method of projection. Even our relationship with it and whether or not the symbol stands for something we personally love or hate will affect our response to it.

Whatever the immediate effect of a logo upon us, we unknowingly multiply this effect in our subconscious. We have seen our energy fields can be increased by making us feel good about ourselves—and with the backing of PR, marketing and advertising, the logo promises that we will feel even better if we ally ourselves with the brand. We then continue to project good feelings back into the logotype, 'loving' it and further increasing its energy or power—and this is the brand experts' dream. We sometimes love a brand so much we will even buy, and proudly display, clothes, for example, inscribed with 'Coke' or 'Vodafone' although Coca-Cola makes drinks and Vodafone makes mobile phones. We pay them to advertise their product on unrelated items! We buy them because a celebrity is seen to endorse them, and somehow we believe that by buying the product, or wearing the logotype, we will steal a little of the feel-good factor via the brand. We could actually say that we don't buy physical products; we buy *energy*.

Managing this intangible resource is a challenge to those in control of branding and design.

CHAPTER FOUR

Keeping the power alive

'What is the most valuable substance known to man? Not gold, coal, railways, oil. The most valuable substance known to man is even less tangible than electricity. It is brands. No one any more asks, "What's in a name?" because we all know the answer. A lot of money.'

STEPHEN BAYLEY, 'HOW DO YOU VALUE A BRAND?' *GQ MAGAZINE*

How do companies manage the energy that is alive in their logotype? This intangible asset can make or break their brand; it is a complex process that comprises constant assessment, control and maintainence.

At an innate level, we may feel and understand the quantum dynamics of symbols and logos. So did our ancestors. The outpouring of grief at the assassination of Thomas à Becket in 1170 by Henry II of England led to the design of symbolic badges that were mass-produced for visitors to purchase in remembrance. Visitors would touch these badges to the tomb and then to themselves as if to connect with the energy of the dead archbishop.[1] Today, T-shirt manufacturers would probably gain licences to print the appropriate symbol so that we might wear it across our chests.

We are aware of the potential effect of latent energy worn near our bodies. Recall the vastly inflated auction prices reached when Princess Diana's dresses sold well above their material value after her death and the auction on eBay of Kate Moss's tracksuit (unwashed for greater value!). A friend auctioned, for charity, a member of the royal family's polo shirt after it was left behind at the end of a game. The money gained for each of these items was well above its intrinsic value. Bristol-based psychologist Bruce Hood once told the story of how he offered a group of journalists a free, attractive cardigan. All of them put their hands up, only to bring them down again unanimously when he revealed it had once belonged to the murderer Fred West.[2] Just a dress, a tracksuit, a shirt and a cardigan—different response, different value.

The money factor

To help us understand logotype energy, it is useful to consider how we view hard cash. Some people see money as a form of energy. In our current economic structure, where money is the standard by which we measure success, it is our understanding and use of this energy that helps us achieve the future we desire. The energy of a logotype is comparable to the energy of money; on their own they are worthless, inanimate objects, but they add credentials and value to that which they represent. Both can be symbols of strength and success.

Like brands though, money can fall out of favour. A charity was forced to refuse a donation because a group of Christians found the source of the money, a theatre production, offensive. An article in *The Sunday Times* headlined 'Christian right threatens Jerry Springer opera' stated a 'militant Christian group forced Maggie's Centres, a Scottish cancer charity, to turn down a £3,000 donation from the show by threatening to picket its premises.'[3]

It appears that money from certain sources can also be 'tainted' by its owners. Donations have also been refused by the British Labour Party, including the rejection of £1 million from Bernie Ecclestone, the Formula One tycoon, when it conflicted with the proposed banning of tobacco advertisements at sporting events.

And yet money is a global language, theoretically neutral in its own right. A recent anti-drugs campaign stated that 99 per cent of all paper money in the UK contained traces of cocaine, but I have heard of no one refusing notes because they may have passed through the hands of a drug user or dealer.

But money, like a logo, can make us feel good. And this feel-good factor can affect us physically. An experiment conducted during Sky1's *Body Language Secrets* series in March 2010, showed that handling money gives us security, status and confidence and makes us feel invincible. The participants were divided into two groups. The first group was given a pile of money to count; the second were given blank sheets of paper. Each group was then given a list of words with one letter missing, which they were asked to fill in. The list given to the first group contained words relating to money, while the list given to the second group comprised random, unrelated words. Each group was then asked to plunge their hand into a large glass of ice-cube-filled water for as long a comfortable. The group of participants who had counted the money kept their hands in for a significantly longer time. The results were 'quite dramatically different.' The experimenters concluded the existence of the physical effect of money, which in this experiment 'hardens you to pain.'[4] Could selected logos increase our resilience to exterior forces?

Measuring the energy of a logotype

Often, we demand scientific proof even when our gut feeling and intuition scream a different reality to the one that presents itself to our logical mind. However, breakthroughs in scientific research enable us to validate many alternative, often ancient, beliefs as well as things we may intuitively know.

In the medical field, diagnostic equipment is being developed to detect abnormalities before they manifest into physical disease (in the way that some medical intuitives can). Could these machines be used for measuring the energy around a logotype, and the effect on its surroundings?

There are specially designed cameras that record people's auras. Subjects are photographed against a neutral background and when the film is developed, different colours can be seen radiating out from the person's body. It is also possible to record the person's aura, live, on a computer screen and monitor changes in the subject's energy field as they occur, for example, when he or she is subjected to different stimuli, such as clothing or logos.

Marco Grove makes angel prayer bowls in England. When photos were taken, using this special photographic process, of subjects alone and then holding a bowl, as well as of the bowl alone, 'the results were quite astonishing, as they showed the immediate shift that occurred as the bowl was placed into a person's auric field.' Even more amazing was the fact that the 'results of the bowl were equally breathtaking.'[5]

Less scientific, but believed by many to be comparably effective, is the kinesiological process of muscle-testing as a measuring tool. This process is based on the premise that our bodies can tell us more accurate information about certain things than our brain, where logic and rationalisation might get in the way. It is used extensively by researcher and physician David Hawkins, MD, PhD, to measure the energy of everything from emotions to television commercials.[6]

I personally experienced the potential validity of this method. Many people seemed to be wearing jewellery incorporating Christian crosses even though, I felt, they were not actually churchgoers. I remarked to a friend that they might have chosen to wear that symbol because they felt it gave them some form of calm or protection in a frenetic world. My friend vehemently disagreed with this conclusion and proceeded to perform a small but effective experiment to illustrate why, in his opinion, I should not wear one of these crosses.

First he drew a Christian style of cross on paper and I muscle-tested weakly. However, when I looked at an equal-sided cross or an Ankh style, my muscle test was strong. In kinesiological terms, this means that I was weakened by my connection with the first symbol. My friend's explanation was that the Christian cross has been associated with so much pain and suffering that this has become embedded in the symbol. Others I have spoken to about this believe that it may be because it is shaped like a sword, a weapon of destruction. I took this information to a very experienced group of dowsers who, after initially scoffing at the apparent absurdity of this claim, returned the following week, having themselves tested negatively using similar processes.

Exploring some of the techniques above, I decided to test the energy of corporate logotypes using a simple experiment.

First, I downloaded and printed out, in colour, logotypes from companies in the FTSE 100 list. I then placed each one in a separate blank envelope and asked a friend, who knew nothing about the experiment, to shuffle the envelopes and pick out 20. We numbered the selected envelopes consecutively for future reference.

Our bodies have an aura, an energy that surrounds and permeates us. The symbols we wear affect our energy and create a specific interface between us and the outside world.

I needed criteria against which the results could be measured. The most obvious one was the share price. Taking the prices from one selected day in the *Financial Times*, I chose to measure the results against the same prices exactly a week later, after the experiments had been completed. The definitive question I asked of those being tested was: 'Will the share price of the company represented by the logo in this envelope increase, decrease or remain the same a week from this date?'

For the first test, I employed someone who used an aura-reading computer. We set it up using a colleague who knew nothing of the procedure. After the machine had settled on the subject's existing aura, to be used as the standard or benchmark, she placed, one by one, each of the envelopes against her solar plexus and we monitored the results. With each envelope a marked difference in her auric field was visible on the screen. The variations ranged from the colourful to the spiky and the dull and also differed in size.

The interpretation of this was difficult because the results did not offer a clear answer to the question. Based on the changes in the subject's aura, however, we believe that we have been presented with some amazing findings and challenges. It seemed that the contents of envelopes, which appeared identical, affected the subject differently.

In the second test I used muscle-testing, as used in applied kinesiology, to check the response. For this exercise I contacted Gwynne Davies, a renowned nutritionist who has successfully used this process over many years to test his patients for food and medicine intolerance. On his recommendation we tested his wife and myself as well.

During this process, we simply asked the question as stated above as the subject held each envelope in the area of their solar plexus. A strong muscle response indicated a rise in the shares; a weak response meant they would go down; and an inconclusive one meant that they would remain the same.

On opening the envelopes at the end of the week, I found that both Gwynne and I had a number of inconclusive results. I scored seven correct out of 20 and Gwynne had 12, but Rosemarie, his wife, got 16 correct. I would like to think that her results were the most accurate because she was the most neutral, and therefore the least attached to the final outcome. However, of course, this might be wishful thinking on my part.

Finally, in search of a dowser, I was recommended someone who had experienced considerable success using a pendulum. She was nervous about the experiment, as she strongly believes that these techniques should not be used to gain money. After I had reassured her that these envelopes would not be opened until the stock market had closed on the seventh day, she agreed—albeit a little reluctantly.

We arranged all the envelopes on a table and she hung the pendulum over each in turn. I recorded a clockwise, anti-clockwise or neutral direction to indicate a rise, a fall or a static position in the share price. The results of this technique were amazing: she scored 19 out of the 20 answers *wrong*, and the one she did get right was that with the smallest change in the share price.

I queried this amazing response with Serena Roney-Dougal, one of the few people in Britain with a PhD for a parapsychological thesis. Serena told me this was a common response known in the industry as *psi reversal*. I thus felt this exercise was a resounding success.

These are small taster exercises and although they do not constitute a scientific proving, they do indicate that the logo holds some sort of imprint that is measurable, an energy that can affect and inform us.

If there is a measurable effect, I want to know more about it and when it reaches me. Some Reiki practitioners are aware that specially designed symbols can effect change in a person or a space. I know of some practitioners who practise the technique of 'throwing' Reiki healing symbols into a space, or even at a person, to clear or prepare energy. Sometimes we may not be aware of this action; sometimes we may not want it. It is also possible to throw a logo at a person or space. Logotypes also have an effective energy with their own values 'charged' through branding and marketing. Both are symbolic devices, specially designed and programmed to manipulate our space. Yet, while Reiki and branding both use symbols as tools for change, one is largely seen as for the greater good, while the other is subjected to all sorts of flak. Do we, as unwitting receivers of this intention, wish to be subjected to others' opinions of what is best for us?

My personal view is that I want to know when these energetic forms are winging their way to me. I want to have a choice; I will decide whether they are beneficial to my wellbeing. But how do we protect ourselves from something invisible to our normal senses?

Traditionally, people have been taught to imagine shields, or bubbles, around themselves and—unlikely as it seems—this may just work.

USA psychologist William Braud completed experiments where participants were told to shield themselves from those trying to influence them. The influence was measured via electro-dermal activity using a lie detector, which works beyond the conscious mind. Those being influenced were able to block any response from their colleagues by using shields as described above. This might help us to deflect the constant bombardment of design and marketing stimuli from ourselves.

Of course, if we are worried about companies entering our mind set, perhaps we can take heart from the fact that *they* may also wonder who is listening in! Once the brand connection is established, it is not a one-way street. Thoughts, impressions and intentions might be articulated in, or stimulated by, a logo, but they can affect the recipient whether they originate from the consumer or the brand company. Former chairman of BP, Lord Browne, attributed the success of the BP brand to the fact that, 'The best way to do business is to consider the mutual advantage between the company and the people you touch.'[7] The two-way communication is vital for the success of a brand; the challenge lies in controlling the quality of the exchange.

Managing the energy

Once a brand is defined and expressed in a logo, the challenge is to control and maximise its benefit to the company that owns it. The logo visually stakes out the brand's ownership. It is vital to control its exposure. Being seen in the wrong place, alongside the wrong 'friends' or 'behaving badly', will damage the fabric of the whole brand.

Logos act as signposts to the brands' boundaries, displaying their presence and keeping out the competition. Where a logo is not visible in a particular country or area of business, it is more than likely that the brand product is not there either. Logos visibly stake out the parameters of the brand field, and their owners will go to great lengths to legally establish their authority. The design, including names, symbols, graphics and even colour, will be registered for their sole use in a defined market. Each of these factors has a bearing in the energy field.

With large companies investing millions in branding, they will register hundreds of potential names—including new possibilities to keep options open for future developments, and similar-looking variations to stop unscrupulous competitors using them. Despite these precautions and the enormous sums paid to company lawyers, there are still occasional clashes. Lloyd's of London, commonly known as just Lloyd's, shares the same name as one of the leading UK banks, Lloyds Banking Group—commonly referred to, even by journalists, as Lloyds. Abbey National, the name of a major building society before it was taken over by Santander, dropped the 'National' because they believed everyone referred to it simply as 'Abbey'. The name doubtlessly became much more user-friendly. Unfortunately, at the time of this change there was an unhappy building company with the short name as well. Not so much confusion perhaps for the average high-street shopper, but it shows how jealously companies guard their names. They cannot afford to share the energy of their own brand.

In our global economy, there are real challenges in defining boundaries. Virtually identical products are manufactured in the same location to be branded differently. Staff will move from company to company, and a look at any major annual report and accounts will reveal that the majority of directors are responsible for more than one company.

Companies overlap. There is no longer an easily definable physical boundary. The identifying device is the logotype; it is this that enables companies to label and stake their claim in the global territory, shared by the businesses before and after them, to attract and secure brand loyalty.

In the corporate world, we are working at energetic levels as never before. With the advent of technology, information such as music, videos and books can be downloaded at the touch of a button. Copyright, for example, used to be relatively straightforward when we had a physical object to register. Ownership of physical property is easier to justify than ownership of information, especially when the information becomes detached from the physical plane and can be transmitted in seconds to thousands of people in different countries.

Paul Virilio describes this trend in his book *The Information Bomb*: 'Only a few centuries after having been, with Copernicus and Galileo, the *science of the appearance* of a relative truth, techno-science is once again becoming a *science of the disappearance* of that same truth with the coming of a knowledge which is not so much encyclopaedic as cybernetic, a knowledge which denies all objective reality.' He goes on to say: 'After the end of "history", prematurely announced a few years ago by Francis Fukuyama,[8] what is being revealed here are the beginnings of the "end of space" of a small planet held in suspension in the electronic ether of our modern means of telecommunication.'

Virilio continues; 'We are not seeing "an end of history", but we are seeing "an end of geography".'

To quote from the book *Digital Aboriginal* by Mikela Tarlow and Philip Tarlow: 'We have entered a very unstable world where information in the form of pure energy can easily fly out of the door and morph into a thousand variations of the product or service we used to think we owned.' This energy escapes traditional boundaries and affects everything it touches—with or without control.

The creation and management of business boundaries is simply good housekeeping. Companies can register and protect the physical design—but they cannot own the emotions that they so carefully link to the logo through the branding process. It really is a case of: who owns the wind? Left unchecked, logos take on a life of their own as brand-hungry consumers vie to label themselves with the graphics, unscrupulous competitors try to copy it, ambitious journalists display it beside flattering or contentious reports in the global press, and fashion fluctuates with randomised regularity. Brand managers must decide on the appearance, tone and position of the logo, and continue to monitor its stance in the ever-fluctuating marketplace. Some boundaries will be created to be firm and immovable, such as the integrity of the logo design; others might be deliberately blurred to gain benefit from the glow of a closely related brand. Modern logos promise more than a guarantee of quality in their seductively tempting offer of a better lifestyle. The display, extent and appearance of the logo are all directly related to the quality of the offer and can both enhance or destroy the brand credibility. Working at invisible, subtle levels, the brand experts will control the selected territory. As corporate objectives and products merge, sharing directors and ingredients, brands that are virtually identical compete. They are bought and sold on the promise of goodwill. The logo is paramount in sealing the deal. The logo ringfences the perimeter of the area to be negotiated.

Branding the parent company

Historically, the product and the company were synonymous: Coca-Cola the company sold Coca-Cola the drink; Cadburys sold Cadburys chocolate, and Ford sold Ford cars. Great companies were synonymous with great products. As businesses became more complex, with branded products being developed, bought and sold, holding companies maintained a lower profile, preferring to invest in promoting the product—the mainstay of the business.

The rewards of the current sophisticated branding processes, which have been successfully applied to products, has encouraged holding companies to adopt their own specialist branding techniques for their corporate benefit.

Jeremy Bullmore of the WPP Group says: 'It is becoming more and more apparent that, far from brands being hierarchically inferior to companies, only if companies are managed as brands can they hope to be successful.'[9] Their market is different but equally important, and this difference is recognised even if the company still shares the same name as its products. The tone of their 'voice' in marketing, publicity and advertising—as well as the way in which they display themselves in print and publicity—will differ as appropriate.

The company brand will have a more limited exposure on items such as stationery ranges and financial documentation through to corporate flags. The product brand must have consumer appeal, and will be applied to a vast range of promotional, publicity and advertising material. Bullmore also states that a brand's 'name, its packaging, its stores if it has any, its vans, its news value can all give people important clues to a brand's character: and in some instances, these non-advertising communications media will be the all-important ones.' He goes on to say: 'The extension of the principles of branding from product to company means opening up the whole marketing strategy to absolutely everyone within that company. It means realising that every corporate action, every corporate decision, every corporate communication will be seen as a clue—as one of those all-important scraps and straws from which people build brands.'

The parent company and the product are inextricably linked for mutual benefit, but the perception of the relationship can vary according to the needs of each.

While the closest relationship between the company and its products occurs when they share the same name and imagery, this creates limited ability to brand other products corporately. Lynx barber shops, Colgate Kitchen Entrees and Pond's toothpaste failed to meet targets.[10] Similarly, it would be difficult to sell Cadbury painkillers or Coca-Cola retirement homes. And it would be confusing if a company other than the Coca-Cola Corporation sold Coca-Cola. Few companies, however, can survive on just one or two product lines, and even those 'monolithic' sounding companies have developed other, differently named, brands. A problem that once hit Perrier water probably did not affect sales of Kit Kat, even though both brands are owned by Nestlé, known for making chocolate. If Unilever's Dove soap hit a crisis, it would not directly damage the perception of its other products, such as Marmite, PG Tips or Flora.

There are exceptions to this, such as Richard Branson's company Virgin, where everything, from wedding dresses, gyms, trains, vodka, condoms and pensions to music CDs, has been identified with the same name. Another exception is Boots the Chemist, with its solid credibility laid down by benevolent founder Jesse Boot. It manages to brand its own-name goods successfully—from sandwiches to tampons.

On branded product items, such as packaging, product stationery and advertising, the parent company can decide on the optimum level of endorsement that will be beneficial to both the brand and the company. The simplest (legal minimum) identification to a holding company can be in small print, which requires the consumer to actively seek the ultimate parentage of the brand. When the relationship is identified with a logo, we get the message and the link.

Whether a business decides to whisper or scream its ownership on a product, the pros and cons of the company name versus the brand name will be considered; the name with the most potential will dominate.

For example, Microsoft dominates Microsoft Word, whereas Birds Eye dominates Proctor and Gamble. Sometimes they are of equal weight, such as in Gillette Sensor.[11]

According to Ries and Ries, authors of *The 22 Immutable Laws of Branding*, the more successful brands are those separated from the parent company so that they may be specifically targeted to their audience. Du Pont does not sell Du Pont petrol; there is no Unilever ice cream, and there are no Proctor and Gamble-named crisps. While it may be a legal requirement for companies to state the owner of the product, what consumer knows or cares that Pearson owns Penguin Books or that Altria owns Philip Morris and Kraft? Once they are named and identified differently, they are perceived differently. Conversely, a company may deliberately brand itself to be associated with its products for mutual benefit. We may know about Nestlé branded chocolate, coffee and condensed milk, but did we know that they also own Herta frankfurters? Heinz may be famous for baked beans and ketchup, but it also owns Linda McCartney meals. The logo clarifies the difference.

A less visible link between the parent company and products allows for more flexibility in business. With brand values being quoted as an asset on the balance sheet, a brand that is visibly separated from its owner, the holding company, has the advantage of being able to be sold as a separate asset without compromising the perception of the parent company. What Burger King devotee ever noticed that Diageo sold the brand; were they even aware of the ownership in the first place? Prospective investors, on the other hand, do need to know the brands produced by a company in order to make an informed choice on their financial portfolio.

Even brand statements vary according to the product. Products may have straplines; companies have mission or vision statements. Coca-Cola the drink may be 'the real thing', but Coca-Cola the company, according to the corporate website, 'exists to benefit and refresh everyone it touches'.

The choice exists for companies to mix and match according to their objectives and stir in the logos into the beneficial pot for an optimum outcome.

Sibling competitors

Competition is a challenge for new brands, as they contend with a finite number of raw resources and a limited number of new potential customers.

Starbucks is one actively competitive brand that has gained remarkable success. It deliberately positions many outlets in locations chosen so as to set up competition, not only with other coffee shops, but also with its own. In just a few years, it became of the USA's best-known and most popular brands. By focusing on a single product, Starbucks has certainly made us more aware of the range of coffees available, and has benefited coffee sales generally.

Would we be so enthralled by buying cola, if at least two major companies ceased to strategically differentiate themselves, identify themselves separately and encourage us, competitively, to drink the stuff?

We feel differently about the coffee or the cola of choice when we see the respective identifying logos, but each will stimulate a desire to drink.

Companies develop competing brands to ensure we are using one of theirs. Danone owns both the Evian and Volvic branded waters; Unilever owns Surf, Omo and Lux soap powder, and Associated British Foods owns two tea brands—Jacksons of Piccadilly and Twinings—as well as Allinsons and Kingsmill breads. These are usually sold side by side, the logo identifying them as two different products.

Each brand is targeted at separate audiences who are usually unaware of the corporation behind the product. The products themselves may be virtually identical. There is a limited range of soap powder ingredients, for example, that can be added to a product before it starts to damage clothes or ceases to clean effectively. Branded separately, their appeal will vary. The mother who wants her children to look smart, the housekeeper who prides herself on whiter-than-white sheets and shirts, or the family that takes eco-friendliness seriously will choose their logos accordingly. This differentiation enables the company to reach a greater percentage of the market, keeping outside competitors at bay, while appearing to be specialists in a defined field.

Branding the brands

When brands strive to be the best in their field, where else can they look to raise their profile even higher? They ringfence themselves into a group and give it a logo representing even better, shared values. They brand the brands!

The organisation Superbrands set up an initiative called Cool Brandleaders with a council made up of eminent experts in the field of branding who invite the public to vote for their own favourite brands each year.

Another scheme identifies brands that claim to live up to their promise; a 'Brand Power' logo is displayed as an endorsement on selected advertisements. From their website,[12] it would appear that the products that form part of this exclusive 'club' are not necessarily claiming to be the best in their field, just that they live up to their brand claims. The site states: 'We're not an independent body—manufacturers pay to use our service. However, all claims made in a Brand Power commercial must be substantiated legally to ensure that they are true. Our objective is to avoid gimmicks and hype in the promotion of products. Instead, we accurately articulate key reasons a particular product is worthy of your attention when choosing at your local store.'

This does not say much for the bulk of the other brand advertising and promotion, or for the standards of the Advertising Standards Authority, the independent regulator for advertisements in the UK!

Young consumers

Companies endeavour to reach out to young children and students alike. Children can influence around 20 per cent of home purchases, and they are less acute than adults at seeing through marketing hype. Most mothers would pay a little extra, for some peace and quiet, for a branded cereal or soft drink rather than a cheaper supermarket version. As children seek to find their own place in society, brands are only too happy to provide appealing standards to alleviate the insecurities of growing up.

One school in the USA made a ten-year $4-million deal with Dr Pepper;[13] a student who wore a Pepsi shirt to a Coca-Cola sponsorship day at high school was suspended for the insurrection.[14] As long ago as the 1960s, I remember being told a story by my college teacher about an American boy who turned up in his school uniform during a casualwear day because, although he had jeans, he 'had no Lees' and refused to be seen by his peers in any other brand.

On a recent trip to Paris, we were frequently stopped in the street by young Chinese people asking us to buy them Louis Vuitton wallets—stating that the store would only let them buy three at a time. Despite their willingness to thrust hundreds of Euros into our hands, we declined, because the queue of young Chinese people, waiting to purchase one particular heavily LV-branded wallet, reached out of the door and into the night air. And all this, according to one of Louis Vuitton's executives quoted in the press, for purses made out of some printed plastic stuck to canvas.

One theory is that these global luxury brands help build the younger generation's fragile self-confidence about the future by creating and appealing to those too young and immature to create their own ideals.

Children are now being encouraged to form brands of themselves in order to market companies' products on the internet. They are given advice on marketing and offered a commission from sales of the products they help to promote. Even children as young as seven are offered the chance to become 'mini-marketers' to their Facebook friends as they are encouraged to mention brands such as drinks produced by the Coca-Cola company, Cheesestrings and the Barbie MP3 player.[15]

Celebrities showing us the way

If we still have doubts about which products to choose, we can look to 'trusted' celebrities, employed by branding professionals, to help us.

While researching for their book *Celebrity Worship*[16] the authors found that about a third of people suffer from what they call 'celebrity worship syndrome'—and that it affects their wellbeing. About one per cent of people interviewed displayed a 'borderline pathological' condition.

Francisco Gil-White, an evolutionary anthropologist from Pennsylvania University, argues that we need celebrities to show us the way to success, and that they provide the educational and entertaining fables once sought in fairy tales and the Bible.[17]

Actors have replaced skilled pensions advisers; celebrity models advise us on the health of our hair, and members of the royal family (seldom seen shopping) endorse products and outlets.

David Beckham's appearance is known to add tremendous value to any product, the bulk of which bear no relation to his professional skills as a footballer. Logos are plastered over expensive, must-have, football shirts. They belong to corporations with operating practices divorced from the game, but for huge sums of money they can identify themselves with the success factor.

Tag Heuer (Swiss watches) directly attributes its success to being seen on some of the greatest names in motor racing—as well as on Steve McQueen, who visibly wore it during the 1970 film *Le Mans*.

Britney Spears has been associated with Clairol shampoo, Polaroid cameras, McDonald's and Pepsi. Venus and Serena Williams have promoted Reebok and Puma as well as Avon, Wrigley's and Sega. These celebrities parade their chosen brands as often as they can. I don't know what brands Jason Taylor, voted the National Football League's Defensive Player of the Year in 2006, is paid to promote, but he stated: 'On Fridays training finishes early, so in the evening I like to dress up in Armani or Zegna and take my wife out on a date.'[18] While we identify with brands, they identify us as well.

Perhaps this rather over-the-top adulation is why Gordon Brown, UK prime minister 2007-2010 pledged to bring an end to the cult of celebrity. Yet, according to journalist Ephraim Hardcastle, this move was scorned by media tycoon Peter Bazalgette, who stated that: 'People have always been fascinated by the famous, whether it's Nell Gwynn or Dick Turpin. Some people have always been famous for being famous and that's the way it will remain. If Gordon Brown thinks he can change human nature, good luck to him. Frankly, I think he's talking b******s.'[19]

When celebrity worship combines with brand worship we have one of the most powerful motivators for sales, which benefits both the celebrity *and* the product brand during the continuing process.

Walking through Trafalgar Square in London, I came across huge letters reminiscent of Stonehenge, which spelt out the name 'Will Smith'. I felt quite excited at having a celebrity about to be dropped into my path and phoned a friend who I was meeting in Piccadilly Circus. She, however, was equally excited, as she was in a store buying Lancôme make-up specials. Lancôme has been fronted by Kate Winslet, Anne Hathaway, Uma Thurman and Julia Roberts. For a moment, at least, we were both seduced by the brand promise. There are times when the temptation overcomes the will to resist—and this is what those in charge of brands hope for.

They will even tap into politics when it suits. A British newspaper, *London Life* published an article on 14 January headed: 'Global brands tap into the Obama "feelgood factor".' It stated: 'Global bands are cashing in on Barack Obama's swearing-in ceremony next week by launching "Obama" ad campaigns. Companies including Pepsi, Ikea, TGI Friday's and Dunkin' Donuts are all trying to tap into the US President-elect's "feelgood" factor to reach new customers. Pepsi is using the 20 January event to launch its "Pepsi optimism project" with the slogan "Yes You Can" and a redesigned red, white and blue logo that strongly resembles the Obama campaign image. Ben & Jerry's have brought out a new flavour ice cream, Yes Pecan, with profits going to an education fund that encourages participation in democracy.'[20]

If all else fails, statistics can be quoted and experts brought in to reassure us that we are buying the best. No stone is left unturned in the pursuit to convince us of the necessity of buying a particular brand, over and above another. Whether we buy it to appease the children, attain a perceived higher level of living or health, or simply because we find we like it, the logo identifies a place where we want to be.

As long as the logo is shining, we want a piece of it. The challenge of a successful brand is to ensure that every time we see the logo, we feel good and continue to want to be associated with it.

Maintaining the energy

A successful logotype is like a seed, full of potential and capable of bearing fruit if it is carefully nurtured. Once a brand is established, the challenge is to maintain and build on its success.

Built on an ideal for a better life, the success of a brand depends on the continuation of that belief for its survival in an ever-changing market. The world moves on and the brand must be seen to be keeping up, or ahead. Sometimes it is necessary to tweak the design of the logotype, often imperceptibly when it starts to look tired and depleted as fashion changes. It can be freshened up, subtly manipulated and relaunched. Depending on the amount of tidying and adjustment necessary, it may be launched as a new and improved brand; more often than not, however, companies are pleased when the cleaned-up image can be slipped in quietly without jeopardising existing goodwill. Perceptions of stability and innovation compete in the ever-pulsating tides of economic change.

Lloyds Banking Group's black horse, Coca-Cola's quirky script, and the GE (General Electric) circle are among those logos that have been revamped to look up-to-date, while retaining the integrity of the original familiar design. Similarly Pepsi and Starbucks have engaged in costly yet relatively subtle changes in their logotypes, both supported by extensive public relations campaigns structured to both reassure and promote the positive effect.

NBC redetailed their existing peacock symbol in an unobtrusive yet powerful way. Betty Hudson, who was then the vice-president of Corporate and Media Relations of NBC Inc, stated that when they were redesigning the existing symbol, they tested the new design against the old and 'more than 90% of the respondents could correctly identify the new design as being NBC and did not notice the difference.'

I recall a similar effect when a major British newspaper was redesigned. Taking some months to complete the assignment, the designer was delighted when she showed it to her mother, who could not see the difference between the new version and the old.

The changes may be subtle, almost imperceptible to the conscious eye, but they are essential for maintaining the design standards in a changing world. As our beloved celebrities go under the knife to remain the same to their audience, so the logo will have its wrinkles ironed out from time to time.

The maintenance and protection of a logo is vital if we are to continue to believe in the integrity of the brand. A poorly applied or inaccurately rendered logo might catch our attention, but we will instinctively know something is amiss. If we have been put off the brand by bad press or an unfavourable personal experience, our minds will override the carefully selected desirable emotions that the marketers have imprinted on the logo and replace them with our own, which might range from dissatisfaction through to loathing. If the logo no longer triggers enough of us to buy, it might be time to change it.

An established logo will be constantly monitored against fashion trends, the brand objectives, and the competition and state of the marketplace as a whole. Everything to do with its application will be considered, from the accuracy of the colours, the placement on a page in a magazine or on a billboard, the space around the logo itself, and the number of times we will be bombarded with the design.

Brand managers will carefully consider if an action or event will add value to the brand by association and secure it for their benefit. Official sponsors at major sporting events will spend millions to be affiliated with the event, usually through the use of logos. This affiliation is stringently protected. Pepsi was an official sponsor at the 2003 cricket match between Australia and India. A businessman who refused to surrender the Coca-Cola can he was drinking from, and the three unopened ones in his possession, was removed from the stadium. Conversely, Coca-Cola was an official sponsor at the 2004 Olympic Games in Athens, and security guards confiscated cans of Pepsi from attendees at the entrance gates.[21]

Furthermore, it was not possible to buy a ticket to the Olympics using a credit card other than Visa, and staff would be on the lookout for T-shirts, bags and hats displaying non-sponsor brands. Even stewards and volunteer helpers, who may have been supplied with their own uniforms minus shoes, were advised not to wear trainers with a bright logo from a sports brand that was not an official sponsor such as Adidas. The latter has also complained that many companies are 'infringing' its trademark by using stripes on their clothing products.[22]

These draconian laws continued into the 2012 London Olympics, where the 2006 Olympics Act made it illegal to combine words such as 'games', 'summer', 'gold' or '2012' in any form of advertising and marketing. Technically, police are able to arrest a taxpayer for wearing a Pepsi T-shirt.[23]

Companies go to great lengths to protect their imagery. The financial benefit of logo recognition is so great that the illegal practice of brand piracy, where the logo (or a recognisably similar version) is applied to a cheap copy of the product. Sold for a fraction of the cost, it can net the perpetrators a handsome profit. We may know that it is not an original Calvin Klein jumper, Kellogg's cereal, Flora margarine or Chanel perfume, but if the logo looks like the original we still feel as if we are buying into some of the brand energy. Those who buy pirated versions might be denied a superior brand 'hit', but the logo identifies the brand from its competitors and is the easiest part to forge. It is the visual trigger for our emotions, which tug us towards the purchase.

CHAPTER FIVE

Falling in love with the logo
*'If people fall out of love with your brand,
you go out of business.'*

RITA CLIFTON, CHIEF EXECUTIVE OF INTERBRAND

If corporations can get us to love their logos, we will want to be aligned with them—buy their products, services and shares, even work for them. We will want to be a part of their success. If they can do this in the first instance, we will be hooked as we continue to seek out and re-experience the good feeling that we enjoyed from the original brand hit.

An experiment conducted by Dr Richard Wiseman, Hertfordshire University-based psychologist, has shown that the best way to make yourself feel happier is to think of something good that happened to you the day before.[1] Dr William Bloom, known as Britain's leading holistic teacher, has revealed a revolutionary method that produces endorphins.[2] People feel better when they focus on an image that has made them feel good in the past. Bloom suggests a strawberry as an example, but the imagery is their choice based on what works for them. It could equally be the sight of a logo that triggers the feel-good response; in the former, *we* have created the link and in the latter, the link has been created for us. But the principles are the same. On this basis, if brands can make us happy, just once, they have established a solid foundation from which to grow the feel-good factor by using the logo as a simple and effective prompt of the initial emotion. The logo becomes our strawberry and just thinking of it could make us feel good and wanting more.

The in-house corporate 'glow'

Logo loyalty starts from within the company and is evident in employees' willingness to be identified with the design on hats, T-shirts and golf umbrellas, or doing their job driving vans, presenting proposals or entertaining clients with logo-encrusted glasses.

When the logo is loved from the inside out, it shows. And when the outside world loves the logo, the workers will be proud to be associated with it. When the Apple store opened in London in 2004, Apple reportedly received more than 4,000 applications for 120 job vacancies.

This loyalty to the logo can lead to the creation of a great deal of resistance to change, so any new design implementation must be delicately handled. This personal attachment is particularly obvious in mergers and acquisitions, where the perceived 'loser' forfeits their logo.

When engineering firms William Press and Fairclough merged, I was responsible for handling their new design, and it was the William Press image that was taken forward by the new organisation. However, as a token gesture to the apparent 'losing team', the corporate colour was changed from William Press red to Fairclough orange (while ensuring that the reddest orange possible was used).

In the case of the merger of Lloyds and TSB banks, the Lloyds' black horse won out. It could be argued that it was the stronger brand—but there was a definite air of success around those at Lloyds that was not enjoyed by their colleagues from TSB. The black horse imagery has gone from strength to strength while it evolves with the company, as indicated in an article in *The Sunday Times* headed: 'Lloyds TSB is banking on the "human cyclone." Terri Dial, an American woman, has been appointed to one of the top jobs at Lloyds TSB bank. About to pack her bags for her return to Britain she has, apparently, already made one request: she wants a model of Lloyds' signature Black Horse in her London office.'[3]

The companies even give us heroes and friends to fall in love with; the Michelin man (Bibendum), Fred the Homepride flour man, Aleksandr Orlov the Meercat from Compare The Market, the Dulux dog, the Andrex puppy, even Richard Branson himself. Gareth Williams, in his book *Branded*, states that in the case of Kellogg's Frosties, 'Tony the Tiger befriends consumers by sharing their lives'.

Animals have existing, attributed characteristics that can be appealing to brands. Wild cats (Jaguar, Slazenger, Puma, MGM and **ING**) hint at power, speed and independence. Lloyds Bank and Ferrari share the black horse, which represents movement and freedom, the life force and manifestation. One of the most attributed powers of the horse is it ability to travel between different worlds – useful for a bank liaising with retail customers on the ground whilst negotiating in international economics and for a car that is built for speed.

In fact, we love them so much we will go to great lengths to protect them. A story from the *Daily Mail*, headlined 'Chubby Little Chef is rescued by fans'[4] stated that the character, called Charlie, who is displayed on the Little Chef restaurant's signs, was about to be made slimmer, as it was felt his overweight image was out of step in the current anti-obesity age. 'Hundreds of letters and thousands of emails' from customers convinced them to retain the familiar chubby image. Similarly, *Metro* reported under the heading 'Fans see red after Jaguar drops green'[5] that motorists felt 'the brand is being stripped of its roots' after Jaguar stated it was changing its classic green for black and replacing the Jaguar icon with a modern version. Gap felt pressured enough to scrap their new week-old logo after an online outcry in 2010. *BBC Business News* reported the fact in October 2010, stating that there 'was an outpouring of comments.' Marka Hansen, President of Gap Brand North America, stated; 'We heard them say over and over again they are passionate about our blue box logo, and they want it back.' They brought the old logo back. We do love our logos!

The seat of our emotions

'In the factories we make cosmetics;
in the shops we sell hope.'

CHARLES REVSON (FOUNDER OF REVLON)

Our hearts are powerful motivators for change. Experiments conducted at the Institute of HeartMath[6] in California have found remarkable evidence that the heart's electromagnetic field is around 5,000 times stronger than that produced by the brain. It can be measured several feet away from the body and can even transmit information between people. If they want us to really love their logo, businesses must appeal to our hearts.

People talk about being 'heartbroken', the 'heart of the matter' and of 'speaking from the heart'; for centuries, the heart has been considered the source of emotion, courage and wisdom. Tribal peoples such as the Sioux understood the importance of seeing with the heart: 'We Indians live in a world of symbols and images where the spiritual and the commonplace are one. We try to understand them not with the head but with the heart, and we need no more than a hint to give us the meaning.'[7]

It is through the heart that logos touch and spread our emotions. A brand needs to inspire passion. Logic and common sense are pushed to one side when our emotions drive our purchases.

Mary Weisnewski, a principal brand strategist at Methodologie, a Seattle-based brand firm, says in her article on *Brandchannel* 'Bypass the Brain and Go Straight to the Heart' that design is one of the most powerful tools for communicating brand emotions: 'It's the glue that connects logic and reason with imagination and feelings. Good design expresses the essence of a brand in ways that speak directly to the emotions. Brands need to make a connection with customers in the first seconds of initial contact and, by tapping into their hearts, consumers will have an instant emotional response that motivates them to act.'[8]

Brand managers are aware of the immense value and strength of this emotional tug. Three schools of thought have developed to explain how consumers are influenced by emotion in their appreciation of advertising and the use of trademarks. The first arose in 1949 and is referred to as the Irrational Weigher; it argues that consumers are misled by emotion and, for example, overvalue branded goods. The second school of thought is known as the Rational Maximiser, and is based on the belief that the emotional appeal is part of the product being sold. Purchasers will choose products that make them feel better. The third is known as the Cognitive Miser, describing consumers who, for example, use emotion as the easiest and most economical way to decide on a purchase, perhaps because the logo is familiar.

Researchers have shown that consumers will use trademarks as a key to decision-taking. They recognise the brand by the logo and buy accordingly.[9] This, of course, is self-perpetuating, as the brand familiarisation strengthens with each purchase.[10]

US attorney Siegrun Kane describes trademarks as ' . . . symbols of goodwill' and states that 'The value of this goodwill increases with length of use, advertising and sales.'[11]

In a decision in 1942, the Supreme Court described the trademark/goodwill relationship thus: 'The Protection of trademarks is the law's recognition of the psychological function of symbols. If it is true that

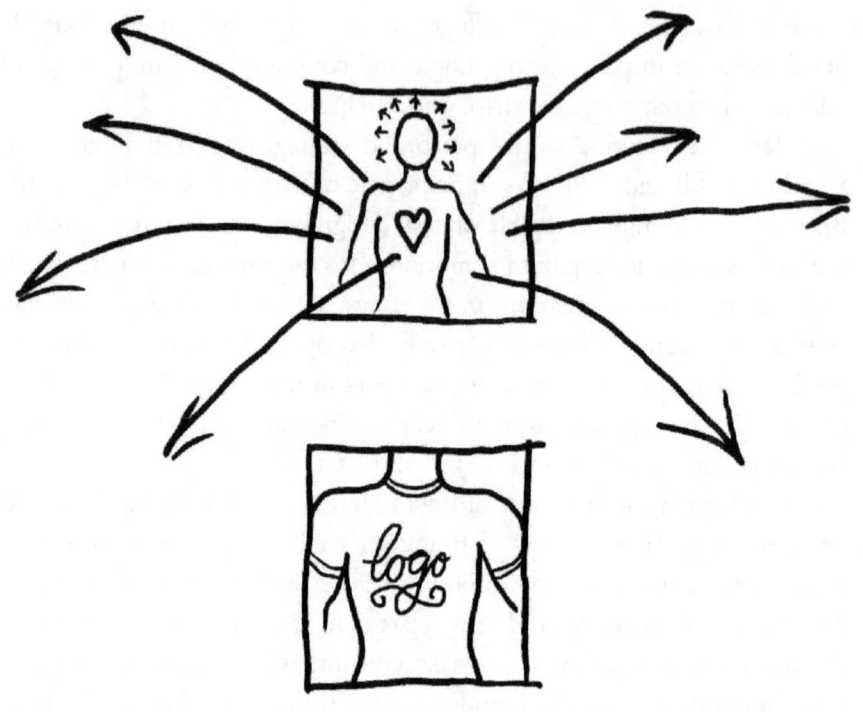

A logo over our heart acts
as a filter between our energy
and the world outside.
The energy of our heart will
be affected by the energy of
the logo

**'The heart's electrical field is about 60 times greater in amplitude
than the electrical activity generated by the brain.'**
Institute of HeartMath

we live by symbols, it is no less true that we purchase goods by them. A trademark is a merchandising shortcut which induces a purchaser to select what he wants, or what he has been led to believe he wants. The owner of a mark exploits this human propensity by making every effort to impregnate the atmosphere of the market with the drawing power of a congenial symbol. Whatever the means employed, the aim is the same—to convey through the mark, in the minds of potential customers, the desirability of the commodity upon which it appears. Once this is attained, the trademark owner has something of value. If another poaches upon the commercial magnetism of the symbol he has created, the owner can obtain legal redress.'[12]

Frank Schechter author of *The rational basis for trademark protection* argued for the recognition that a mark was not only a simple method to identify a producer, but also to 'identify a product as satisfactory and thereby to stimulate further purchases by the consuming public', calling it 'an agency for the actual creation and perpetuation of goodwill.'[13]

A first-class emotion

'The idea that business is just a numbers affair has always struck me as preposterous. For one thing, I've never been particularly good at numbers, but I think I've done a reasonable job with feelings. And I'm convinced that it is feelings—and feelings alone—that account for the success of the Virgin brand in all of its myriad forms.'
RICHARD BRANSON

The value of emotional intelligence is realised as being equal to, and perhaps more important than, the rational, learned type of intelligence that we are taught in schools and institutions. Our gut feeling and heart have much to offer in informing us about the world.

Daniel Goleman, author of *Emotional Intelligence,* states: 'A view of human nature that ignores the power of emotions is sadly shortsighted. The very name *Homo sapiens*, the thinking species, is misleading in light of the new appreciation and vision of the place of emotions in our lives that science now offers. As we all know from experience, when it comes to shaping our decisions and our actions, feeling counts every bit as much—and often more—than thought. We have gone too far in emphasizing the value and import of the purely rational—of what IQ measures—in human life. Intelligence can come to nothing when the emotions hold sway.'

In *Power Vs Force,*[14] Dr David R Hawkins states that the difference between power and force is that power 'appeals, uplifts, dignifies and ennobles' and 'energizes, gives forth, supplies and supports.' Force, on the other hand, always moves *against* something, it 'always creates counterforce', and it 'has an insatiable appetite, it constantly consumes' . . . 'Power gives life and energy, force takes these away.' He explains that power attracts; force repels. So, emotions such as love, compassion and forgiveness are very empowering—whereas revenge, judgement and condemnation make us weak. Eventually, Hawkins argues, in the long run the strong prevail—as can be seen in history.

Author and lecturer Wayne Dyer illustrates this aspect in his lecture *There is a Spiritual Solution to Every Problem*; he asks a volunteer to think about various emotions such as shame and love while he measures their responses through muscle-testing. It becomes apparent that emotions we see as negative, including shame, guilt and anger, weaken us, whereas positive emotions, such as love, joy and thoughts of beauty, appear to empower and strengthen the volunteer.

Brands tap into this. Coca-Cola's 2005 advertising campaign incorporated the word 'love' written in the brand lettering style. The ad included a man giving out free bottles of the drink as well as hugs. If simply writing or thinking a word can affect water, the magnitude of the effect of this 'heart-warming' style of advertising on the effect of the drink on us is probably immeasurable.

Even in the world's poorest societies, people will seek out and pay more for branded products rather than locally produced equivalents. I have witnessed people buying branded over-the-counter painkillers many times the price of supermarket brands, even though they have exactly the same ingredients. We really want to believe that the big brands care for us more; we want to trust them.

Companies spend fortunes to ensure that we fall in love with their logos. Branding experts have developed sophisticated methods of attaching extremely desirable values to a logo that effectively delivers and elicits the feel-good response; even a mere glimpse can touch our emotions and stimulate our desire to buy. Branding, through advertising and marketing, imbues a logo with feel-good factors, so that we wish to be associated with it—whether we wear it, eat it, use it, display it or invest in it.

Even when we are faced with death, brands can reach out to us. An article on the fashion industry by journalist Liz Jones (who has worked at publications including *Marie Claire*) tells of the story of one fashion editor who was diagnosed with cancer. She said: 'At least now I'll be able to wear Chloé.'[15]

It prompts the question of whether companies create or fulfil our dreams and desires, and whether brands really add value to our lives.

We buy the promise, based on lifestyle or emotional values. FedEx has a 'purple promise' that vows to make every customer experience outstanding across the entire organisation. Häagen-Dazs ice cream was built on the promise of sex, whereas Ben & Jerry's is more natural. Stolichnaya vodka promises Russian authenticity; Grey Goose vodka promises elegance. The Rolls-Royce promise of quality was so successful it has been made illegal for any other company to call themselves 'the Rolls-Royce of' whatever.

Can the purchase of a mere product really bring us happiness, fulfilment or even enlightenment? Perhaps it is not unthinkable that we could buy goods on a more informed basis such as on the ingredients, quality, ethical stance or price, but these qualities alone do not sell the quantity of goods required to keep companies in business.

As our basic *needs* are met in the consumerised world of plenty, it is our *wants* that become our driving motivator to purchase.

Does the product itself ever truly live up to our expectations as promised in the advertising? For how long? The feel-good factor is due to the advertising and marketing effort, which promises to enhance our lives. Perhaps we could be forgiven for believing the hype, as we are tempted to search for elusive lifestyle and emotional values. Who cares about ingredients when much more tempting, emotive brand promises are on offer? And when the companies have succeeded in convincing us to buy their products, the subsequent challenge is to encourage us to continue to

Home-grown fun has lots of flavor

The family circle is one of our cherished institutions. In the happy world of home life, simple pleasures light smiles on the faces of young folks and parents. The wholesome quality of Coca-Cola fits so properly into this picture —delicious and sparkling, always refreshing.

Serve
Coca-Cola
REG. U.S. PAT. OFF.

A logo, layered lavishly with brand messages via advertising and marketing, can stimulate our desires, regurgitate a host of memories and stir a range of emotions that extend far beyond our primal need for food or drink.

use them. Some aspect of the brand promise must resonate within us, to make us confident that this product will continue to change our lives for the better. Of course there are products that *are* good for us, but few are sold on physical benefits alone.

When we buy a prestigious item—a Ferrari, Jimmy Choo shoes or a Hermès necktie—would we be so satisfied with the product if the branding was not obvious, hopefully triggering the envy of our friends or the admiration of our colleagues? Would we feel the same about them if they were not recognisable brands? As long as the brand is in favour, we believe that we can buy our way into the hype. The brand promise *is* the product we buy.

Referring to an exhibition at London's Victoria and Albert Museum about branding, journalist Richard Benson called those susceptible to branding 'label-whores.' In his interview with Jane Pavitt, one of the curators at the V&A, Benson states: 'It used to be the case that the brand was built on ideas inherent in the product. Now it is often the case that a set of brand values will be pushed and the product just becomes the way of people buying in to the lifestyle.'

'Quality is important, but brands are not built by quality alone.' This is so inherent in building a brand that this is quoted in the book by Ries and Ries as one of *The 22 Immutable Laws of the Brand*. While we may think that we can detect the quality of a product or service, in reality this is not so. We know that competing products are often manufactured in the same building, to be stamped or labelled with different logotypes at the end of the production process, and yet we are still drawn to spending more for a name in the belief that we are buying something better.

Two frying pans were given the highest marks in consumer tests. The first, Jamie Oliver's branded frying pan, cost £44; the similar unbranded version, objectively just as good, retailed at £17.[16] The market for so-called luxury brands (the stuff we don't really need but do really want) was worth nearly € trillion at the end of 2010, and this market segment is growing stronger.

Designer Karl Lagerfeld states that handbags 'make your life more pleasant, make you dream, give you confidence, and show your neighbours that you are doing well.'[17] He is obviously not talking about the Primark brand here. In fact, I have a friend who saves her superior-branded plastic bags to put her Primark goods into when she shops there. An English journalist wrote during London Fashion Week in 2006, 'Everybody—everybody—is talking about handbags with the intensity of cardinals appointing a new pope.' Finally, the article states that some Japanese women work as prostitutes to earn money to buy Louis Vuitton, Hermès and Chanel bags and that in 2005, some victims of Hurricane Katrina used their Red Cross cards to buy $800 bags at the Louis Vuitton store in Atlanta.

On a saner note, in order to get my young children to eat more healthily, I would put (my approved) breakfast cereals into another box, one that they recognised from the ads on TV. They would munch these happily in the belief that they were aligning themselves with the kids having fun in the advertisements.

In the case of those who buy counterfeit goods to display the logo to make them feel good, is the desired outcome achieved without the purchase of the original brand? When only an expert can tell the difference between an original and a fake, the temptation is great to avoid paying full retail prices for a Gucci handbag or a Burberry coat. The logo will identify you with the brand virtues. The key to letting the outside world be sure of this status is reflected in a trend whereby labels are left on the outside 'to make it clear that your designer gear is not one of the many excellent fakes on the market but the real thing, and that you can afford to pay for it.'[18] Perhaps the next opportunity for the counterfeiters is simply to produce realistic brand labels.

Worshipping the logos—symbols of a new type of religion

'The reputation of the brand is carried almost exclusively by the logo'

GARETH WILLIAMS, *BRANDED, ON GUCCI*

Our deep relationship with logos is such that we wear them as we might wear Christian crosses or Jewish Stars of David. Wearing them turns us into altars from where we can worship the brand. Associating ourselves with these logos is similar to gazing at a tattwa (geometric symbols that represent the five universal energies) or yantra (a symbol designed to balance or focus the mind): we try to reach different moods, worlds and states of consciousness through the symbols we buy into.

Martin Lindstrom, in his book *Brand Sense*, cites the case of Sydney-born teenager Wilhelm Andries Petrus Booyse, who, in 2004, underwent an operation that marked the end of his obsession with the Gucci brand by removing a tattoo from the back of his neck. The tattoo comprised a barcode with the letters G-U-C-C-I underneath 'carefully duplicated from the Gucci Corporation's guidelines.' He describes how Will believed that Gucci had become more than a brand and was, in Will's own words, 'My one and only religion.' He summed up his experience with the brand thus: 'The admiration I had for the Gucci brand was stronger than any other person I knew. For me, Gucci was more than a brand—it was my personal companion. When I entered a Gucci store, I felt like I was in heaven . . . In the time that I wore the Gucci tattoo, people approached me constantly and made me feel like the centre of the universe.'

Another Australian was reported on the front page of a national newspaper headed 'Give me a job and I'll give you my face.'[19] It described a man offering to sell part of his face for advertising space, saying he would work for the company that wins the right to tattoo his bald head. At the time of writing he had already received some offers.

Lindstrom believes that brands are trying to fill the gap where religions are failing. People need something more to believe in, and brands are trying to provide it. He labels this phenomenon the 'Holistic Selling Proposition', believing that: 'HSP brands adopt religious characteristics.' He states that: 'Each holistic brand has its own identity, one that is expressed in its every message, shape, symbol, ritual and tradition—just as sports teams and religion do today.' He lists fundamental components that underpin religion and can serve as the ultimate role model for marketing:[20]

- A unique sense of belonging
- A clear vision with a sense of purpose
- Taking power from your enemies
- Authenticity

- Consistency
- Perfection
- Sensory appeal
- Rituals
- Symbols
- Mystery

A gold-leaf statue of David Beckham exists at Bangkok's Pariwas temple in Thailand. The monks defend it, stating: 'Football has become a religion and has millions of followers. So, to be up to date, we have to open our minds and share the feelings of millions of people who admire Beckham.'[21]

There is, however, no need to travel to another country in order to worship the successful Japanese brand Hello Kitty. An easily accessible website was set up called 'Praying for Hello Kitty.'

A special report on brands stated: 'Brands are so powerful, it is alleged, that they seduce us to look alike, eat alike and be alike. At the same time, they are spiritually empty.'[22] But we still look to them for spiritual sustenance; perhaps it is spirituality with a small 's', but it is a starting point.

Loving and hating the symbol

'Reason leads to conclusions, emotion leads to action.'
SAATCHI & SAATCHI

A logo acts like a visual barometer, displaying the condition of the company. If we see it and feel good then the company is probably in good shape. Symbols prompt numerous responses; most bypass our rational mind.

Flicking through channels on a television in the USA, I came across a Christian-based programme, where the commentator was articulating the importance of the cross symbol; he stated that, while 'Christ is the source, the cross is the means.' The power of even a small cross to create an impact is evident in the scale of the revolt when a member of staff at British Airways was suspended for wearing the Christian symbol on a necklace at work in 2006. One newspaper headlined its front page: 'BA cross: the revolt grows.'[23] The article described how the ongoing battle to enable a check-in worker to wear a cross at work had led nearly 100 MPs to join the backlash against British Airways. In a further article in the same paper, journalist Michael Dobbs pointed out that the flag used to brand British Airways consists of the crosses of three Christian saints—St George, St Andrew and St Patrick.

Another newspaper reported that Prince Harry, wearing a Nazi armband at a fancy dress party, prompted a Europe-wide ban on the public display of the swastika.[24] As it happens, at the same time, Britain's Hindus were campaigning to save the swastika as one of their religious symbols. For similar reasons, the EU also considered banning the hammer and sickle and the red star! Banning these symbols could drive them underground and it would alter our perception of them, not necessarily for the better. It could actually increase their effect. It certainly illustrates how shapes, lines and curves can carry powerful messages.

Similarly, when we wear a Lacoste crocodile, a Nike tick or the French Connection FCUK we are saying as much about our beliefs as when we identify ourselves with a cross. The edges between commercialism and the attainment of enlightenment become blurred, as symbols jostle to connect with our spirit. By associating ourselves with certain symbols we feel as if we belong; we feel protected, part of the gang, loved, and so on.

On BBC Radio Four's programme *Woman's Hour*,[25] the subject of banning the Playboy bunny symbol from children's items, from pencil cases to clothing, was discussed. Applied to a specially designed range of items, the cute bunny appeals to young children. Some adults consider this wholly inappropriate, as they believe this symbol stands for anti-feminism, pro-sexual exploitation and the like, effectively sanitising the porn industry. On the one hand we have the cute bunny, reminiscent of Easter and fluffy toys; on the other, there is a real belief that this symbol could contribute to corrupting our young.

Successfully branded companies understand this layering of values onto symbols. They know how qualities can be subtly woven into the fabric, or psyche, of the imagery so that we can receive it at some level and get the brand message instantly—whether or not we fully understand it, or agree with it.

A single symbol distinguishes a product from the crowd, makes all the difference to our perception, and prompts subsequent action. Even modern architecture no longer necessarily identifies the use of a building through its structure—for example, a church can look like a commercial centre until we glimpse its cross. We can only be sure when we see the symbol. Logos identify much more than a physical product. Competing products may appear virtually identical until we spot the identifying logo and form a completely different view of them.

Falling out of love with the logo

Of course, the carefully laid out brand values can be hijacked, for example, by the press and the public. When a business behaves badly, it is the brand logo that is held up to identify the culprit. Repeated often enough, the logo can take on unwanted, undesirable traits. The *Metro* newspaper displayed a full-colour Norwich Union logo beside an amended version of its strapline headed: 'How we quote you *un*happy . . . '[26] to go alongside an article stating that it had been named the worst insurer for motorists in a new survey. The BP oil spill in the Guf of Mexico in 2010 prompted news editors to design a new logo, comprising the familiar sunflower symbol dripping oil, to identify the frequent progress reports. Too much of this kind of negative input could lead to the dissipation of positive brand values that have been carefully built onto the logo.

Bad feelings about a company might be attributed directly to the logo. The original Proctor and Gamble logo of stars and a man in the Moon was used on many of the company's products from 1882 to 1985. Proctor and Gamble was forced to drop the symbol after a story began circulating that the company was controlled by Satan-worshippers. Whether the rumours are true or not, it is fascinating to see how the symbol became the forefront of this belief. Danone's current corporate imagery comprises a young face looking up to a star in a blue sky within a circle of blue, which is somewhat reflective of the controversial imagery in the Proctor and Gamble identity, but has not attracted a similar response.

When the sight of the logo sparks feelings of dissatisfaction, irritation or anger, we cease to want it in our lives. We simply will not buy.

The product: 'Made with real logos'

Dr Abraham Maslow (1954) researched human motivation, what energises, direct and sustains us, and structured his conclusion in his hierarchy of human needs. It states that once our physiological needs for survival are met, we re-prioritise and begin to focus our attention on different, as yet unfulfilled needs. We no longer drink and eat simply because we are thirsty or hungry; we have a choice. Even daily essentials such as food, toilet paper and soap powder have an identity which we will favour—yet, how much softer can toilet paper or towels be, how much whiter can our teeth or sheets be, and how much creamier can yoghurt or chocolate get? From herbal extracts to sugar replacement (or added *natural* sugar) or vinegar or baking soda, ingredients may be highlighted or added or defined as natural, organic, ethically sourced, healthy or tried-and-tested. While some of these procedures may have a basis in reality, claims that Red Bull can give us wings or that Heineken can reach the parts that other beers cannot reach are dubious to say the least—and barely, if at all, based on the effectiveness of the contents.

With so many identical ingredients in each product, claims of overall product benefit may be difficult to substantiate. However, by incorporating and promoting specialist ingredients, displayed alongside the logo, companies appeal to our senses and pander to our egos. They encourage us to believe that we have made an informed choice as well as taken a personal stance. Even if we decide to drink cola because we like the taste, we will buy Coke or Pepsi because their promise resonates with a part of us. As we continue to be motivated by our unsatisfied needs, our emotions are powerful drivers in making choices. Whether the marketing experts decide to kickstart our purchasing through fear, love, desire, aspirations, envy, and so on, they have a huge armoury of effective tools from which to choose.

Of course it matters what is in the bottle or package. There are cases where brands have completely flopped because the product was no good, as in the case of vaginal deodorants, which were medically dismissed. But there are many more brands that have failed because the image was not right.

Contagious emotions—spreading the good feelings

Brands build on our desire to belong in a desirable group. They will even create the tribe for us with its own values and badge. The right exposure is paramount in the success of a brand, and if a celebrity, or someone else that we admire, tickles our egos and aspirations we will want to belong to it. Malcolm Gladwell, author of *The Tipping Point*, cites the example of the ailing Hush Puppy brand, about to close down as sales reached rock bottom, when the shoes were adopted by some young people who chose to wear them to be deliberately different; the trend spread to become fashionable in the bars and clubs in Manhattan, eventually spreading to every mall in America within two years. If it had not been the 'hip' group that took up the Hush Puppy brand, the fashion world would have been less than happy to buy into the logo. It is highly unlikely that the brand would have survived with the endorsement of some subculture or other undesirable group.

Non-conscious processes drive much consumer behaviour. Mimicry is one way in which we make choices, by following someone else's lead unconsciously. Participants in an experiment were engaged in a task with a confederate who was casually eating one of two snacks from separate bowls in front of him. There were two similarly filled bowls in front of each participant. Whichever snack the conferate chose to eat, the participants followed suit in every example. And they were not aware of doing it.[27] Similarly, the more our friends wear or display a chosen logo, the more likely we are to follow their lead.

Emotions such as happiness can be passed on. We talk about laughter being 'infectious'; now there is evidence to support the truth behind this statement. Psychologists Elaine Hatfield and John Cacioppo state in their book *Emotional Contagion* that mimicry is one of the means by which we 'infect' each other with our emotions. For example, if one person smiles at another, the other person will not only smile back but will feel happier in the process.

Even the charisma around people is infectious, as illustrated by an experiment conducted by Howard Friedman at the University of California at Riverside.[28] He paired charismatic people with those who had less charisma, and showed that the former affected the latter. The situation could not be reversed: it was only the charismatic person who had the capability to infect others. The power of this ability is seen in the fact that this experiment was conducted without moving or speaking, only by *being in the same vicinity*! The charismatic participants in the experiment did not have to perform any carefully choreographed tasks; they simply had to be present.

Daniel Goleman cites another example of emotional contagion in his book *Emotional Intelligence*. During the Vietnam War, in the midst of fighting, as an American platoon was huddled down in some rice paddies, a group of monks walked into the line of fire. Calmly, they proceeded across the field, looking neither right nor left; they simply walked through. One of the American soldiers stated that, after seeing this, the fight went out of him and he just did not want to do it anymore. The fighting around them stopped.

The above examples indicate that emotion can work from outside-in instead of inside-out. Someone else *can* affect our mood. Those of us who are good at expressing our emotions and feelings tend to be 'emotionally contagious'; psychologists call these types 'senders.' If the branding experts succeed in enrolling people like these, and in investing logos with this positive sort of 'charisma' or 'aura' or 'loglo', then they are on to a winner.

A successful logo will have its own charisma, representing desirable emotions. If it makes us feel depressed (owing to bad press, the wrong peer attitude, or something similar), we will not feel good when we see it and we will refuse to buy it or recommend it to our friends.

One of the ways in which companies use this contagion factor is via appropriately named 'viral marketing', where, for example, emails go out that are specially created in the hope that they will be passed on. They usually amuse the receiver, who is tempted to pass it on again. I don't know how many of the friendly junk emails I receive are started by the companies themselves, but here are a few examples of hypothetical 'proposed mergers' that I personally found witty and sent on to other people:

- Polygram Records, Warner Bros, and Zesta Crackers join forces and become Polly Warner Cracker.
- Zippo Mfg, Audi Motor Car, Dofasco, and Dakota Mining merge to become ZipAudiDoDa.
- Federal Express is expected to join its major competitor, UPS, and consolidate as FedUP.

If these examples make us smile, they have gone some way towards endearing us to the names, at least, of the companies.

Fear the consequences

Happiness, love, humour and other desirable emotions may attract us to a logo, but there are many other equally powerful emotions that can be called into play as part of the branding armoury. None of these is greater than fear. We might worry that our neighbours will ridicule our greying laundry, that we will be unrecognised or rejected by our friends, or even that we will die penniless; the brand nudges these fears and presents solutions to alleviate them.

Joseph LeDoux, a neuroscientist at New York University, carried out experiments to see how threatened rats responded. The rats were conditioned to associate a particular sound with an unpleasant sensation, such as an electric shock. Rats, and many other animals, are known to initially respond to an outside threat by freezing still. But when the rat learned that freezing provided no prevention from the shock, it tried to avoid it by moving, even climbing up the side of the cage. 'At this point, the rat makes the transition from being an emotional reactor to an actor, capable of making choices and trying different strategies.'[29]

On this basis, the marketers must not scare us too much, but enough, and for a time, so that eventually we will be prompted to action.

A brand's success depends on reaching a large enough sector of the marketplace to create a profit—and quickly. Emotional values are the tools of choice. The tone of voice and the emotions behind the logo are as important to the success of the brand as the product, if not more so. Branding has turned into a complex procedure with emotion at its heart. Marketers might not know the intricacies of the workings of the brain, but the benefits of controlling our minds outweigh any misgivings about detrimental effects. Specially designed, researched, targeted and often complex campaigns help to get the message out to a lot of people; subsequently, even a quick flash of the logo helps perpetuate the brand message in our mind.

Experiments have identified a phenomenon known as priming, which is similar to subliminal influence. Subjects are exposed to a stimulus, such as a sound or an image, so fleetingly that they are not consciously aware of it and cannot recall it later. Yet tests show that the stimulus has been imprinted on the brain at some level. In one set of experiments, subjects are shown a list of words too briefly for it to be stored in short-term memory. Later the subjects are asked to guess what the full word is after being prompted by the clue 'o-t-p-s'. Those who have previously been exposed to a list of words containing *octopus* are much more likely to guess correctly, even though they cannot explicitly recall whether it was on the list.[30]

The majority of advertising exposure occurs when the audience's attention is focused elsewhere. Whether we are flipping through a magazine or browsing the internet, we get the message. The more we see it, the more we like it, and we don't know why. In an experiment, 'researchers discovered that even if people could not recall the content of the ad, repeated exposure led to familiarity, which then led to positive feelings.'[31]

A logo combining a picture with a word is a powerful combination for firing our brain cells in a predetermined and effective sequence. As the design embeds itself into our brain, we might recall it without knowing why. And as the design gets filled with emotions and memories, the logo jostles to claim a part of our memory, creating a pattern of neuron functions that might keep out other designs by stopping them from imprinting our minds with the same effect. There is evidence that shows that once a brand is imprinted in our minds we will reject newcomers. Scientists have discovered that brand loyalty heavily influences consumers' responses to marketing from competing brands. 'When loyalty is high, consumers search for evidence that a competitor brand is not a good brand, contrary to the advertisement information.'[32]

Tribal elder and author Malidoma Patrice Somé from West Africa describes how parts of our mind can be used up to become inaccessible to further learning. On his return to his tribe, having been removed for some years, he considered being initiated even though he was past the normal age for this procedure. He realised, however, that parts of the initiation process would not be open to him, as his Western school education prevented him from receiving the training: ' . . . It dawned on me that literacy, from the traditional point of view, occupies a space within the psyche that is reserved for something else. So my knowing how to read and write meant that I would never be able to access certain traditional knowledge as long as I lived.'[33]

One of the main ways we learn is by seeing others do something first. But we do not have to physically perform the task for our brains to react appropriately. Simply watching someone else stimulates the watcher's neurons in exactly the same firing sequence as that occurring in the person physically performing the task. This 'mirror system' was first noted in the brains of monkeys; the neurons that were activated when a monkey executed a specific hand movement were also activated when the monkey observed another carrying out the same action. Furthermore, it is likely that symbols can be created to stimulate a similar response.[34]

This mirror system also works empathically; when we see someone cry, our neurons fire up similarly; when someone pricks their finger, an observer will experience the same neural response. It is as if we are able to read the minds of others.[35] We are repeatedly exposed by advertisers to clothes being washed whiter than white, children laughing as they eat their favourite breakfast cereal, and workplace disasters that are potentially life-threatening. Our neurons will be firing again and again, forming new ways for us to think and act as we are prompted to empathise with the brand.

Our brains are incredibly plastic. Grey matter can shrink or thicken; neural connections can be forged or severed. One of the most important findings of recent research is in how closely connected our senses, such as our hearing and vision, are to our memory and cognition.[36] Brands reach out to us through our senses, which are stimulated when we recognise the value-imprinted logo. It is evident that our brains can adapt to extraordinary circumstances. Even on a day-to-day, second-by-second basis, our neurons are adjusting to, and analysing, the minute changes in our world and adapting to get us what we want. If we can be convinced to buy a particular brand, the logo will remind us of the purchase and wedge its way into our minds to punctuate our own experiences with brand values.

Those in charge of brands are literally helping us to form new ways of thinking and being. As our physical brains respond to our brand-stimulated emotions to form new neural pathways, we begin to see the world according to the brand values. We perpetuate this process by continuing to match these established patterns and share them with others. We trust brands and are only too willing to believe the promises of fulfilment.

Logos are magical little icons that are designed to work themselves into our unconscious so that we might share the dreams of the brand owner and play a part in making them come true.

CHAPTER SIX

Beyond the physical world

'All that we see or seem is but a dream within a dream.'

EDGAR ALLAN POE

In order to understand how a small logotype can have a profound affect on us—mentally, physically and energetically—we need to understand about a new and emerging viewpoint on the construction of our world. It is not as 'solid' as it may seem.

Historians and archaeologists have found evidence of a higher belief held by humans since the development of humankind. Mystics have known from the Indian Hindu Vedas of 2000 BCE that 'separateness is an illusion.' Patanjali's *Yoga Sutras*, from 400 BCE, outlines detailed instructions for looking at different places and into the future, just like similar scientifically practised procedures today.

As new views develop about the nature of the world, including how we fit and are affected by it, it becomes apparent that our comfortable viewpoint of a reality that is firmly embedded in space and time is shattered; it simply does not exist.

The difference between early Chinese and Indian philosophers and modern-day scientists is that the former came to their conclusions through psychic ability and meditation, while we depend on a mechanistic scientific 'proving.' Our brains are probably the most advanced 'computers', but we use only a small proportion of them. Most of us strongly focus on the part that demands logic and scientific proof before it will accept the existence of anything at all.

Dissection and microscopes cannot prove the existence of much beyond the physical world. Despite leaps and bounds being made by science into the workings of the mind, our mental world still remains largely a mystery. Few physical tools exist (yet) to prove the existence of 'something more out there.' While science is able to prove many ancient beliefs about the state of the universe, this exploration is limited by the speed in development of increasingly sophisticated equipment.

Those who do sense an alternative reality, perhaps via intuition and gut feelings, can take heart from the fact that Galileo was arrested and tortured for saying that the world revolved around the sun, and John Logie Baird, inventor of the television, was told that it was absolutely impossible to send pictures down a wire.

Quantum physics for beginners

Quantum physicists believe that everything is part of a larger energy field, *absolutely everything* is just energy, and that our view of a solid, real world independent of us is simply not so. They state that the universe comprises a matrix of energy patterns, that there is no such thing as a 'thing', and that we all exist as parts of a sea of quantum particles that are formed into three-dimensional 'reality' by our minds.

But we like to think of things either being there or not being there. If we can see or touch them, we conclude that they exist. If we can't see or touch them, we need a lot of convincing to believe in their presence. Despite the simplistic explanation of everything being energy, which we manifest into some sort of reality, it is a virtually impossible theory for the average person to comprehend. Indeed, Niels Bohr, one of the founders of quantum physics, said: 'Anyone who is not shocked by quantum theory has not understood it.'

Nevertheless, our left brain demands reasoning. In order to find some logical and understandable definitions (words not readily applicable to quantum theory), a group of physicists met in 1927 to discuss what quantum mechanics really meant. Their conclusion became known as the Copenhagen Interpretation, which stated in essence that we were never going to understand the quantum theory using logical left-brained processes based in linear time and definitive space. Rather, we were going to have to use our right 'irrational' brain to sense it, rather than define it. They were ' . . . forced by their own findings to acknowledge that a complete understanding of reality lies beyond the capabilities of rational thought.'[1] This makes logic an adversary when we try to connect with and understand the quantum field at large.

University of London physicist Dr David Bohm states in his book *The Implicate Order*: ' . . . one is led to a new notion of unbroken wholeness that denies the classical idea of analysability of the world into separately and independently existing parts.' This implies that location ceases to exist at the quantum level; nothing is separate from anything else.

This information is not new. In *The Upanishads*, one of the great ancient yogic texts, we are reminded:

As is the atom, so is the universe.
As is the human body, so is the cosmic body.
As is the human mind, so is the cosmic mind.
As is the microcosm, so is the macrocosm.

Creating our world

Since Einstein presented his now famous formula $E=mc^2$ (where E is energy, m is mass and c is the speed of light), our scientific understanding of the world, especially at the sub-microscopic level, has been revolutionised. This theory directly relates energy to matter, showing them to be interchangeable—matter being described simply as slowed-down or crystallised energy. Furthermore, Einstein used his Theory of Relativity to prove that time is not linear and space is not three-dimensional; that they are interconnected to form a four-dimensional continuum, which is known as 'space-time.'

Physicists have discovered that if matter is broken down into smaller and smaller pieces, a point will eventually be reached where these pieces no longer have the traits of objects. These quantum particles are not 'bits' as we know them; they have no mass and their lifetime is incomparable to ours. As one example, a single such particle version known as a sigma, part of the baryon family of particles, has a lifespan of 80 trillionths of a second!

We might think of more familiar-sounding electrons as being little particles whizzing around a nucleus—but they too possess no dimension.

Even more remarkable is the fact that an electron can manifest as a particle or a wave; this is common to all subatomic particles.

Physicists believe that these subatomic phenomena should not simply be classed as waves or particles but as something else, hence the name *quanta*—and they believe that the universe, the quantum field, is made from these.

Scientific evidence shows that although these quanta can manifest as either particles or as waves, they only ever become particles when we are watching them. We alter the properties of what we observe—the act of observation is the act of creation. For example, when an electron is not being looked at, it is a wave. As soon as we observe it, it becomes a particle, but then only until we withdraw our observation, when it becomes a wave again. The longer we look, the more it changes. Scientists at Israel's Weizmann Institute of Science documented this phenomenon, showing that: ' . . . the greater the amount of "watching", the greater the observer's influence on what actually takes place.'[2] It seems that our very thoughts create the world around us. This field, in which we do our creating, could be described as the space where nothing exists but everything is manifested.

Physicist Nick Herbert supports this theory; he likens us to King Midas, who turned everything he touched into gold. He says: 'Likewise, humans can never experience the true texture of quantum reality because everything we touch turns into matter.' Bohm (see above) does not support this theory wholly, but he does believe that we exist in a sort of illusion with different levels of reality.

We create the familiar world that surrounds us from a sea of energy, where we learn our lessons from cause and effect in a timescale that we understand. Quantum theories are mind-boggling to most of us; they expose a world that makes more sense of boggles than it does of mind.

No wonder this field is also known as the *ex nihilo* ('out of nothing'), from where ' . . . human perception occurs because of interactions between the subatomic particles of our brains and the quantum energy sea. We literally resonate with our world.'[3]

We create our reality through our thoughts and observations. What we pay attention to is what fills our world. We create our reality merely by looking at it; we see the effect of the construction of our thoughts only when we pay attention to them. We see what we believe and we believe what we see. Winston Churchill articulated this concept simply when he said: 'You create your universe as you go along.'

This means that if we believe the logo hype, we play a major part in its creation. Furthermore, if we continue to buy into it via the branding, we increase the probability of its perpetuation. We co-create the success of the logo simply by paying attention to it.

Jahn and Dunne, of the USA based Princeton Engineering Anomalies Research laboratory, believe that subatomic particles do not even have a distinct reality until consciousness enters the picture. They cite cases where particles have been discovered that seem to exist only after physicists have thought of their possibility. One such particle is known as an *anomalon*. Its properties vary from lab to lab, appearing to support their theory that it changes to fit the expectations of the physicists observing it.

The existence of a *neutrino* was simply proposed in the 1930s by the theorist Wolfgang Pauli, in answer to solving a problem concerning radioactivity. The neutrino remained nothing more than an idea until 1957, when scientists discovered evidence of its existence. As a massless particle, it still did not solve some of the problems the scientists had hoped for, but with further attention, the neutrino appeared to gain mass. This supports Jahn and Dunne's theory that we create particles out of our expectancy. Today neutrinos are at the forefront of experimentation by particle physicists at CERN. Chosen beause of their ability to pass through matter completely, they might be able to able to travel faster than light and can be 'seen' through closed eyes.

Similarly, the physicist John Hagelin believes that if we speak of illness, we have it; if we speak of prosperity, we have that instead. We are like magnets, attracting and shaping everything we think about. Whether those thoughts are stimulated through remembering, observing or acting something out, whatever is going on in our mind is attracted to us and our thoughts become things. It really does become a case of mind over matter.

It is easy to see the value of bombarding us with logos: constant reminders of a host of brand values to perpetuate a belief. The more a logo fills the spaces in our minds, the less we will be tempted to drift away from the brand dream. The more we are exposed, through marketing exposure, to a logo, the more we aid its growth in the quantum field.

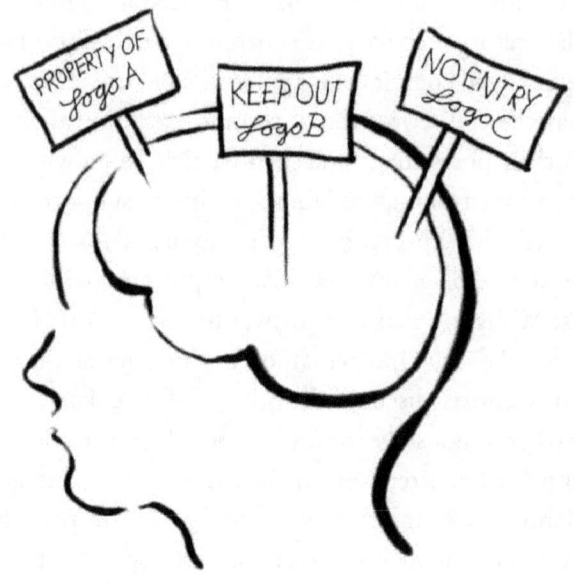

Brands secure our thinking process by creating and consistently triggering specific neural pathways in our brain.

The saying 'I will see it when I believe it', begins to take on more weight when we note the following events surrounding several hypnotists. The first is where a family friend was hypnotised to believe that his daughter was invisible; when she stood in front of him and the hypnotist held up a watch behind the girl, the father was able to read the details on the watch. The second, based on the sense of taste rather than sight, was explored by British physicist Sir William Barrett. He showed that when another person was hypnotised to taste whatever someone else was eating, she would accurately taste salt, sugar, mustard, ginger and so on. Further experiments have shown that sight, smelling and hearing are able to be experienced by one person while another performs the actions.[4]

When the early American settlers arrived in the Caribbean, the Native Americans were unable to see the approaching ships because they had no knowledge that clipper ships existed. Eventually the shaman in the tribe noticed the ripples caused by the ships and wondered what was causing them. After a time, he was able to see the ships and told everyone else. His people then became able to see the ships since they trusted the shaman; they too saw the world differently.[5] When logos become familiar to us, pathways of recognition become established in our minds. Once the brand merchants have highlighted our awareness of the brands we will continue to see them.

Jude Currivan, PhD, in *The Wave*, states that the cumulative results of relevant scientific experiments ' . . . are undeniably far beyond chance and are demonstrating what metaphysical traditions have always maintained—that we individually and collectively co-create our realities.' She continues: 'In scientific terms, the resonance of our attention and intention causes the quantum field of free-wave possibilities to harmonise into the coherent standing waves of realised materiality.'

Fields of consciousness

The ideas of theoretical biologist Rupert Sheldrake build on Jung's idea of the collective unconscious, which he takes a stage further. Rather than fields of consciousness being primarily applied to people, he believes that 'societies have social and cultural fields that embrace and organize everything within them.'[6] He believes that new fields are initiated by a minor change in an action or thought. This change acts as a catalyst of effects influencing future actions and thoughts, over and over, constantly gathering momentum until the energy in this field increases to a point that enables a shift to occur. This creates what Sheldrake calls a *morphic field*—a field of energy with its own structure and pattern as well as its own memory. He believes that even crystals have morphic fields that determine their form. As scientists endeavoured to crystallise new compounds in their laboratories, it was noted that it was really difficult to succeed the first time but became easier and easier with subsequent attempts. Sheldrake reasons that a morphic field emerges through time; each crystallisation is influenced by previous successes, as the memory of prior crystallisations becomes increasingly embedded in the field.[7]

In his book *A New Science of Life*, Sheldrake describes how, in 1921 in Southampton, blue tits discovered how to get the tops off the milk bottles standing on doorsteps so they could drink the cream. This action was quickly taken up by blue tits 50 miles away and eventually spread throughout Britain as well as to Scandinavia and Holland. Since blue tits do not travel far from home, it would have been impossible for this to occur through imitation. Curiously, and lending more weight to the theory, the habit ceased in Holland during the war, due to the fact that there were no milk deliveries, but resumed when milk was again delivered. No blue tits could have survived the length of the war and so this habit is assumed to be dependent on a kind of collective memory due to morphic resonance.[8]

Even further back in history is an example observed by Jung in 1906. He noticed one of his patients, who suffered from paranoid schizophrenia, standing at a window looking at the sun and moving his head from side to side. When asked what he was doing, the man replied that he was looking at the penis of the sun and moving it from side to side so that the wind would blow. Jung thought no more of this until he came across a 2,000-year-old Persian text outlining a series of rituals and invocations to bring on visions. One of these was that if a participant looked at the sun, he would see a tube hanging down from it; if this tube was swinging from side to side, it would cause the wind to blow. Jung believed that this had bubbled into the man's mind from the collective unconscious.[9]

Possibly the most famous evidence for morphic fields came from another example when it was noted that individual members of a species performed identical actions, regardless of their geographic location and within a timespan which made it impossible for them to communicate physically. When monkeys on the Japanese island of Koshima began washing the sand off the sweet potatoes thrown to them by scientists on the island, there came a point where others in distant places spontaneously started doing the same thing. The phrase 'hundredth monkey syndrome' was coined; the number 100 being an arbitrary number given by Dr Lyall Watson as the number of the critical mass reached for a field to be created allowing communication over time and space.

In the field of branding it may therefore be just one extra person buying into the brand who could tip the balance in the way that the last straw proverbially breaks the camel's back. The last in the line can make a difference. I believe that the huge success that celebrity chef Jamie Oliver experienced in changing the content of school dinners, known by many for a long time to lack substantial nourishment, cannot be attributed to Jamie alone (although in the main it was). Without the previous efforts of many people who had tirelessly worked behind the scenes to change the way we feed our children in school, and building up the field of energy over the years, his initiative might have had little chance of getting further than the television screen. This effect may be simply the result of someone voicing something that is already obvious but being denied for whatever reason—rather like the child in the story of the Emperor's New Clothes, who finally stated the obvious, giving the rest of the population permission to do likewise. The obvious might be apparent, but it remains inactive until one small event tips the scale into action.

Malcolm Gladwell outlines this principle in his book *The Tipping Point*. A magic moment occurs when trends, ideas and social behaviours cross a threshold and spread with incredible speed. This, of course, is the dream of those in charge of brands: how to reach this elusive tipping point. It is dependent on the right people at the right time in the right place, and can be tantalisingly difficult to attain.

Gladwell describes three laws of epidemics that enable this to occur. First, there is the 'law of the few', when exceptional people adopt a trend and others want to follow. We have seen how a brand's profits can be boosted when celebrities become associated with the logotype. Second, there is the 'stickiness factor', which describes how a contagious message becomes memorable. Again, step forward the logo, as the single most identifiable device on a brand. Finally, there is the 'power of context.' This is about the sensitivity of people to their environment and the importance of delivering a message in the right area. Advertising and marketing experts spend fortunes to ensure that the logo is displayed in the right magazines, the right environment and on the right people.

An experiment conducted in 1983 in Britain illustrated how a memory held in the quantum field can be picked up in other parts of the world. 2 million television viewers were shown a picture that had an image hidden within it. Many failed to see the image. Several thousand people in other parts of the world were subsequently tested with the same picture and the percentage recognising the hidden image increased substantially.

On this basis, it would seem that the successful launch of a brand need only be a major campaign in one country, with minimal supporting 'prompts' in the rest of the world. Those prompts could be as simple as flashing the logotype around, to carry the imprint of the whole campaign.

In corporate design we have created a field with a new language, composed of words and pictures, which we recognise even if we do not understand it at a linguistic or artistic level. Through the branding process, we can create a very powerful and influential field, at the heart of which is the logo. This is how we recognise and build on this field in the world.

The logo enrols people into a controlled collective consciousness, a common cause that benefits the brand it identifies. In a sense we can look at brand values, whatever they are chosen to be, as fields of consciousness that are coordinated into a whole. This collective consciousness is important in the area of branding: we create a 'unique' field around a product or concept, and if we can convince enough people to buy into it, it tips the balance to become mainstream.

We create communities of Gucci, Starbucks and Ferrari, some of which are more exclusive than others, but their success lies in the fact that many people yearn to become members. Whether or not they can afford to join, people continue to 'feed' the energy of this field through the attention they pay to the label, by drinking the coffee or poring over the glossy magazine ads. Each community was started by a single thought; a concept that fired a possibility.

I have found that artists are among those who really understand the concept of these fields of energy. They seem to tune into the universal field to find inspiration to create a piece of art that can be shared physically with the rest of the world; through this sharing it can effect change in people's thinking and even their actions. Tracey Emin stated about her famous unmade-bed piece of work titled *My Bed* that: 'My bed now exists in the national psyche.' Whether we like the piece or not, it is now in our personal field of consciousness, as well as in the field of art and in the national consciousness as well.

We can consider that branding is one process that helps builds these fields-within-fields, by increasing and linking brand values with other desirable fields or values. Taking one product—breakfast cereal, for example, it may be aligned with the fields of health, family, childhood, colour and taste; it may even influence these fields in much the same way that Domino's Pizzas influence our perception of pizzas.

Can we really *see* the qualities of 'quality and responsibility' when we look at the Amec symbol, or 'Joie de vivre, passion and dependability' in the Vodafone symbol? At a conscious level, I would say absolutely not. But if we look at some religious and national symbols, such as the Christian cross or the swastika, then we do find that we experience emotions. These will arise depending on the information we have gathered from reading spiritual texts, attending a place of worship, watching television or via the media at large. Through marketing exposure, these emotions will already be firmly attached to the symbols and pre-exist in the fields of energy that surround and influence us.

The 'overall' or universal energy field has the ability to permeate all space and connects everything to everything else. Everything in the universe, whether inanimate or animate, has its own form and energy imprint, which is determined by its relationship to the overall energy field.

Changes in the universal energy field occur when it encounters the energy radiating from an object. These changes can thus be used to measure the force, or energy field, of the object itself—such as in the case of a person's aura, or a logo.

Synchronicity or coincidence?

Once a concept is sparked in the quantum field by a thought, it is there to be accessed and available to anyone tuned into a similar wavelength. Proof of this capability is evident when virtually identical new fields are created at the same time. Professor Gary Schwartz[10] of the University of Arizona states that because potential is invisible, most people think it is not there. But since the whole universe is just one 'big quantum soup of potential' in which possibilities already exist, two or more people, focusing on a specific outcome, may be able to find the answer in this huge database. This is why some of history's greatest inventions have been discovered by two or more people, often countries apart, at the same time.

Inventions and discoveries including the telephone, photography, the telescope and the planet Neptune were all made more than once and at similar times. More recently, it was noted that Richard Desmond's *Express* newspapers were about to launch a new women's weekly with the snappy name *Take 5*, which the 'insiders were especially chuffed with'. Then they discovered that Australian media rival Kerry Packer was ' . . . planning a launch of his own, his first in Britain. It's a women's weekly and will hit the shelves in a few weeks' time. Even better, it's called *Take 5*.'[11]

Professor Karl Pribram, developer of the holonomic brain model of cognitive function, stated in an interview in *Psychology Today*, about the quantum field of coincidences: 'It isn't that the world of appearances is wrong; it isn't that there *aren't* objects out there, at one level of reality. It's that if you penetrate through and look at the universe with a holographic system, you arrive at a different view, a different reality. And that other reality can explain things that have hitherto remained inexplicable scientifically: paranormal phenomena synchronicities, the apparently meaningful coincidence of events.'[12]

Thousands of brands, selling similar products and services, vie for our attention. This leads to a tremendous amount of overlap from the production source through to the customer base. Whether the brand is a specialist business in London or New York, a telesales organisation in India or an Asian manufacturing company, the competing products can be virtually indistinguishable. The likelihood of two or more designers coming up with similar solutions for a logo is inevitable.

According to the laws of quantum physics, this could be more than a coincidence; it can occur simply when we see familiar things in a new light—which opens up the potential for others to see them likewise. Once a new field is created, it exists for anyone to tap into. I would often think of a design concept, which of course I believed to be unique, and would subsequently see a similar one produced by someone else, sometimes in a different country. These coincidences happened far more often than could be explained by the logic of fashion, and were frequent enough to lead one design magazine to put the 'copied' (or so they thought) design side by side with the original for the rest of the design world to scoff at.

A particularly famous example of this occurred when NBC television commissioned a large and successful design agency to come up with a new image. After months of design and research, they presented the new design—at more or less the same time as a small radio and TV network in Nebraska adopted an identical design solution for a fraction of the cost using one designer. The symbol was finally adopted by NBC at great expense in an out-of-court settlement.

These sorts of coincidences make it difficult to protect the boundaries of a logo. The physical reproduction of the approved design on specific products in selected countries can be set out legally and according to a defined schedule. But thoughts can be transmitted instantly and similar logos can be launched simultaneously. Time and space might appear controllable, but design managers are unable to control this quantum field effect.

Influencing the energy field

'Whether you think you can, or you can't,
either way you are right.'

HENRY FORD

From Gary Zukav's book *The Dancing Wu Li Masters* comes the following quote: ' . . . the inescapable conclusion is that if the statistical predictions of quantum theory are correct, then our commonsense ideas about the world are profoundly deficient . . . this is quite a conclusion because the *statistical predictions of quantum mechanics are always correct.'* He also says: 'Reality is what we take to be true. What we take to be true is what we believe. What we believe is based on our perceptions. What we perceive depends upon what we look for. What we look for depends upon what we think. What we think depends upon what we perceive. What we perceive determines what we believe. What we believe determines what we take to be true. What we take to be true is our reality.'

We have already seen how the human field and the universal field are inextricably linked and how quantum physics supports this theory. By default, therefore, when we influence our minds with our every action and thought, we create a change in the field.

Bohm's hologram theory helps verify this: if everything in the world is based in every part of the world, then there is no separation and every action, every thought, affects the whole. Scientists refer to thought forms as being real structures, occupying a dimension in space-time, not merely a reflection on reality, but also a movement of that reality itself. It follows that by controlling our minds we can influence the world around us. We can see the potential of controlling the minds of a targeted group.

Psychokinesis (PK) substantiates the power of our minds at a physical level. Described as 'the influence of mind upon matter' and 'the use of mental "power" to move or distort an object,'[13] psychokinesis is also known as remote influencing, distant influencing, remote mental influence, distant mental influence, directed conscious intention, or 'The Force.'

Robert Jahn, Professor of Aerospace Sciences and Dean Emeritus of the School of Engineering and Applied Sciences at Princeton University, was asked by a student to oversee an experiment involving PK. He was so impressed with the results that he was inspired to set up the Princeton Engineering Anomalies Research (PEAR) lab in 1979. It was there that Jahn and his associate, clinical psychologist Brenda Dunne, found that people were able to affect the results of actions such as the number of times a coin would fall heads up.

In today's scientific world, we like to prove things by measuring and recording them with machines. Therefore it was logical to test a machine as an object to be influenced, in order to prove that we can affect our environment with our intention. Jahn and Dunne proved beyond doubt that ordinary people could affect the random movements of machines simply by an act of will.[14] I can attest to this; I have a friend who is banned by his colleagues from coming near their computers during busy periods, because they tend to crash—particularly when he is storming around in an agitated frame of mind.

It follows that if logos trigger our minds in a common cause, we can influence the future of the brands they represent.

Believing in the power of others to influence

Regardless of the quality of the product, it might just work if we believe it enough. Women pay substantial amounts of money for facial creams that promise to make their skin look younger and yet they are little or no more effective than the creams that are much cheaper. But if the women that pay high sums for their cream believe that it really does work, then there is the distinct possibility that it *will* work. That is until someone disproves it and destroys the brand claim.

A placebo is any medical treatment that has no specific action on the body; its effect is well documented. In some cases, a placebo can rival the success of the drug being tested against it. It is usually given as a control in a double-blind experiment—a study where one group of individuals is given a real treatment and another group is given a fake treatment (sugar pills or a saline solution injection, for example). In such experiments, neither the researchers nor the individuals being tested know which group they are in, so that the effects of the real treatment can be assessed more accurately.

A study of 46,000 heart patients published in the *British Medical Journal* in 2006 found that those taking a placebo fared as well as those on a heart drug. At a Methodist hospital in Houston, Texas, patients who were given a sham operation reported better results in helping their osteoarthritis than those who actually had the surgery.[15]

The case that remains most vivid in my memory is one reported by psychologist Bruno Klopfer about a man dying of cancer. Because he was only expected to live a matter of days, he was not chosen to be tested for a new cancer drug called Krebiozen. On pleading, the patient was given the drug, and days later his tumours had 'melted like snowballs on a hot stove.' He recovered to the point where he was able to resume his normal life, apparently cancer free, until the results of the final drug test were announced. The drug turned out to be ineffective in curing cancer and it began to spread once more through his body. At this stage his doctor tried an experiment and told the patient there was a new improved form of the drug available and once again the man's tumours shrank. The doctor had given him water.[16]

Doctors, dentists, lawyers and a range of other credible experts are frequently enrolled to convince us that a branded product is efficacious. If we believe them enough, the promise might turn out to be true. Subsequently, we share the success with our friends and the belief spreads.

Influencing others

First we choose to be associated with a brand—but in order to maximise the value of this association, we will enrol and influence our friends and colleagues in the benefits. Brands stroke our ego and our ego depends on positioning us favourably with those around us. We spread the 'goodwill' of the brand and co-create our reality. Ultimately, we can create a tipping point of group consciousness and we become swept forward to share in the success of the brand. Of course, it is the brand that creates this potential in the first instance and encapsulates it in the logo.

In their paper on the speed of thought, USA research scientists Rauscher and Targ state that highly significant double-blind clinical studies in distant healing, published in *The Western Journal of Medicine* and *The Annals of Internal Medicine*, show how we can affect the wellbeing of other people, or places, by the way in which we feel about them. They declare: 'In the twenty-first century, the evidence has become overwhelming that our thoughts and bodies can be directly affected and influenced by the thoughts of another person, or by events and activities at a distant location blocked from ordinary perception.'[17]

In 2005, a group of researchers from Bastyr University and the University of Washington conducted an experiment where couples were divided into *senders* and *receivers*. The former were asked to send an image or thought to the latter at a specific moment. During the time of transmission, the receivers experienced an increase in blood oxygenation in the visual cortex of the brain. Furthermore: 'The receiver's brain reacts as though he or she is seeing the same image at the same time.'[18]

Two people, in separate rooms, were asked to sense each other's presence, and eventually their brainwaves began to synchronise. However, the one with the more cohesive brain patterns was able to influence the other—possibly by picking up their colleague's information as if it were their own. This could be compared to what companies do, in that they present desirable concepts about their products and services that we readily pick up and accept as our own.

William Braud,[19] along with Marilyn Schlitz,[20] provided evidence of the success of healing by illustrating how other people can have as much influence over the subject's personal response as the subject themselves. One of the ways they measured the response of the receiver to the conscious influence of the sender was via the electro-dermal conductivity of the skin, similar to techniques used in lie detector tests. These record unconscious fluctuations in emotions; the results showed how the nervous system of one person could be affected by another, whether they were aware of that person or not. They found that: 'In statistical terms, it meant that other people could have almost the same mind–body effect on you that you could have on yourself. Letting someone else express a good intention for you was almost as good as using biofeedback on yourself.'[21]

It is interesting to note that during this experiment, mental images were used as part of the study. The influencer imagined and visualised the desired outcome on the target person. While the imagery included vigorous exercise, listening to energising music or visualising scary circumstances, it might not be unreasonable to hypothesise that a logo stirring similar emotions (a sports brand, a hip-hop brand, and an insurance brand, for example) could also have a measurable effect.

Rupert Sheldrake cites ample evidence of the awareness people experience when others focus on them in his book aptly named *The Sense of Being Stared At*. At the extreme end of using the power of our minds, Jon Ronson describes in his book *The Men Who Stare at Goats* how it is possible to stop the heart of a goat (or even a person) by intent alone. The experimenter, a member of the American military, simply imagined the goat's heart stopping—and it did. Obviously, the objective of the military was in learning to stop more than a goat's heart. However, when we start to explore the power of our imagination, the possibilities are awesome.

In 1997, William Tiller, physicist and Professor Emeritus of Materials Science and Engineering at Stanford University, conducted an experiment that proved that intention could affect the wellbeing of a living object. Using fruit flies as a test subject, he constructed two black boxes. One box was imprinted with an intention to increase the health of the flies; the other box remained untouched. Both boxes were sent to a place where fruit fly larvae were normally hatched; the box with the health intention produced healthier and faster-growing flies. Perhaps most remarkable was Tiller finding that successive experiments produced stronger and quicker effects. Like Rupert Sheldrake's field of consciousness, once established, it exists to be plugged into. Tiller further reported that the environment around the black box with the intention also seemed to have been charged: 'Somehow his lab was beginning to manifest different material properties, almost as if it were a specially charged environment.' Even when all traces of the experiment were removed, there was still measurable evidence that Tiller's laboratories had undergone some long-term transformation: 'The energy from intention appeared to "charge" the environment and create a domino effect of order.'

Similarly, researcher Graeme Watkins and his wife Anita recruited participants with psychic ability and asked them to help anaesthetised mice recover more quickly than usual. Not only were they able to do this, but other mice placed on the spot where the experiment had taken place beforehand also recovered more quickly. It was as if the space itself had developed a healing charge.[22] This, of course, may be precisely what happens in sacred and healing sites around the world. One person has an experience and others visit and add their belief to the energetic space.

Measuring group consciousness

In 1993, Roger Nelson developed a machine that could measure the energy of a group or event, to see if he could pick up evidence of a collective consciousness. The Global Consciousness Project (GCP) that resulted from this development is an international effort involving researchers from several institutions and countries. Designed to explore whether or not the construct of interconnected consciousness can be scientifically validated, it has resulted in the discovery of evidence that the physical world and our mental world of information and meaning are linked. By 2006 they had had studied 205 top news events; they found that when people reacted to these events, the machines responded too.[23] Peaks in huge events were evident including the death of Princess Diana and the World Trade Center disaster, as well as during global celebrations such as New Year.

Nelson's machine could also measure the energy of locations. The energy levels recorded at sacred places, for example, were shown to be high, whether people were present or not. It is worth noting, however, that while a group at an event such as a play created energy, business and academic meetings had no effect on the machine. This might indicate the ability of the right, creative, emotional brain to connect with the quantum field, whereas our left brain demands logical constraints in our pursuit of hard physical facts.

A brand launch may not be a particularly momentous event. However if, as I believe has been considered, a logo were beamed on to the surface of the Moon for all Earth-bound beings to see, could it not create a measurable response? Especially if it stirred our emotions.

Closer to Earth, a special-effects engineer has launched 'flogos'. Francisco Guerra, an entrepreneur from Alabama, has come up with a way to form logos out of foamy clouds, up to 4 feet across. As reported by the *Associated Press*,[24] Guerra said: 'It's a shock factor when you look up and there's a logo over your head.' Of course, in order to see these flying logo clouds, we have to look upwards, a movement known to trigger a specific brain response.

With the ability of a logo to deliver messages effectively and quickly, in a way that can affect our energy field, which subsequently affects the energy field as a whole and meets with other fields to influence them, it is possible to see how powerful the logo is in creating, maintaining and building new ways of being.

Avoiding the hype

Marketing experts are committed to creating, growing and strengthening these fields of brand consciousness that affect us collectively. The logo prompts the brand values, enabling them to seep into the psyche of our society. There are many ways this can happen, with or without our participation or awareness.

Many people are waking up to the power wielded by companies and are taking action. They too are using the logo as a powerful tool for change and are turning the tables.

One mother, distraught by the commitment of her children to branded clothing, was publicly broadcast, on *BBC Radio Four*, ritually cutting ties with the brand by removing the logos from all her children's clothes while they watched. We have already read of parents removing the Playboy bunny symbol from children's items such as pencilcases, as they feel it represents the wrong values for youngsters. Despite the fact that these parents admit their children are too young to know what it means, they still believe the children could be affected.

Neil Boorman, author of *Bonfire of the Brands*, ritualistically burned all of his branded goods. Before the event, Boorman said: 'To be honest, I think it's going to be a relief. For the past 20 years, I have relied on the Ralph Lauren pony, the half-eaten apple and myriad other badges of status to prove to myself and all around me that I'm worth something. Call me lazy, but it's easier to express your hopes and dreams via an embroidered logo on your chest rather than articulate who you are/want to be. (I wanna be creative and successful and, er, cool.)' He concluded: 'Richer or poorer, the one brand that remains is the real me.'[25]

These people have chosen to pull their own strings rather than have them jerked by the brand merchants. They recognise that, whether we want to protect ourselves from a cult-like movement, or from vastly inflated prices, action at the level of the logo is an effective means.

CHAPTER SEVEN

The creative challenge

'Creativity is the defeat of habit by originality.'

ARTHUR KOESTLER

Weber's Dictionary of Psychology defines creativity as 'a term used to refer to mental processes that lead to solutions, ideas, conceptualisations, artistic forms, theories or products that are unique and novel'. When we create a logotype, this process becomes quite intangible, since we are creating a symbol that represents an ideal part of something else—rather than a literal representation. We are creating a creative solution to a creative solution.

The creation of symbols to effect a desired destiny taps into an ancient resource that was used by our ancestors. Throughout history, art has been used effectively to transform the fate of society.

According to an article by Helen Phillips in *New Scientist*: 'People have speculated about their own creativity for centuries . . . because creative thought just seems to "arrive", the credit has been laid at the feet of the gods or spirits or, recently, the id or subconscious mind. Whatever it is, it is thinking at the edge, at the very fringes.'[1]

While creativity has long eluded scientific study, Jordan Peterson, a psychologist at the University of Toronto, Canada, believes that the brains of creative people seem more open to incoming stimuli than other, less creative, types. This makes creative people more open to possibilities and ideas.

When we connect with our creative mind, we are able to access the power of our imagination. This is the key to freeing our mind from the constraining limits of our logical thought processes and allowing us to connect with the universal field. In this state of mind, we have access to infinite possibilities for creating different futures.

Design is where our imagination and our conscious mind meet to visualise a potential that can be created in reality. Graphic designers combine creativity and logic in a common cause to envision a future in a symbol that enables brands to deliver solutions to our desires.

Without this ability to imagine a future and then create it, we would not have the world we live in. Commercial designers are employed to use their imagination to help create an environment that will benefit their clients.

The challenge begins with the creative mindset.

Connecting with the creative mind

The creative mindset does not necessarily respond to a traditional 9am Monday-morning start; designers and artists find their own personal ways of getting into the mood. Before starting to write or compose, various famous people are reputed to have inspired themselves by stroking fur, sniffing rotten apples, shining shoes, writing only with special ink or walking. The aim of these exotic rites is to connect with the creative flow; to reach a mental state where new ideas are able to germinate. Sometimes just going to sleep can be enough. James Brindley, responsible for pioneering a whole new transport system for the country via a set of waterways, went to bed for three days after he had been briefed on the project and before coming up with the idea. Frederich Von Kulke, who had been struggling with the structure of carbon for some time, only realised the solution when he took a nap and had a dream about a snake biting its tail and realised that the structure of carbon was a ring. Mozart described, in a letter to a friend, how he heard music in his imagination, stating: 'All this inventing, this producing, takes place in a pleasing lively dream.'

More recently there is the success story of Frank Warren, who set up the highly profitable company PostSecret based on people sending in postcards confessing their innermost secrets. These get posted on the internet and the site is in the top ten visited by students. Warren was inspired to start the company when, after a visit to Paris where he bought three postcards, he dreamed that they were covered with cryptic messages including one about a 'reluctant oracle.'[2]

The phrase 'sleeping on the job' begins to take on a completely new meaning and brings new possibilities.

Designers are usually born with a creative flair that gets developed, even constrained, at art school where we learn the logical process of design including choosing and reproducing typefaces and colours, presentation skills, computer and print techniques, budgeting and so on. Successful designers enter the commercial design field with both of these abilities: creativity (the design) and logic (business-related skills). The latter, being more structured, can perhaps be more easily learned than the former.

While the design process comprises complex physical stages including analysing a brief, defining design requirements and justifying the result, creativity comes from a deeper source. But in the commercial world, creativity and logic must work side by side to achieve a logo design that will prompt us into action.

Research has indicated that the most effective solutions arise when *both* sides of the brain are utilised. The left, rational side will consider and digest the requirements of the brief, while switching to the right will open the creative, exploratory process. Finally, the left side will logically analyse the ideas and discard those that do not meet the brief, are impractical or creatively unacceptable, and eventually focus on the remaining potential solutions.

This is what we do as designers. In creative meetings, I am aware of constantly switching from my conscious to my subconscious mind, as if I 'pop out' from the briefing at one level to gather a basket of possibilities, which are then consciously rationalised and may be discussed or sketched out during the meeting. This is like a sort of 'soft journeying' in the shamanic sense, and I think many of us do it all the time unconsciously. During daydreaming we may be physically present but our mind is elsewhere, checking future possibilities or making sense of past events or places.

Colin Martindale, a psychologist from the University of Maine in Orono, made one of the first studies of the creative brain at work.[3] It was shown that creativity has two stages: inspiration and elaboration.

While people were dreaming up stories, their brains were surprisingly quiet; the dominant activity was in alpha waves, indicating a relaxed state as though the conscious mind were quiet while the brain was making connections behind the scenes. However, when these quiet-minded people were asked to work on their stories, the alpha wave suddenly dropped off and the brain became busier, revealing more corralling of activity with more organised thinking. Strikingly, it was the people who showed the biggest difference in brain activity between the inspiration and development stages who produced the most creative storylines.

'It's as if the less creative person can't shift gear,' said Guy Claxton, a psychologist at the University of Bristol, UK. 'Creativity requires different kinds of thinking. Very creative people move between these intuitively.'

In a later study, Martindale found that this change in activity was particularly noticeable on the right side of the brain. But people who had the connections severed to treat intractable epilepsy, for example, seemed to become less creative, indicating that communication between both sides of the brain is important.

Talented designers are able to tap into the collective subconscious, wherein lie our thoughts, memories and dreams. From this powerful standpoint they consciously construct a symbol that attracts us like moths to a flame. Thus we become willing participants in the success of the brand.

The word *inspiration* originally meant receiving a breath of divinity. Artist and photographer Man Ray (1890-1976) said: 'Personally I always preferred inspiration to information.'

In *A Space for Silence* by Alen Macweeney and Caro Ness, the sculptor Arlene Shechet says: 'When I am sculpting, I find that there are moments of meditative consciousness close to the Buddhist experience. Working with a medium that requires immediate action requires you to suspend conscious planning and enter a state of not thinking—just doing.'

Actors are known for immersing themselves in their role long before filming begins. Johnny Depp, when chosen for the role in the movie version of Roald Dahl's *Charlie and the Chocolate Factory*, sat in Dahl's shed for some days to get a deeper sense of the author.

Similarly, I would often 'know' the symbol of an organisation as I sat in the reception area waiting for the design briefing to begin. The actual briefing would then serve as a confirmation that allowed me to detail or fine-tune my previous gut feeling. The bulk of the design budget would then be spent in preparing a lengthy post-rationalisation to justify the design concept. And it made sense.

Of course, the more 'logical' approach is to assess the situation, review the competition, complete extensive market research on the organisation, internally and externally, including staff, managers, suppliers and competitors as well as the position of the relevant market as a whole. Even using the latter method, I would defy any designer worth his or her salt to deny that the glimmer of a concept had not evolved long before the final results had been gathered.

A well-known Australian designer told me he would know the design solution before he got back to the studio after the client's briefing, and brief it immediately to the designers. A design director friend told the story of the time he presented a concept that had taken weeks to prepare. When the client informed him that he had already rejected something similar from another design group, he created an alternative solution immediately, on the back of an envelope, which the client accepted and paid for! These concepts are the priceless part of the imagery, sometimes taking seconds to conceptualise, but weeks or months to actualise.

Where does this information come from? There are many theories, including gut instinct, intuition and universal fields of consciousness where we all pick up responses from 'out there'. It is certainly not entirely from the logical, rational part of our thinking process. Does the image already exist out there somewhere waiting to be recognised and grasped from the future ambitions and objectives of an organisation? Or are we subconsciously guided by key personnel in the organisation who are unable to interpret the information graphically and manifest the design themselves? Do designers channel a solution from a higher source, on behalf of the client?

When we truly begin the design process, we enter a sort of commercial dream world: like Einstein's beam of light, we travel into the ether on a vision quest, searching for the innovative design solution that does not come readily from logical left-brain thinking. As designers, we tap into the world of the subconscious, using the right brain, without its time and space constraints, where we are able to 'dream' the imagery. It is as if design, through its creation and subsequent application, can ground the very core of an unformed idea, bringing it into our consciousness as a tangible inspiration for our physically based objectives. When we get the design right, the logo is more likely to resonate with the rest of the world.

Research and technology versus creativity

Do research and technology sanitise or support the creative process? They may certainly help focus on the desired design outcome—but do they encourage inspiration?

According to Winston Fletcher in *Tantrums and Talent*: 'Compared with most other consumer industries, the creative industries engage in comparatively little market research; they rely to a very great extent on experience, intuition, flair, hunch and judgement.' In design, unlike the logical system of analysis in research, ideas will pop up almost at random. Gut feeling and intuition play as great a part, if not more so, in the creation of a design as the logical processes and educational qualifications of the designer.

Theoretically, a computer could be programmed to design a logotype, based on the findings of the commissioned research. An interesting exercise was undertaken, and displayed in a Sunday magazine, where a face was made up of all the 'best' features (according to research findings) of famous people. Lips, eyes, nose, hair and face shapes were selected and compiled into the 'perfect' face. The resulting image was one of complete disharmony; there was nothing 'wrong' with the final face, it just did not gel, despite having the best features as defined by research. We can use this process to design a logo, but the result can portray a soulless design and we cannot put our fingers on why it does not work. If it is designed solely with head-based logic, without the passion of the heart, it cannot reach out to the hearts of others. We just won't love it.

As corporations expand and become more complex in structure, it becomes increasingly difficult to measure the potential effect of one small part. For example, as the globalisation of brands grows, companies need to be increasingly vigilant about cultural differences.

Coke, Marlboro and McDonald's may have made the leap to global acceptance, but many colours, symbols and names have potentially disastrous political, historical or cultural implications. The consequences of getting it wrong have, understandably, led designers to stick to some boring typographical solution with a bland name that is inoffensive in any culture. This is why many corporate image programmes reach for the lowest common denominator: it is safe and the stakes are too high to risk getting it wrong. Companies will become increasingly dependent on research to minimise the risk of failure.

By depending heavily on this practice, however, we only use half our brain; the spontaneity and wisdom of our intuition and gut feeling is rejected in favour of 'proven' market trends. It is remarkable that companies continue to play it safe in this way considering that many of the most successful designs seem to have occurred after little research.

Anita Roddick believed that: 'Running a company on market research is like driving while looking in the rear window.' London based graphic designer Adrian Shaughnessy states: 'Business life has become so hazardous and competition so intense that risk has been eliminated from most areas of commercial activity. If we follow this no-risk philosophy to its logical conclusion, all communications will eventually look the same.'[4]

Advanced wind tunnel research, for example, determines the efficiency of the performance of a car at speed on the road—but it does mean that most cars end up looking similar in shape as they reach for this single ideal. On the other hand, innovative designs can seem traumatic to the outside, commercial world—as can be seen from the effect the YBAs (Young British Artists, including Tracey Emin and Damien Hirst) had on the British art world in the 1990s. (The YBAs were noted for their shock tactics, use of throwaway materials, and wild living.)

Today's designers may be fed a diet of research and technology, but the creative spark comes from somewhere else. While market research and creativity work hand in hand, it is the input of the latter that provides the design with magic and memorability. The production process is very logical. It can be split into stages, planned and monitored. The creative process is less tangible, much more difficult to plan or to force into a tight schedule, and is immensely subjective.

Differentiation in a world of similarities

The logotype is how a company is physically recognised in the world; it symbolises everything it does and is. More than this, a well-designed and implemented logotype will project the brand *values* to staff, shareholders, customers and the public at large.

Cleverly handled in print and advertising, the logotype is a constant and familiar reminder of the brand, and we soon learn to recognise the design as we would the face of a good friend. In the right hands, a logotype can encapsulate the essence of the company, well beyond its physical activities alone.

This presents a challenge for designers at large. In a world filled with competitive products, brand values are often abstract, idealistic concepts to which many companies aspire. This renders them difficult to articulate in a simple piece of commercial art, and can provoke designs that can be applied to almost any business. This becomes apparent in the case of some advertisements, which are so generic that they can even be sold to promote different products in other countries. Nevertheless, a logotype is an extremely effective way of communicating abstract concepts.

For example, when BT changed its symbol, it attributed a whole new set of brand values to it. It is doubtful whether we would easily see these merely by looking at the symbol, but when supported by marketing they can become synonymous with it. These values were stated as:

- Trustworthy—keeps its promises
- Helpful—listens and responds
- Inspiring—creating new communications possibilities
- Straightforward—keeps things simple
- Heart—cares and is committed to what it does

These are part of a whole branding process signified by the new logo for BT, known as the 'Connected World' symbol and representing a more 'dynamic, colourful approach to communication'. These values describe how BT needs to be seen as an organisation (brand values) and how they need to behave to achieve this (people values). Most, if not all, of these would probably be desirable to most businesses. The logotype linked to these values differentiates BT, ensuring that it stands out from its competitors.

Fiona Gilmore, managing director of the design company Lewis Moberly, states that, 'The majority of people continue to misunderstand and think that it is just a logo, rather than understanding that a corporate identity programme is actually concerned with the very commercial objective of having a strong personality and single-minded, focused direction for the whole organisation . . . it's like planting an acorn and then a tree grows. If you create the right foundation then you are building a whole culture for the future of an organisation.'[5]

All brands have logotypes by which they are identified, but not all logotypes are brands. Using Gilmore's analogy of the oak tree, all oaks must have an acorn to start with, but not all acorns turn into oak trees.

Umpqua Bank, a small local chain in the American Pacific Northwest, was an unlikely pacesetter for a design-led revolution, but this is exactly what the company did when it looked towards retailers for hints on selling products. It started calling its bank branches *stores*, using large displays to 'productise' its services and inviting customers to 'sip', 'read', 'surf' or 'bank'. Umpqua branches looked more like plush hotel lobbies than banks and at least one store stayed open in the evening for poetry readings, book clubs and movie nights. All this enticed customers to stay longer and buy products. Although it was seen as a risk, it paid off, with much of the credit going to designers. Lani Hayward, Umpqua's Vice President of Creative Strategies, said: 'Without creativity, we wouldn't be where we are today. Creativity drives vision and fuels implementation.' Ray Davis, President of Umpqua, says: 'Without the design, it wouldn't work.'[6]

Who takes design responsibility?

Who actually runs the design of a logo and related graphic material in a company? Who takes the final decision? It is not always someone who understands the heart and soul of the business and who can also aid the integration of this into a design. Those who really understand the brand understand the company at its deepest levels. Those who control branding imagery hold many of the cards in the future of the company—and yet this task is sometimes passed to inexperienced employees, or design coordinators, who have little interest in the long-term success of the company.

Originally the person who held the vision for the company, the managing director or owner, was also responsible for organising the symbol for the company and would probably have had some input into the final solution. Now, a whole range of specialised businesses help determine the visual future of brands.

In his book *Tantrums and Talent*, Winston Fletcher points out that creativity begins with the manager: he or she is the person who decides on the designer, is responsible for the brief, outlines the requirements and 'recognises and puts the appropriate value on creative quality, style and technique'. The book quotes Jeremy Isaacs saying that by inviting them to do the job, ' . . . You've made your creative decision, which is which creator to work with.' In the same book it states that designers need to meet face to face with clients; a written paper brief alone will not suffice.

The constant cry of designers is that they are only as good as the client allows them to be. But Colin Forbes, founder partner of the international design group Pentagram, stated in his Design Museum lecture in March 2007 that he believes there is no such thing as a bad client, only bad designers.

Logos drive our world

In the beginning, we ate whatever food was available when we were hungry; we wore simple clothes and lived in basic dwellings to keep us warm and sheltered. As we became more civilised, our awareness of our surrounding world increased along with a desire for more choice in our lives.

With the development of a more commercial age, businesses grew beyond the point where the owners or manufacturers could personally liaise with the individual customer. New methods were needed to communicate the value of their products or skills. The corporate promise was developed, and identified with a mark that guaranteed quality.

This was not an entirely new concept: Tutankhamen was buried more than 3,000 years ago with jars of wine labelled with the name of the winemaker, the vineyard and the year of bottling. Soap-makers in ancient Rome were fined for selling unbranded soap. Hallmarks on silver have been a form of consumer protection for more than 700 years. The branding of animals has been practised for at least 5,000 years. Stonemasons have their own marks—there are more than 15,000 different marks in Strasbourg Cathedral alone. There have been watermarks on paper since the 13th century and there are no doubt many more early examples of branding.

The word 'brand' has its roots in Old Norse and meant 'burn', because cattle were 'burnt' or branded to signify ownership. Those farmers with a good reputation for quality would find people seeking out his brand. Jeremy Bullmore, a long-time director of the advertising agency J Walter Thompson, says: 'Brands were the first piece of consumer protection—you knew where to go if you had a complaint.'[7]

Discovery of the first tribal 'logo' was reported in *The Northern Echo* in 2007: 'Tribal marker unearthed by archaeologists.' The markings on a stone, discovered by archaeologists near Whitby Abbey in North Yorkshire, are believed to have been an instantly recognisable logo with a specific meaning to the people of the time. Project direct Sarah Jennings said: 'It's possible it has some sort of symbolic importance that needed no explanation in the same way that the well known logos of today do.'[8]

The main function of the original trademarks was identification. They signify much more in present times, as ancient symbols take on an identity of their own in modern-day usage.

We might have much in common with other animals, but one trait that sets us apart is our ability to rely on symbolism. We have done this for thousands of years. Symbolic engravings have been found in South Africa that date back to 77,000 years ago. It was noted: 'The Blombos Cave motifs suggest arbitrary conventions unrelated to reality-based cognition . . . and they may have been constructed with symbolic intent, the meaning of which is now unknown.'[9]

Graphic design itself is not such a new profession. Again in South Africa, archaeologists unearthed 270 pieces of engraved ostrich eggshell dated to around 60,000 years ago. An article in *Scientific American* titled 'Engraved Ostrich Eggshell Fragments Reveal 60,000-Year-Old Graphic Design Tradition' stated 'The fragments constitute what the researchers say is the "earliest evidence of a graphic tradition among prehistoric hunter-gatherer populations." As such, the finds help to illuminate the emergence of symbolic representation—a hallmark of modern human behaviour.'[10]

We have learned to trust symbols, whether they are road traffic signs or musical notation. Mathematicians, engineers and electricians are among the professions that have their own set of symbols to ensure their efficiency and wellbeing. These symbols set out a certain standpoint in time and space and we follow them knowing that we will reach a desired conclusion. At a glance, symbols guide us instantly and we follow their intention without question, trusting that they give us information and guidance for our own good.

Brands started to develop into the symbols and processes we know today during the late nineteenth and early twentieth centuries, with the growth of the industrial revolution. This enabled the mass-production and marketing of products. Some successful early brands established in this time still survive today and include Coca-Cola, Quaker Oats and American Express.[11]

They have come a long way since the first commissioned brand designer. This title is usually attributed to Peter Behrens (1868-1940) because, retained as an artistic consultant by AEG, he designed the entire corporate identity, including the logotype, the product design and the publicity. The AEG website states: 'Peter Behrens was not only the father of German industrial design—he was also the founder of corporate identity. Working for AEG, Behrens was the first person to create logos, advertising material, and company publications with a consistent, unified design.'

It was only around 50 years ago when the first documented evidence on the positive effects of branding appeared, illustrating the fact that people were prepared to pay more for a branded product even if the quality was the same as another, similar, product. Psychology began to play a part, as material content was no longer enough to sell products above a competitor's. The experts were challenged to get into our minds and change them.

There may still be a basic assumption that we buy things because we benefit from them. However, the act of shopping, rather than fulfilling needs, is now an end in itself—to the point where psychologists have identified a pathological condition: oniomania, or 'compulsive shopping'. This is defined in *The American Psychiatric Association's Diagnostic and Statistical Manual* of mental disorders as an obsessive-compulsive disorder.

Fulfilling our dreams or creating them?

Today, our purchasing power is motivated by imagery. Brands help create our futures.

The brand identity is now recognised as one of the most valuable assets of any organisation in distilling and promoting its ethos and personality. When we buy a product or service, we are buying much more than that; we are buying a part of the company promise. People will pay much more for a brand name, despite the fact that they may know that it possibly came off the same factory line as something much cheaper. In fact, in our world with numerous brands it is difficult to think of a case where the cheapest is also the market leader.

The survival of the existing economic world is dependent on corporate growth. Since the 1980s, the development of technology, cheap manufacturing and aggressive business tactics in an ever more competitive global market has led to the growth of the brand as we know it—products that are sold solely on the basis of their label rather than their price, quality or usefulness.

Companies have switched from manufacturing products to marketing lifestyles. Potential customers are arranged into target groups depending on their age and their social, emotional, prestigious or aspirational status. Whether they are exuberant teenagers, conservative elderly people, or romanticists there will be a logo to suit them.

Nowhere is the statement 'a picture is worth a thousand words' more valid, especially when taking into consideration the cost of advertising time and space.

The corporate, or brand, promise is singularly identified by a consistent mark: the logotype. It is how we recognise it. A photograph or illustration of a product may remind us that we are thirsty or hungry. But a logo, layered lavishly with brand messages via advertising and marketing, can stimulate our desires, regurgitate a host of memories and stir a range of emotions far beyond our primal need for food or drink.

Most successful logo designs are deceptively simple. When millions of pounds or dollars are cited in the press as the cost of implementing a new design, the cry usually goes up that a child, or at least an art school student, could have done it for much, much less. And yet the art of creating a logo has turned into a complex, creative, ritualistic process that can make or break a brand.

Jim Hytner, Group Brand and UK Marketing Director of Barclays, states: 'Imagine Coca-Cola without a logo. Imagine Apple's iMac as a grey rectangular box. Imagine Nike without its TV adverts. Design is intrinsically linked to the bottom line.'[12]

USA graphic designer Mark Fox says: 'A logo represents the company, and transfers its inherent meanings to the company which is then perceived as hip, or dynamic or stable.' He continues: 'What if I encounter a logo before I know anything about the company?' (That is, before branding exercises have linked it with corporate values.) 'In this case, all I have to form my opinions—to gather meaning—is the name of the company and the way the identity is articulated by the designer.'[13]

In the book *Corporate Source II*, an annual publication of Wilcord Publications Limited, it states: 'Perhaps the most influential trend in graphic design as a tool of corporate communications is the notion that a designer can bring to a corporation much more than a system of decorative symbols and appealing brochures. When the designer's work is created as a communication of a corporation's objectives, personality and style, it has the power to dictate how the specific audience will perceive that company.'

A logo is the place where the corporate spirit interfaces with the commercial world and entices us to share the brand dream.

Left and right designer brains

To be successful, a designer must have the ability to tap into both sides of the brain, to blend left-brain logic with right-brain creativity and intuition. The dominant use of one side of the brain can lead to the creation of designs that, although they may meet the research criteria and answer all the other prerequisites, are unmemorable and unexciting; or to designs that may be beautiful but completely miss the point of the brief.

Experiments have shown that the two hemispheres of the brain are responsible for different ways of thinking. The left brain is logical, rational, analytical, objective and looks at parts. The right brain is more intuitive, subjective, deals with feelings and creativity and looks at wholes.

Evidence of the difference in the workings of the left and right hemispheres of the brain was reported thus: 'Three neuroscientists from America set 23 volunteers a series of tests, which involved plugging either their right or left nostril with tissues. With the right nostril blocked, the subjects did better at visual tasks (which use the right half of the brain). With the left one blocked, they did better at verbal reasoning, a left-brain task. This proves that you can control how your brain works by choosing which nostril you breathe through.'[14]

A corporate image or product logotype must straddle two worlds: the boundless world of the brand dream as well as the limitations of the business world. The designer brings the invisible world (the concept) into the visible world (the actual design).

Dr David R Hawkins, in his book *Power Vs Force*, states: 'The visible world is created from the invisible world, and is therefore influenced by the future.' It is one thing to have a brilliant concept such as the London Eye, for example, but then we need to build it. This requires motivation, which, according to Hawkins, is 'derived from meaning'. He concludes: 'Therefore the visible and invisible worlds were linked together.'

Designer and typographer Adrian Frutiger states that: 'One can say that the artist or craftsman is in reality a mediator between two worlds, visible and invisible. In former times, craftsmanship in itself was regarded as something "miraculous". The more completely the work brought its content to expression through its aesthetic perfection, the greater its symbolic value became and the more worthy of worship it was.'

In my own design business, I became acutely aware of the dilemma of switching from creative to logic modes. At times I would be sitting silently, meandering in the dream world of the right brain, trawling for juicy concepts, when someone would come through the door and ask something relatively mundane such as whether they could take the following day off.

The pictures forming in my mind would instantly pop into oblivion like bubbles in the air, often to be irretrievable.

Graphics have a language of their own and have the power to inspire and excite us well beyond the simple relaying of commercial messages. A successful symbol or logotype must be both inspirational and practical. While research and practical experience can provide the logic for a design solution, a true expression of the corporate dream in a piece of commercial art requires creative intuition. Richard Ward, designer and founder partner of the design group The Team, states: 'You know a symbol is right when it flows.' Paul Klee apparently knew when a painting was completed when, after looking at it, it started looking back at him.

David Puttman, in *Tantrums and Talent*, says: 'The good manager constantly stresses the relationship between creativity and society, the social responsibilities of the creative individual. The more creative the individual is, the greater that responsibility.' Wally Olins, founder of the design group Wolff Olins, is quoted in the same book, aiming at designers: 'I try and explain to them the enormous significance of what they are doing, the enormous power that they have in the world, the fact that what they are doing is going to be seen by everybody, and it is their work. It is their imprint, if you like, on mankind. It may only be a very small imprint, but it is their imprint. I try to make them feel a sense of responsibility for what they are doing.'

Perhaps the greatest attribute for the designer is his or her ability to tune into the client's space and out of his or her personal designer ego. Lawrence Llewelyn Bowen stated in the television programme *Changing Rooms* that designers are merely facilitators of the client's dreams. (He also claimed that being a designer is being a 'control freak'.)

I personally feel that the design field has succumbed to the left-brained fast-track world where everything is wanted here and now, and usually by yesterday. Designers seem no longer to be the magicians of the past, weaving the corporate dream, qualities and aspirations into a logo to share with the rest of the world. More often than not, they seem to be pressured into producing more for less, are often referred to as 'creatives' and organised by a 'creative head'. This could be an apt description for a profession that is in danger of losing its heart.

Design qualifications and computer skills alone do not create a successful logo designer; deeper skills of innate creativity are required if the resulting logo is to turn us on.

As an example of the importance of individual design input, we can look to the art world. The value attributed to a two-dimensional interpretation of an object varies vastly, depending on who the artist is. It is not so hard for any competent artist to render a picture of irises. What makes Van Gogh's version so desirable and attractive? Although an extreme example, we can look at children's art versus art displayed in the Tate Modern. To the untrained eye, many works are comparable.

Avoiding a well-trodden discussion of what makes good art, we do know that a recognised artist can command vastly higher fees. If Picasso drew a simple line on a canvas and authenticated it with his signature, it would be worth thousands of pounds. It may be something anyone could do, but it is the energy associated with the identity of Picasso, the quality of the artist himself, that makes it special. A logo, the signature of the brand, turns an ordinary handbag into an expensive desirable object. And with fame being self-perpetuating, more people will want to own or visit a famous painting. This alone increases its desirability, adds to its 'glow', and so on.

Consider the following, extracted from Alan Fletcher's book *The Art of Looking Sideways*: 'Sol LeWitt, American conceptual artist, believes in the superiority of idea over object. In 1987, he sold an intangible concept (an idea for an artwork that doesn't actually exist) for the concrete sum of $26,400. Legal ownership was indicated by a typed certificate, which specified that the artwork ('10,000 lines about 10 inches long, covering the wall evenly') should be executed in black pencil. The owner has the right to reproduce this piece as many times as he likes. If you reproduce it without permission you'd only have a fake—despite the fact that LeWitt would not have picked up his brush in either case.' A logo, reproduced without permission, is also a fake.

Corporate image design may not be categorised as fine art, but its success depends heavily on the use of the creative mind. Despite the sanitisation and formalisation of the research and design development process, ultimately the mark itself is a piece of commercial art with the potential to become famous and desirable.

Good design versus bad design

'Good design goes to heaven, bad design goes everywhere.'
ANON

How do we know if a design is good when the quality of design, including art, is so subjective?

D&AD, the Designers and Art Directors Association, lays down the following standards for the judging of its annual design awards: 'Great Idea, Brilliantly Executed and Appropriate.' Alan Fletcher stated that: 'To be effective, a trademark should fulfil criteria: utilitarian values of being relevant, appropriate and practical; intangible qualities of being memorable, attractive and distinctive; and that visual tweak which creates a unique personality.'[15]

The designer Paul Rand prefers to use the term 'effective design.' In his article 'Logos, Flags and Escutcheons', he says that the effectiveness of a good logo depends on distinctiveness, visibility, usability, memorability, universality, durability and timelessness. He states: 'Design, good or bad, is a vehicle of memory. Good design adds value of some kind and, incidentally, could be sheer pleasure; it respects the viewer—his sensibilities—and rewards the entrepreneur. It is easier to remember, with good feelings, a well-designed image than one that is muddled. A well-designed logo, in the end, is a reflection of the business it symbolises. It connotes a thoughtful and purposeful enterprise, and mirrors the quality of its products and services. It is good public relations and a harbinger of good will.

'It says "We care."

'If, in the business of communications, "image is king", the essence of this image, the logo, is a jewel in its crown.

'The ugliest flag is beautiful if it happens to be on your side. "Beauty," they say, "is in the eye of the beholder," in peace or in war, in flags or in logos. We all believe our flag the most beautiful; this tells us something about logos.'[16]

Nicholas Green, chief executive of digital solutions experts Tangent Communications, says: '[Bad design] probably won't make your business perform poorly—that's down to people and service. But bad design is hardly going to make your business grow, is it?'[17]

Many designers believe that the best logotype of all is the Coca-Cola signature. But what makes it so good? It is successful, but can we really say that this is due to the logotype design or the branding that has heightened its perspective? If we presented a similar logo today, would it be hailed as a milestone in the design field? There is no way today that I would suggest, to a major beverage manufacturer, that we look to anything akin to an accountant's sign-off for inspiration.

The children's brand Nickelodeon changed its logo in September 2009. A post by Stephanie Startz on *brandchannel.com* states: 'Nickelodeon is now armed with a forward-looking logo to effectively market their brand across all platforms. Renaming The N and Noggin creates a powerful visual presence, and reinforces the brand identity to their demographic. In a crowded, oversaturated market, the simplicity of the new logo stands out.' Further comments on the site, however, differ from this positive outlook, claiming it to be 'bland, boring, driven by MBAs and irk, nick, nirk, eewh!'[18]

Displayed in the *Daily Mail* (and most other national newspapers) on 5 June 2007 was the new 2012 Olympics logotype. It had taken a year to produce, cost £400,000 and was designed by one of the best-known design companies, Wolff Olins, which specialises in corporate design. But despite all this, I could not readily find one word of praise, either from the design fraternity or from the public. According to the newspaper: 'Critics of the new logo described it as a "broken swastika", a "scribbled joke", a "toileting monkey" and even the logo for the Nazi SS. Within hours of its announcement, an online petition had been set up condemning it as an "embarrassment" that represents Britain in the "worst possible" way and calling for it to be scrapped. It attracted 10,000 signatures.' Four years after the logo was launched, Iran threatened to boycott the impending games, claiming that the symbol read as the word 'Zion', used to refer to its arch-rival Israel.

Contemporary British designers were near-unanimous in their disapproval of the logo, describing it as 'confusing' and 'embarrassing'. Stephen Bayley, founder of the Design Museum, called it a 'puerile mess, an artistic flop and a commercial scandal.'

So we think we know good design, and many of us are prepared to protest against design we believe is bad. And bad design can have hidden effects and provoke negative responses.

Curious about this unsurpassed deluge of negativity about a logo, a friend decided to perform a small, casual muscle-testing exercise to discover any underlying effect the Olympics logo may have on ourselves. Into four envelopes, subsequently sealed, we placed an Olympics logo, a Coca-Cola logo, one from Oxfam, and a blank piece of paper. After testing the effect of these on a group of participants, it turned out that the Olympics logo was the only one that delivered a single unanimous result. My friend believed that this was because its fragmented design scrambled the brain response.

The prime minister at the time, Tony Blair, said optimistically: 'When people see the new brand, we want them to be inspired to make a positive change in their life.' Olympics Minister Tessa Jowell, stated: 'It takes our values to the world beyond our shores, acting both as an invitation and an inspiration.'

New logos often challenge viewers and, more often than not, we just get used to them. But while we visually skim over their presence, they might continue to prompt a negative stab in our unconscious mind.

The effect of a physical negative response to this logo might not appear so strange when we consider the findings reported under the title: 'Beautiful art eases pain.'[19] Scientists found that volunteers, who were given a pricking sensation, felt less discomfort when looking at an attractive work of art than at an ugly painting or blank canvas. A team from the University of Bari in Italy asked 24 volunteers (12 men and 12 women) to select 20 paintings that they found either beautiful or ugly. As they gazed on these, the team administered small laser pulses on their hands. The volunteers stated that they felt the pain a third less intensely when gazing at a beautiful painting compared to when they were looking at either a blank or an ugly picture. The research leader, Dr Marina de Tommaso, stated that: 'Hospitals have been designed to be functional, but we think that their aesthetic aspects should be taken into account too.'[20]

While we can discuss the importance of 'good design'—and most designers spend much time on this—the perception of design quality is one that can vary, and ultimately it resides in the eyes of the beholder.

Nevertheless, while a good design, professionally implemented, may not be a guarantee of corporate success, it is certain to have a more positive impact on a company than a poorly applied, unattractive design.

We feel measurably good when we visit a great work of art. Carl Jung emphasised the importance of the human spirit in art; the artist finds order in apparent chaos. So, it is possible that a logotype that is well designed, with attention to colour, spaces, form and mathematical principles, will appeal to people's senses.

CHAPTER EIGHT

Creating a new image

'Design is important because if it were not designed it would not be made.'

ONE OF 50 DEFINITIONS PUBLISHED BY THE BRITISH DESIGN COUNCIL, THIS ONE BY A TEN-YEAR-OLD, IN *THE ART OF LOOKING SIDEWAYS*

Anyone can make a mark that identifies a brand and with a little computer savvy it can look good. But a successful logo must project the authentic core values of the brand; it must hold the soul of the business that it represents and share it with the rest of the world. Without this depth of reach, we might not connect with it, we might not believe in it, and we probably would not wish to be seen with it.

The challenge for designers lies in how to formalise the brand dream without losing the magic that tempts us to buy it. Anyone who has worked alongside good designers will note how they straddle the two worlds of imagination and reality, and weave the essence of the company into the graphics. No idea will be ignored as the details and content of all the elements—colour, type, symbols and layout—are intricately combined, with consideration given to the tiniest hairline space and virtually imperceptible comparison of colour shades, until the final design seems to click into incarnation.

The designer, with the help of key people in the company, is literally dreaming a future for the organisation or product through the process of designing a symbol. The logo might look deceptively simple, but the journey to the final design is a complex, lengthy and ritualistic process.

The design challenge

As businesses reach for a common solution in a given market, creative boundaries become so tightly set that there is often little room for artistic manoeuvrability.

Using a combination of creative skills and logic, the designer's challenge is to weave through the findings of the research, the opinions of the client, the requirements of the corporation as a whole, and the pros and cons of current trends—and still produce a design that he or she feels proud of, that satisfies the artistic ego, and that might even win a design award.

Despite the copious amounts of research, rationalisation and logic applied to the development and application of logotype design today, it is still a subjective, creative process. Everyone will have their own personal opinions about the appearance of the design, including colour, shape, typeface and style. This makes design a relatively safe forum for the expression of feelings; the likes and dislikes of individual managers and staff members get a chance to be aired in what can be an otherwise fairly sterile business environment.

Sometimes it feels that corporate identity design is a form of visual therapy as the designs get pushed around and heated feelings are often expressed about the theme of the concept through to the details of the elements. A logo design is an extremely powerful method for a manager to make a mark on a business; one that will reverberate through everything and be seen by the rest of the world, for years to come. A sensitive designer will take great care to build rapport with the client and not only provide a safe hearing space for this information to be vocalised but will manage and judge the value of the dynamics and their relevance to the design. One designer I know calls this process 'building bridges'; another refers to it as 'putting the client in the comfort zone.'

It gives a voice to the individuals responsible for the implementation of the image, allows selected staff the opportunity to participate in the design process with a sense of involvement and ownership, and enables designers to seek valuable pointers towards acceptable creative approaches. Without this personalised process, there is a real danger of the design being rejected at a later stage.

Shortcutting this design-led rite of passage can lead to massive resistance to the acceptance of any change—and change itself is one of the things we humans resist most, especially in a challenging financial environment. Design concepts that are bulldozed through by management can even lead to dissent and resentment within the organisation. To be fully successful, any new branding must be accepted and embraced by those who use it; they need to feel part of the 'baptism.'

Ultimately, it is the designer's job to pull together all the threads of all the relevant information and visually articulate this into one, simple, memorable graphic device that encapsulates the core of the organisation, expresses the dreams of its managers and captures the imagination of its clients.

History and track records will be taken into account but, in the main, design is a forward-looking aspect. Designers are challenged to visualise and imagine a future from where they can pull the imagery required.

We are becoming an increasingly visual culture, and the power of the designer as a communicator has never been so great. And yet, with the design process already transformed by technology, websites now exist that will promise a range of new or improved logo versions, from a variety of qualified designers, for a few hundred pounds; all they need is a brief company outline or even an existing logo. How can the result ever truly and accurately reflect the ethos of the business the logo represents, when the designer has no chance to conduct some in-depth personal research and to connect with the business at a gut level? It is comparable to sending a list of the symptoms of a disease in the post and waiting for some stranger to deliver the appropriate remedy. It may work, but there could be serious repercussions.

In the words of Wally Olins in his book *Corporate Identity*: 'The problems in developing symbols are complex. In addition to avoiding negative connotations, technical, creative, fashion and cost requirements all have to be considered. Creating something that is unique to the organisation for which it is devised, that will encapsulate the idea behind the organisation, that won't go out of date, that is flexible and cheap in use, and that will evoke strong, positive emotional feelings in all those who come into contact with it, is actually a very difficult thing to do.'

The long design process

'The details are not the details. They make the design.'
CHARLES EAMES

The process of designing logotypes has changed dramatically over the last 50 years, owing to the growth of competition and technology.

The design identification of companies and products used to be relatively simple. Up until the 1980s, in my experience, designers would work closely with key people responsible for the running of the organisation—possibly the chairman or chief executive. Initial meetings would be set up to formulate the project, discuss the brief and tease out the design requirements. Usually the end result would be affected by their personal tastes; many a wail would go up from designers when chief executives and chairmen alike would ask for a copy of the design presentation to take home, for opinions to be gathered from friends and relations.

As a result of this informal process, the visual identities of some of our older, established businesses are attributed with quirky and endearing beginnings. It has been reputed that the symbol for Shell was conceived when the founder, driving home from a family beach trip, checked his rear-view mirror and saw shells that had been collected by his children laid out to dry on the back shelf. However, according to Alan Fletcher and Germano Facetti, in their book *Identity Kits*, the Shell company image came from the fact that shells were used as ballast in ships when they returned empty; when oil took their place, the company adopted both the design and the name. In *Marks of Excellence*, the author Per Mollerup claims that Marcus Samuel chose the Shell symbol when he formed the Shell Transport and Trading Company in 1897. The company name and symbol were chosen in memory of his father, who had had a small shop dealing in decorative oriental seashells. And these stories all differ from the one on Shell's website, which links the symbol to the pilgrims travelling from Santiago de Compostela in Spain to Rosslyn Chapel in Scotland; they carried a shell from the former to the latter to indicate that they had completed the pilgrimage. According to the website, the family of one of the original directors had a coat of arms incorporating the scallop shell after their ancestors made the trip. The shell is one of the eight emblems for good luck in Chinese, and a sign for a prosperous journey.

Whichever is the true inspiration for the design, each adds a human value to a vast organisation.

The Coca-Cola script logo is based on the common handwriting of the day, and may have been taken from the signature that the company accountant used when he signed off the early accounts. The familiar Citroën symbol was designed to represent the 'herring-bone' gear made in the factory established by Andre Citroën. The Renault diamond was derived from the diamond-shaped hole cut into the bonnet to cool the engine.

This relatively spontaneous and informal response to design requirements is rarely adopted today as the logo becomes ever more important in the success of a business. The risks are too great. Design groups, research companies and specific in-house teams responsible for developing and marketing brands all combine to create a process of brand development that leaves little to chance. Personal opinion (if anyone is brave enough to express one) is almost inevitably sidelined in favour of research findings.

Design ritual

The rituals used to complete a design have changed dramatically in only 30 years. The designer used to be the conductor of an orchestra of specialists, managing and fine-tuning the process until the final result matched the conceived and approved design. Type was carefully selected from printed catalogues, specified and ordered from a typesetting company that would first supply a draft proof to be checked by the designer. Finally, high-quality final typesetting would be manually cut and pasted on to a (designed) grid by a specially trained artworker, who could prepare the design for reproduction. A photographer or artist would be selected via agents and briefed at length by the designer, who would oversee all the work during its process. Eventually, everything to appear on the final piece would be a part of, or attached to, the artwork board and briefed to another company responsible for preparing it for print. Finally, the designer, the printer and the client would each check, just to make sure that nothing had fallen off the boards between the time it left the studio until it was printed, and that all instructions were clear and understood.

Not that long ago computers were relatively scarce in graphic design, and very expensive. I remember learning how letters and pictures, made of metal, were physically arranged into words, sentences and a layout before inking and printing. There were specially formulated slabs of metal so that individual letters could have varying spaces between, and there were superior figures and inferior figures. Designs and layouts would have to be carefully calculated beforehand, as a mistake could be costly. A 'journeyman' was the name for a typesetter even up to 1977, and it was understood as a craft. An older friend of mine, still in the printing business, said wistfully that: 'It was like creating a stained glass window.'

Today, most of this process can be completed on a computer, but the stages remain the same. Many designers, usually the older, more experienced, ones, bemoan the lack of depth and care in today's fast-track world of electronic design and production. One such designer, Richard Ward, believes that: 'Technology has completely devalued and destroyed respect for creative work since it is perceived that technology can do anything now; technique has replaced the craft.'

Colin Forbes (one of founders of Pentagram design), on the other hand, believes that computer technology has freed up designers. At the click of a button, numerous typefaces can be tested, optional layouts can be manoeuvred in the blink of an eye, amendments are virtually immediate and artwork can be delivered to the printer in seconds.

Graphic design has moved a long way from the circuitous process where the final delight at getting the printed result was unsurpassable. Today, the first concept looks so polished that it often looks identical to the final product. The leap in the design process in the last 20 years is staggering. Few designers would swap the immediacy and ease of modern technology for the laboured process of earlier years, and fast turnarounds of design and implementation are now the expected norm. But without some space to reflect, backed by a rich process of ritualistic steps, we are in danger of churning out a plethora of meaningless designs.

In recognition of this, the laborious ritual of physical production has been replaced with equally lengthy sophisticated rituals of research and presentation to entrance and convince clients of the efficacy and quality of design.

Most large corporate design programmes will demand some sort of formal procedure—if not led by the designers, then requested by the client—so that a deeper understanding of the process can be absorbed and understood. Whether the presentation comprises a simple design for a stationery range or a large-scale concept constructed so that the designers can 'walk through' the design implications with the client, some ritualised structure of presentation is important in order to get a sense of the final proposal—a taste of the dream and new potential.

All this time and effort is not wasted; every stage, every consideration and every feeling during this process from conception to birth will go towards building up the power of the logo, layer by layer, and its position in the energy field.

Developing a logotype

The process of designing a logo has always been the same—the intention, the concept, the rationalisations, the detailing, the presentations, the agreement, the application, the implementation and the launch. The techniques have changed; the technology that supports the design process has been turned on its head and specialist professions have sprung up to deal with the complexity of the modern world of branding. Clients might demand designs for the logo, the ultimate goal, to be completed at a moment's notice, but the final result can take months to achieve.

Step One: Research

'Today, the starting point for articulating the brand is to really understand the organisation's identity. This is the role of research.'

LIVING THE BRAND

With so much to lose, businesses cannot afford to trust to creativity alone. Research is often commissioned at strategic stages before, during and even after the design process. Specialist companies, usually commissioned by the client, can define the design requirements and specify information on consumer, shareholder and company attitudes as well as competitors, and the relevant state of the world at large including economic opinion, market gaps, fashion trends and future projections.

Qualitative or quantitative research may take place, where either a selected group is interviewed in depth about the company or product, or a wider range of people are approached for their opinion. The latter can extend to thousands of people, and could include approaches by telephone, the internet or in person. Key staff and management may also be questioned about their impressions and opinions and their future strategies and wishes.

Whether research covers a relatively limited group, such as 12-15-year-old boys with computer skills, or a group as extensive as those with a bank account—the findings will establish a set of criteria, against which the pros and cons of potential imagery can be measured. The history of the company, as well as its ambitions, will be taken into account so that the foundations for a successful future can be laid. The research conclusions help the designer tune into the dynamics of the project and the quality and intensity of the research begins to build the energy.

Research is not a guarantee of success. McDonald's conducted a huge amount of research into a new product: a hamburger aimed specifically at adults. It appeared that McDonald's had another winner—but the product quickly flopped. The concept sounded good to people, but the reality of buying more sophisticated food at McDonald's did not stand up in practice. Henry Ford remarked that if he had asked his customers what they wished for, they would have asked for a faster horse. But when we note that a brand flop can cost millions (the failure of Unilever's Persil Power, for example, cost over £200 million), market research, or anything else that can minimise risk, is a sound investment.[1]

By making educated assumptions about customers' desires and their potential responses to a product, brands hope to benefit by fulfilling those customer expectations—the reality is that customers don't really know what they want, and cannot predict (or accurately express) what they will do anyway. But this might not matter. Steven Quartz of Caltech and Tim McPartlin of LA-based Lieberman Research have created a functional magnetic resonance imaging (fMRI) service that can discover what we really think about logos. The marketers can know what we like even before we are aware of it. FMRI is being used by marketers for studying consumers' emotions and motivations by detecting 'the ebb and flow of blood to the brain's centers of pleasure and memory'. Ford has already run a market test in Europe, and Hollywood is interested as well.[2]

Step Two: Choosing a designer

Today, the development and control of visual imagery is delegated to experts in the company, more often than not headed by a specialised person such as a corporate identity, or brand development, manager. The value of this role is reflected in the fact that every FTSE 100 company has a communications manager, of one sort or another, on the board.

A designer or design group will be selected according to size, reputation, ability and relevant expertise. Huge one-stop shops have grown up that provide design, advertising, research, PR and marketing, and speak corporate language such as share price, profit and market share. They are often chosen over smaller, creative design groups as large companies veer towards the safety of the 'no-one got fired for employing IBM' principle.

Initially, several groups may be invited to present themselves to the relevant branding specialists in the corporation and might be asked to tender design concepts. These are often huge presentations and can include an actual proposed design outcome. This may not provide the ultimate solution, but it will give an indication of how accurately each designer has understood and interpreted the brief. Finally, one group will be commissioned for the project.

Step Three: Briefing the designer

The chosen designers will be subjected to further in-depth briefings and meetings. They will become privy to all relevant internal and external research, including the historic and current values of the company as well as its future aspirations and plans. There might be a series of relatively informal meetings, to enable the designer to connect more deeply with key individuals and the internal dynamics of the company, and to gain important clues to the varying driving forces within.

Only someone who understands the company in depth, who is passionate about its future and is connected to its wellbeing, can impart a vision of the corporate spirit to a designer and enable him or her fully to encapsulate and express it in the corporate image. Lack of this deep understanding can often lead to a disconnected solution; it may be a fashionable or even award-winning design, but it has little to do with the business it represents.

This process involves the consideration of tangible, physical characteristics such as the applications, the market and the competition. It also has to take account of less tangible issues such as whether the business wants to be perceived as warm, approachable, dynamic, laid-back, cool or professional. Some of these values may be historically inherent in the company, through its founders or management, while other characteristics may be instilled through the design and branding process. Using a combination of intuitive and practical skills, the designers will begin to piece together initial creative concepts.

Designer Andrew Crane says: 'We go to the client, we pick his brain, we ask all the right questions, and we come away with a "feel" for the job. This "feel" combined with the hardcore facts is all we have.'

During this initial stage, budgets, key areas, schedules and requirements will also be discussed and agreed.

Step Four: Meeting the brief

Back in the design studio, a specific team, dedicated to the project, will often create a dedicated forum to enable the birth of a concept. Individual designers will have their own personal methods of kick-starting their creative skills, and ideas will be conceptualised and shortlisted according to their aesthetic appeal and compatibility to the brief.

Designers will trawl the research in an attempt to glean elusive inspiration from a relatively sterile rationalisation process. Within the defined constraints they will search for any tidbits that might justify and validate a new and innovative design solution.

Computer technology enables the viability of prospective design concepts to be tested on applications before they are presented to the client. Various details including variations in colour, on different media, animated and in print, can be tried out on a selection of applications such as stationery, advertising (including press and television), labels and vehicles prior to the final design choice.

Step Five: Presentation stages

Depending on the brief and on the client's requirements, design proposals will be presented at various stages to relevant personnel. Large corporations will usually have a separate department for monitoring and controlling visual imagery within the company, and this will normally be the primary interface between the designer and the rest of the company.

Design concepts will be bandied back and forth before they are finally presented to the rest of the company. Initially, the first people to see the proposed, final design may be the chairman or the managing board; once it has their seal of approval, it will be rolled out in a series of presentations throughout the organisation, in the most effective manner to ensure that the new image is fully understood and embraced by those it represents.

Sophisticated design presentations can include large-screen animated displays, in specially hired conference venues, incorporating a range of applications illustrating the use of the final design. Specially designed gifts emblazoned with the proposed new logotype may be presented as 'sweeteners' to the major decision-takers in the client team.

Presentations may be individually tailored for different groups of personnel within the corporation, from management to those on the shop floor. While this process is, hopefully, rewarding on both sides—the designer's and the client's—it can also be nerve-wracking. The risks are high with brands rising and falling with increasing regularity, and there is a lot to lose or gain. However, the process is exciting: each design presents new potential for the company, and these rituals and presentations are a vital part of the birthing process of any new logo.

Denise Linn notes the importance of this process, in a more esoteric sense, in her book *Sacred Space*. She believes that, while symbols are powerful in their own right, it is important to *consecrate* them. All sorts of rituals can be used, including passing them through fire or bathing them in water while stating out loud the intention behind the symbol.

Step Six: Design application

The agreed, final logo design will be detailed and applied to relevant items—flags, clothing, pens, vehicles, packaging, websites, brochures and stationery, to name a few. All the details of the final design including colour, typefaces, approved sizes and even the control of the space around the logotype will be carefully established and managed.

The quality and control of the applications can make or break a design. Whether the logotype appears on television electronically or in black and white newsprint, it must be instantly recognisable to the viewer, in the appropriate context for the brand, through its consistency of design appearance regardless of the differing formats. The relative size, position, typeface and colour will all be considered in detail and recorded for future reference in a design manual in a way that leaves little to chance. Even legal or descriptive text on documentation or on the back of a label will be considered in terms of its layout and grammar, according to the agreed corporate tone of voice.

All this, everything the company produces, says something about the company. The logo itself may reign supreme, but it must be supported by a complete, overall design strategy in order to succeed fully.

Huge effort is spent on ensuring that the agreed company logotype is consistently and accurately applied according to stringent standards set by the designers. Design manuals are produced covering every detail of logo implementation—from stationery to corporate clothing—and will include guidelines and specifications on colour, type, position, size, acceptable and non-acceptable variations and protected space.

Brand managers know that deviation from these standards can severely dilute the impact of the logotype, and this manual is distributed to everyone responsible for implementing the logo.

Henrik Poulsen, Executive Vice-President for Markets and Products at LEGO, stated that: 'The difference between a LEGO Fire Truck where the design is exactly on the mark and one where the design is a little off may seem subtle, but it makes a big difference in terms of consumer perception, play value and sales.'[3]

Malcolm Gladwell in *The Tipping Point* tells of examples where participants who were asked to pick the best out of a selection of options would get it wrong, because the context would throw their judgement. One experiment encompassed viewers who were asked to judge the quality of two teams of similarly talented basketball players. One team was playing in full light, the other in dimmed light. Those who could see the ball played better, and the audience judged them to be the better players regardless of the environmental disadvantage. However well designed the logo is, if it is not applied and displayed in the appropriate *context* for the brand it represents, it could well be perceived as being inferior to its competitors.

Consistency of extensive and controlled exposure of the identifying logo is the basis for establishing and ensuring ongoing familiarity that is the prerequisite for successful branding.

Step Seven: The production process

The designer no longer has to leave his or her seat in front of the computer in order to create the final design and artwork for print. Typefaces can be purchased and stored on computers and layout grids can be created at the touch of a few buttons. Photographic and illustrative sources exist via the internet and can be selected from thousands of pictures, reproducible for a fee.

Cutting and pasting type and pictures, manipulating design options and selecting ranges of colour can be done in seconds and printed out for final approval by the client. A few more depressed buttons will deliver the approved artwork via electronic technology, directly to the printer's desk.

Step Eight: Public launch

The new logo will have its own ritual of baptism when it is time to expose the design publicly. This celebration can include anything from a simple local announcement through to a full-scale national, or international, television and advertising campaign including free gifts, offers and celebrations that cost millions.

'The difference between failure and success is doing a thing nearly right and doing it exactly right.'

EDWARD SIMMONS

The logo encapsulates and delivers the brand guarantee. In order to do its job effectively, it must appear efficient, consistent, authentic and trustworthy. Undisciplined implementations during its life can lead to shoddy, inconsistent reproduction, which ultimately dissipates the energy of the brand.

The strict guidelines and definitive design standards recorded in the design manual will be referred to when any new application is required. Whether a transport manager requires a vehicle to be painted, a temporary secretary needs to produce a letter, or a salesperson is preparing a new presentation, the corporate style specifications in the design manual are in charge of how it is done. Designers used to joke that the larger the manual, the better—as it provided a hearty tool with which to hit those who deviated from the design standards contained within.

During its lifetime, a brand will be constantly monitored against relevant criteria such as changes in the condition of the parent company, the rise and fall of celebrities, and developments in the world of fashion. Issues from pack size to manufacturing locations will be assessed for their branding values, not just for their economic advantages. The logo will be tweaked or changed accordingly to reflect these changes.

Design, advertising and marketing will be used strategically to deliver the updated message keeping the brand up with, or ahead of, the times, ensuring it remains our loyal friend through our own life changes. The logo identifies the continuing brand promise.

Details behind the scenes

Corporations display their logos on as many items as effectively possible— stationery, flags, uniforms and signs—each with its own technical requirements and presenting unique challenges to the designer.

Different styles of applications include variations in colour such as monochrome, spot colour and the four-colour halftone process. There are also print finishes such as embossing, varnishing (matt or shiny), thermography and die-stamping. Even more specialist application techniques on media other than paper can include film and TV, sand-blasting on fascias, cut-outs for stencils on crates, etching into granite, or foil blocking on the barrel of a pen. Logotypes may be woven into a variety of materials such as carpets or uniforms, painted onto buildings or vehicles, projected during PowerPoint or cinema presentations, on websites and emails, or even using skywriting or applied on grass during high-profile sports matches.

Each of these will have a different feel and quality about it, of which designers are aware. These differences will affect our perception of the logo as well as its impact on us. Care and attention to minutiae underpins the logo design from its inception. Richard Ward, the designer of the cover for the Beatles album *1*, used a traditional wooden printer's block of the number one. He rolled and printed it manually, using different techniques and surfaces until he was happy with the result. Even then, it was scanned in black and white and digitally enhanced until he achieved what looks like a very fresh image of the letter in a bright yellow, printed on a red background.

I worked on a whisky label design that incorporated a signature as a feature. In order to get it looking 'spontaneous and authentic', the designer signed the name over and over, filling an A4 pad with many signatures on each page. Even then, selected letters were chosen from various versions and cut and pasted together until he was satisfied.

These rituals add to the depth of the design—certainly in the eyes of the designer—but this detailing also reaches out to the viewer. It imbues the logo with an authenticity that reaches beyond the eyes.

Whether we see a logo on the side of a building or surrounded by numerous other symbols on a joint venture document, we will absorb its meaning differently. The manual may designate a 'no-go' protected area around the logo, but at some point it will meet with the rest of the world. Like the same letter used in different words, the logo can deliver various meanings to the viewer, depending on where and how it is seen or heard.

I heard the directors at Pentagram Design tell a story to prospective clients, which illustrated the importance of context. The story was about a man who, walking down a country lane, came across two signs. The first displayed the words 'farm fresh eggs'. The sign was rendered in a beautiful classic, detailed type, perfectly ranged left, in clean black text, on a pure white board. He did not buy any eggs. Further along the road, the second sign identified a small flying school with a sign saying: 'flying lessons here'. This sign was painted roughly in a rustic-style handwritten type with a paintbrush, obvious from the drips at the bottom, on an old plank of wood. Again, the man felt disinclined to take up the offer. Finally, the client would be shown the sign styles transposed—with the rustic, homely sign advertising the obviously home-grown eggs and the clean, professional-looking flying lesson sign, reassuring any potential pilots.

Covering all angles

Brand managers will tempt as many of our senses as possible in the pursuit of success. Martin Lindstrom, author of *Brand Sense*, articulates this multi-sensory approach of brands. He explains how image, sound, smell, touch and taste are all exploited by marketers. Even the pleasing new-car smell, lasting about six weeks, exists in aerosol cans that are used to spray inside the cars. The glug of a bottle and the click of a pen have all been incorporated into products to make them user-friendly. In the 1990s, Daimler Chrysler established a department with the sole function to work on the sound of the doors shutting.

According to Lindstrom, Kellogg's has spent years researching crunch and taste—even to the point of working with a Danish commercial music laboratory that specialises in the exact crunchy sensation of a breakfast cereal. They wanted to patent their own crunch.[4] And it worked. The day the new crunch was introduced, they moved up the brand ladder.

Smell, with its ability to trigger powerful emotions, is used to promote brands: 'Big global brands set the trend which spurred scent marketing in Brazil. Brazilian brands, big and small, are now creating their olfactive logo, a scent signature which helps generate brand recall,' explains Elaine De Oliveira, olfactive marketing consultant for Biomist, one of the pioneers of scent marketing in São Paulo, Brazil. Marcelo Ginzberg from Air Berger, a French consulting firm that established an office in Brazil in June 2008, says, 'A wide variety of businesses have been adopting olfactive logos— hotels, spas, medical facilities, pharmacies, gyms, restaurants, banks and supermarkets have capitalized on scent marketing to attract consumers.'[5]

And if it is not enough to beam logos from neon signs, television screens and iPods then they can emit their own light from the page they are printed on. In San Jose, California, in 1998, a physicist reported using an ink-jet printer to create the first polymer-based light-emitting logos.[6]

Lindstrom's evolutionary scale shows how brand-building has changed with the times by moving from a two-sensory approach to a multi-sensory approach:[7]

USP (Unique Selling Proposition)—where no two products are alike.

ESP (Emotional Selling Proposition)—where products are perceived as different because of an emotional attachment.

OSP (Organisational Selling Proposition)—where the organisation, or corporation, behind the brand becomes the brand.

BSP (Brand Selling Proposition)—where the brand is stronger than the product itself.

MSP (Me Selling Proposition)—where we see consumers taking ownership of their brands.

HSP (Holistic Selling Proposition)—including those brands that not only anchor themselves in tradition but also adopt characteristics of religious sensory experience to leverage the concept of sensory branding as a holistic way of spreading the news.

Getting it absolutely perfect

The amount of detail that designers put into a logo is remarkable. I can recall numerous arguments with printers as, between gritted teeth, we explained that the colour they had produced was not exact. The attention to the detail between letters, even whether serifs should be shaved to fit or completely redrawn, can be all-consuming.

Every single feature of every individual element will be considered again and again, and combined to create one final irresistible, perfect logo design. Only by researching, detailing and combining the best ingredients can the perfect 'dish' be created; one that pleases our senses, one that we will remember forever, and one that we will reorder time and time again.

Sometimes, at the height of my design career, I would think that anyone outside the scene, looking on, would probably have thought us insane! But, somehow, we inherently knew that every component in the logo was capable of delivering a profound message, and that only the perfect design combination would deliver the perfect brand message.

When we understand the power that each element contains in its own right, we can begin to realise the ultimate strength and ability of a whole, specifically designed, logo to transform us deeply.

CHAPTER NINE

Naming the brand destiny

'A trademark is a symbol of a corporation. It is not a sign of quality . . . it is a sign of the quality.'

PAUL RAND

In his book *Marks of Excellence*, Per Mollerup states: 'A design programme should be a dynamic statement of aspirations that inspires employees, helping to improve company performance and customer satisfaction. When it succeeds in serving that goal, the design programme becomes a self-fulfilling prophecy. The aspirations come true.'

Corporations, in conjunction with branding experts, have shown us how they—and we—can be transformed via the logo effect by creating an influential interaction between their brand and each of us. Companies dream their dream, manifest it in a piece of art (the logo) and deliver it worldwide to create a new way of thinking, demonstrating a methodology that is capable of changing our economic world.

Each design element in the logo plays a part in this process. In order to understand the full effect of a logo, we need to look more deeply at the elements that make up the design: type (including the name), symbols and colour. Each of these is a motivator for change in its own right and has been used throughout history to affect individuals and communities alike.

Name and destiny

'Spoken words are symbols of mental experience. Written words are the symbols of spoken words.'

ARISTOTLE

Able to be heard as well as seen, the name of a company is one of the most memorable parts that make up the logo. An estimated 80 per cent of brand communication is auditory or visual; this is the language of the logo and secures its ability to affect the success of a brand through our reaction.

What makes a company choose a particular brand name? As a parent, I know how difficult it can be to choose a name for a child without even knowing how she or he will look, what his or her ambitions will be or what peer group will be selected or why. While it was easy to quickly reject names that came with personal, unacceptable preconceptions such as Muriel, Egbert or Percival (too 'English') or Charlene, Darlene or Raylene (too 'Australian/70s') or Gay, Dick or Randy (could be open to ridicule), there was still a huge amount of choice. We found ourselves trawling through family history, specialised books and the names our friends had chosen for their children for inspiration. It felt wrong to choose the same as the latter; the books gave us too much choice, but were helpful on meanings—as we would rather have a courageous child (Andrew) than a pale one (Blake); and the family choice was riddled with problems. Apart from this, we wanted a good future for our children and the choice of name was one starting point where we felt we had some influence. We did of course, eventually decide; our children do have names and we now cannot imagine them being called anything else. It is as if they have grown into their names.

Roland J Fryer Jr, a black economist analysing the black–white gap in the USA, noticed that black parents gave their children names that were starkly different to those given to white children. Fryer believes that the reason behind this is that each gives a name to their children that ensures solidarity with their community. Deja and Shanice, for example, are predominantly black names: out of 626 girls named Deja in the 1990s, 591 were black; of the 318 babies named Shanice, 310 were black. Levitt and Dubner state in *Freakonomics*: 'The data shows that, on average, a person with a distinctly black name—whether it is a woman named Imani or a man named DeShawn—does have a worse life outcome than a woman named Molly or a man named Jack.'

Similarly, parents from different socioeconomic backgrounds will generally choose names that reflect this. The most common 'high-end' white girl names include Alexandra, Lauren and Katherine; the most common 'low-end' white girl names include Amber, Heather and Kayla. Levitt and Dubner say: 'Broadly speaking, the data tells us how parents see themselves—and more significantly, what kind of expectations they have for their children.'[1]

Similarly, names are chosen for brands that will align them with the best possible outcome within their chosen tribe.

Many actors have changed their names to ensure, as far as possible, future success. Doris Day's original surname was Kappelhof; Kirk Douglas was Issur Danielovitch, and Michael Caine was Maurice Micklewhite. They chose the way they wanted us to read and hear about them.

While being interviewed by British chat-show host Michael Parkinson, Michael Caine, commenting on his blossoming career success in later life, pointed out how his friend Roger Moore had changed his accent, kept his own name and had no work—while he (Caine) had changed his name, kept his accent and had lots of work.[2] Rock Hudson's name was specially chosen by his agent, who was inspired by the Roc (a powerful mythological bird) and the mighty Hudson River. And would the success of these famed actors have been enhanced by the name of the birthplace of celebrity worship? Hollywood might not be so important today if it had not been named thus by Mrs Wilcox, in 1903, after Mr Wilcox registered a development of 700 inhabitants in the state of California? She named the place Hollywood because, as she remarked, holly brings good luck.

The choice of names for people can even be inspired by brands including Lexus, Armani and Bacardi, professions such as Judge and Senator, or places like Harvard and Princeton—as well as Brooklyn. In the main, however, it is the neighbours, relatively local, who have larger houses or better cars, whom people aspire to. Levitt and Dubner also noted that popular names change throughout time. As high-end names become popular and credited with high income status, they gradually filter down the socio-economic ladder to those hoping that some of the success will rub off on them—rather in the same way that we might wear a logo hoping to be bathed in the aura of its status. They summarise from the California research, which produced the data above: 'An overwhelming number of parents use a name to signal *their own expectations* of how successful their children will be.' Just as our own parents try to secure a good life for us through their choice of name, so the parent company of the brand will do likewise.

These social and cultural differences, signalled by the choice of name, have led to the discovery of some interesting statistics. *Schotts Almanac 2006* refers to an analysis by Churchill Insurance of their database in 2005 that indicated the likelihood of driving certain models of car by various first names. Those driving a Ford Fiesta are most likely to be called Anthony, Gareth, Dennis, Audrey, Kate or Laura; whereas the names of those driving a Volkswagen Golf are more likely to be Jonathan, Daniel or Nicholas.

Curiously, Hannah was the top name for winning Premium Bond prizes in 2006, as it was in 2003 and 2004. Emma came second, with the only male name, Sean, third.[3]

Hermeneutics ('hermeneutic' means 'interpretative') is a branch of philosophy that emerged in the fifteenth century; it is concerned with the interpretation of written texts believing that words, as information, act within our body. The word 'hermeneutics' derives from the Greek god Hermes in his role as patron of communication and human understanding. This 'corporealisation' of words was initially recognised by Wilhelm Reich, a physician-scientist born in Austria in 1897 and a student of Sigmund Freud, and later by Jacques Lacan (1901-1981), an influential French psychoanalyst. In this sense, words are not passive carriers of information but are 'made flesh' and exert an influence on how we think, act and perceive.

By choosing our words and their context, carefully and with intent, we can sculpt our future. The person who is saying the words is directly affecting the listener, including himself, and weaving into it a reality through the careful choice and control of the words spoken.

The choice of a brand name presents even more complicated difficulties. While companies too want a name encapsulating a vision that a brand will grow into, competitors, target markets, geographical locations and the product itself can combine to create impossibly constricting parameters. As with children's names, corporate names are inspired from many sources and getting it right can make the difference between success and failure. As soon as we hear or see a name, we will form an impression about the brand well before the brand gurus begin to attribute it with chosen values through marketing strategies. With brands coming and going with increasing regularity, the name is a vitally important first point of contact that can incline us towards choosing a product above its competitors. The *name* of the company is what makes it *sound* different from similar products.

On one small stretch of highway, I noted the following car names: Diamanté, Legacy, Soul, Avalon, Focus, Echo, Tundra, Frontier, Sequoia and Yukon. Whether chosen to appeal to the romantic or the rugged, each word would have been carefully selected to trigger emotionally based values. Words are powerful motivators for provoking our emotions, and an effective way of jerking our purse strings. This can stem from how they sound (flowing or clipped—compare *bitty* to *gooey*); their appearance (the length of the name as well as the design), and the images they evoke (eagle, purple or kangaroo poo).

Words evoke responses and carry imprints of meaning that have been embedded into them through varying usages in different cultures. Knowledge of these details enables companies to choose appropriate combinations for a favourable global outcome.

Companies can use the name to tell the customer about the product. 'Coca-Cola' may have originally referred to the cola leaves used in the flavouring, but this quality is now virtually irrelevant. 'Vodafone' describes the fact that the company deals in telephones, whereas 'Orange' does not. 'Holiday Inn' tells us we can stay there, but 'Hilton' does not. Some names echo the symbol: Mitsubishi's name means 'three diamond shapes'—relevant to the logo design, but not particularly relevant to the car design. 'Apple' says little about computers, but a lot about the symbol that identifies it.

The letters

The origination of our current 26-letter alphabet is attributed to the Phoenicians, who lived around 2000 BCE on the eastern shores of the Mediterranean. The simple consonants they developed are today recognised as the prototypes of all alphabetical scripts. In many traditions, including Kabbalistic, each letter has its own special meaning with the power to affect us beyond human consciousness. Similarly, the simple ancient letters of the Irish alphabet were used in magic or divination.

As abstract shapes, letters will prompt different responses from us, whether inherited from our ancestors or adopted through personal experience. Sometimes this response can be conscious; for example, we might just prefer the shape of an O over and above a P. Other times we might be affected and not know why.

Some businesses simply use initials to identify themselves. United Airlines and Unilever use the U, and Volkswagen uses only the V and W in their identifying images. Although all these letters rely on a similar drawing path in order to create them, the rounded lower edge of the U, which can be created by using one continuous line, contrasts with the sharp edges of the V and W, which rely on a pause and immediate change in direction. We feel different when we draw them; we feel different when we see them.

X really marks the spot to call our attention in some brands. Halifax, the building society, uses the X in its name for branding purposes, as does the Apple Mac's operating system 10 (X). A delightful 'x' story is included in Alan Fletcher's book *The Art of Looking Sideways*: A lady, sitting next to the designer Raymond Loewy at dinner, struck up a conversation. 'Why,' she asked, 'did you put two Xs in Exxon?' 'Why ask?' he asked. 'Because,' she said, 'I couldn't help noticing.' 'Well,' he responded, 'that's the answer.'

Gucci and Guess both use the letter G to identify themselves, but when Guess interlocked the Gs to make a pattern, Gucci accused them of trademark infringement.[4]

In *Graphis Corporate Identity* by Martin Pederson, Robert Schulman states that, in the NASA logotype, the letters n-a-s-a ' . . . are reduced to their simplest form, giving a feeling of unity, technological precision, thrust and orientation towards the future.'

Exposure to certain letters can affect us simply by their presence. A study carried out by Dr Keith Ciani and Dr Ken Sheldon at the University of Missouri, USA, found that exposing the letters F or A to students before an exam could affect their performance. Dr Ciani said: 'The letters A and F have significant meaning for students: A represents success and F, failure. We hypothesised that if students are exposed to these letters prior to an academic test it could affect their performance through non-conscious motivation.' The A group performed significantly better than the F group. 'Exposure to the letter A made the students non-consciously approach the task with the aim to succeed,' said Dr Keith Ciani.[5]

This therefore poses the question of how the clothing company Fat Face compares with Adidas, for example. Each, according to this, could make us feel differently. We are, of course, not in an examination setting, but nevertheless the imprint exists.

Our own initials can affect our performance in grades. Students whose names began with 'C' or 'D' earned lower average grades than those whose names began with 'A' or 'B.' Students with the initial 'C' or 'D', presumably because of an unconscious fondness for these letters, were slightly less successful at achieving their conscious academic goals.[6]

Brand managers know the value of making the logo familiar to us so we learn to automatically reach for it in confidence that it will deliver the continuing brand promise. It seems that we even seek out this familiar reassurance when we look for a job. We are more likely to want to work for a company that has our own initials in its name. Psychologists Frederik Anseel and Wouter Duyck from Ghent University, Belgium, were interested in testing the extent of the name-letter effect and whether it is potent enough to affect where we choose to work. The researchers looked at the employees' names and how often their first initial matched the first letter of their companys' names. They demonstrated that 'people are more likely to work for companies with initials matching their own than to work for companies with other initials.'[7]

The type

Typefaces are specially chosen for their characteristics and what they can add to the overall design concept. Every typeface and every letter-tweak brings its own values, affecting the whole in the same way that the amount of salt and pepper added to a recipe can make or break the success of the final dish. Braun and Dell, for example, both use fairly simple typeface designs to identify their brand but a tilt of the E in Dell and an increase in the size of the A in Braun makes these logos distinctive.

Different styles of typefaces include bold and light, serif and sans serif, roman and italic, capitals and lower case, and so on. Each of these variations delivers a different tonality, which can further be varied by the use of scale or colour.

One typeface, Helvetica, has had such an impact on design that its 50th birthday in 2007 was celebrated by a documentary. While the general public may be unaware of the choice of type used, Gap, Currys, Evian, Toyota, Orange, Hoover, Lufthansa, Tupperware and numerous public institutions use Helvetica. Its clean lines deliver a message of safety, reliability and honesty. Some designers even hate Helvetica because of this, calling it bland. Finlo Roher, in his article 'Helvetica at 50' in *BBC News Magazine*, 9 May 2007, says: 'Helvetica's message is this: you are going to get to your destination on time; your plane will not crash; your money is safe in our vault; we will not break the package; the paperwork has been filled in; everything is going to be OK.' He quotes the designer Neville Brody as saying: 'It's bland, unadventurous, unambitious.'[8] One simple typeface, diverse responses.

Numbers

Numerology is the ancient science of numbers. Each number is believed to have a life and meaning of its own that can influence us in different ways. Like letters, numbers also have abstract shapes; some we will warm to more than others depending on our personal preferences. But our responses to different numbers can be triggered from our deeper subconscious. The zero

Those who see an A on their examination paper perform better than those exposed to the letter F.

is known as the unmanifest; many brands tap into this potential, including O books, Oprah Winfrey and O2. They invite us to become part of their formation in order to make them manifest. The number 2 represents a relationship. Did the designers of O2 realise what a powerful combination of shapes they were putting together? (Zero and O are the same shape and share similar dynamics.)

Pythagoras and Plato were both fascinated by the eternal truths of mathematics. Pythagoras believed that numbers are living realities and that we would actually be able to see 'God's breath or spiritus' in everything if we identified it in numbers. Scientists including Copernicus, Descartes, Galileo and Newton took this a stage further and expressed the idea that numbers, proportions, equations, and mathematical principles are more real than the physical world we experience.

Those who chose the identities for 3M (previously the Minnesota Mining & Manufacturing USA) and Nestlé (who changed the number of the birds in its nest from four to three in 1988) may be interested to know, if they don't already, that three is a perfect number according to the Chinese. In many religions and traditions including Christian, Persian, Hinduism and Buddhism, the number three is endowed with magic and meaning.

Sound

Sound can affect us even before we are born. The ear becomes functional by the 16th week and the foetus begins active listening by the 24th week. Babies have their first language lessons in the womb, where they respond to different sounds. Loud sharp noises can disturb them, while soothing sounds, such as lullabies, will calm them. As they become exposed to more sounds they learn to accept those that are repeated as the norm. They remember them as non-threatening and 'safe.' This is called 'habituation.'[9]

Infants as young as seven months are sensitive to the emotions in the human voice.[10] Dr Alfred Tomatis referred to the ear as 'the Rome of the body' because almost all cranial nerves lead to it and thus it can be considered our primary sense organ. He also believed that, because embryonically the skin is differentiated ear—babies' ears develop from skin folds, we listen with our whole body.[11]

It is not unreasonable, therefore, to hypothesise that numerous pregnant women, bored and tired of waiting for the imminent birth of their child, might spend time in front of the television, unwittingly enabling the foetus to absorb and become familiar with brand names as they are repeated over and over, as well as listening to them incorporated into catchy tunes. After the birth, many mothers put their babies in front of the television to be entertained—carefully positioned so they can see the logo and hear its name spoken, or sung, in syrupy tones or surrounded with catchy tunes, backed with laughter and colours.

Different languages stimulate different parts of the brain. Chinese, with thousands of pictorial characters that need to be learned independently, stimulates the visual, bringing in both the left and right sides of the brain. The English language, however, with only 26 characters, tends to be read as sound rather than pictures, thereby stimulating very different parts of the brain. This creates a very powerful effect on how we see the world once we have learned to read. Socrates did not want reading and writing to become available to the masses because he believed this would create a different relationship to memory.[12] Logos combine words and pictures, securing a position in both the verbal and visual centres of our brains.

Sound has the ability to transform us and our environment. In religions such as Hinduism and Buddhism, various sounds are chanted in order to help people on the road to enlightenment. These mantras are used to access universal energy and the subsequent alignment with one-ness. Today, there are organisations where employees chant the company name before commencing work. No doubt this helps to align them with the core energy and 'one-ness' of the company. At the very least, it would appear that they could be chanting in the intended future of the brand as expressed in the logo.

Deepak Chopra says the Vedas maintain that if you recite a mantra out loud, its pattern of vibrations creates its own effect, which can create physical effects in the world. This historic power of the spoken word is evident in the word 'abracadabra'. It originates from the Aramaic language and translates almost exactly as 'I will create as I will speak'.[13]

Master of Voice and Sound Healer Stewart Pearce tells the story of a group of talented musicians, imprisoned in a Nazi concentration camp, who alleviated their suffering by organising themselves into a group to perform some of the romantic operas of the nineteenth century. Since there were no women in the camp, the men sang the female roles—only to start developing female characteristics including breasts and a lack of facial hair. As soon as they ceased playing these roles, their hormones returned to normal.[14]

Our ancestors knew something about the link between sounds and symbols. Caves in southern France, including the Grotte du Pech Merle, have been found to be enormous natural echo chambers. Drawings, including representations of bison and female figures, are scattered throughout the caves and positioned at areas where the natural echo is greatest. The most effective echo chambers are also identified by a pattern of painted red dots. Since bone flutes roughly the same age as these cave paintings have been found at several Palæolithic sites in Europe, it is possible that musical rituals took place in these caves.[15] The carefully positioned symbols combined with the power of sound could create a potent resonance to aid the manifestation of game for food, fertility and so on depending on the intention.

When we speak a word, we are expressing more than the sum of the vowels and consonants. The order of these—the accent, tone, volume, history and culture of each—combines to form a sound that captures and carries the vibration of the essence of the whole meaning, to reach out and influence us in ways beyond our conscious hearing process.

From Aboriginal songlines, tribal drumming and Tibetan chants through to classical and modern music, sound is created with the intention and ability to move our emotions and inspire new ways of being.

Voice trainers such as Chloe Goodchild, Jill Purce and Stewart Pearce help people use the power of their voice to effect profound change in their lives. This resource is what the marketers use to benefit the brand. The sound of the spoken name of a logo can affect us at levels that reach beyond our ears; what we hear will influence the way in which we perceive the brand.

Christian Kyriacou, chartered architect, interior designer and Feng Shui consultant, uses sound to transform space in buildings. He states that the ancient Greek architects were trained in musical harmony and geomancy and understood that if the proportions of a building were not in harmony, you would 'perceive the noise of an orchestra tuning up' when you entered the building.

I experienced this effect during a weekend workshop with Christian, where he enlisted the audience to make the required sounds. Using the musical scale, we reached particular notes that were based on the mathematics of the figures in sacred geometry. The objective of this exercise was to raise the energy level in the room. According to the attendees, it worked. If the sounds that the vowels and consonants of the name of a logo are in harmony, specific harmonics could be created that raise the energy of the brand.

Zacciah Blackburn is a sound healer and director of education of the Sound Healing Network, an international community of practitioners, healers and others interested in the field of sound healing. He utilises sounds in a therapeutic manner to enable individuals to come into a greater state of wellbeing, and to embrace their authentic self. His school is one of the most extensive training programs in therapeutic application of sound in the USA. He believes that sound can be used in many ways, with focus on physiological, emotional, psychological, or spiritual wellness. One of the primary ways this works is through the nature of entrainment— all living organisms seek community and they will find it through the strongest resonance within that community. Zacciah believes that if that is resonating integrity in its purest form, then it will assist that community to come into that high ideal.[16]

At the moment, commercial brands and their accompanying lifestyles have some of the loudest voices in our Western communities. We only need to look at the state of our current society to see the results of this aspiration, as we seek our ideal community and display our commitment through visibly embracing the logo.

Hans Jenny (1904-1972) was a Swiss medical doctor, natural scientist and pioneer of Cymatics, the study of wave phenomena. He found that sound creates shapes, and showed that certain vibrations hold a form of geometry that have sacred proportions. Masaru Emoto (see Chapter 1) clarifies how certain sounds create beautiful and highly proportionate geometrical shapes in water crystals as they freeze.

In sacred languages, such as Sanskrit, Tibetan and Hebrew, there is an essential quality inherent within the sound vibration of each spoken word, which holds tremendous potential, and which affects us when that language is used with pure intention. These and other cultures suggest this is how the universe was brought into creative manifestation. The Bible says: 'God said: "Let there be light, and there was light."' In Hindu culture, the phrase 'Nada Brahma' is used, meaning *all is sound*, or *all is created through sound*, with the sound of 'Om' being the universal causative sound of creation.

The ancient Egyptians may have known about this aspect of sound in detail. John Reid, acoustic engineer, designer, and long-time Cymatics researcher, carried out Cymatic experiments in the Great Pyramid. First he stretched a plastic membrane over the whole four-ton sarcophagus on the floor of the King's chamber. He then sprinkled sand over the top. As the membrane was exposed to different sounds, one by one a whole series of ancient Egyptian hieroglyphics appeared. At another time, John was working in his laboratory to discover the effects of very pure low-frequency sounds. The shape that formed in the sand was a pentagram around a circle. He was particularly excited to see these two shapes, since the five sided figure contains Phi, a mathematical constant of the universe, and Pi is a constant concerned with circles.[17] The logo of Texaco is created using both a circle and a pentagram.

David Elkington, in his book *In the Name of the Gods*, states that, for the Egyptians: 'Hieroglyphs were most certainly a living link between the cosmic mind and the human mind,' and ' . . . an emotional expression of a universe built upon patterns of sand.' He cites the example of how chanting 'Om' (a mantra of power and the word of creation) produces a mandala in the sand and a male voice sounding an 'O' produces a circle with a dot—the glyph representing Ra the sun god. The latter has become of particular interest, since the Soho satellite, a joint collaboration between Europe and USA, launched in 1998, confirmed that the sun does 'sing' at a very low resonance.

It would be fascinating to see the symbols formed when the name of a chosen logotype is vocalised and subjected to this process, and then to compare the compatibility of that shape with the approved logotype design.

Stewart Pearce tells the story in his book *The Alchemy of Voice* of the time when he was facilitating a training session in the USA. He explained how, in some cultures, it was forbidden to utter the name of God unless it was by an authorised person such as a monk, rabbi or priest, and in a sacred space, as this would evoke the deity. Encouraged by some of the attendees to prove this, Stewart sounded the name *Yahweh* (the Jewish form of the name); the doors swung open and a squall arose outside, leaving the participants with a feeling of awe. Before he uttered the name, Stewart suggested that the notion of evoking the presence of God should be fully respected, and advised those present to be prepared for anything.

Often we casually speak God's name in our daily life, whether blasphemously or in passing; when it is spoken with the intention and belief that something profound and awesome will happen, that is when we see the results of the spoken invocation. Stewart states in his book: 'Naming the things around us channels our intentions in certain directions to make sense of the environment we live in and how we think, feel and perceive it.'

Alan M Webber, founding editor of the magazine *Fast Company* and former managing editor of the Harvard Business Review, states: 'If you change the conversation, you can change the future.'[18]

Hearing that name of a brand spoken with intention, will, the brand managers hope, channel our thoughts and feelings in that direction.

Joseph Rael, an indigenous American, has researched the transformational power of sound. His life mission is to build domes at strategic points on the Earth's surface, which can be used to emphasise sound and bring harmony into the area. He says: 'When chanting, the repeated sounds of the consonants direct the power of the vowels in such a way as to create an energy design. Vibration impacts the physical body, bounces back, and on its return, the original form has changed into a new form. Next, as it once again bounces on the newly formed body, it designates the extent of the growth achieved and connects that change with the self.'

He believes that the vibratory essence of sound affects the inner walls of nerves, blood vessels and cells—and that the power of vibration (sound) affects not only the physical aspect but also that of the mental, emotional and spiritual.

According to Rael, the vowels in any given word reveal the power of that word, and are sufficient for chanting, but it is the consonants that conduct the power of that energy into a healing current and give it a physical, mental, emotional or spiritual impulse.

Marks & Spencer produced a series of extremely appealing television advertisements, which were so successful that other food manufacturers quickly copied them. The beautifully photographed food was supported with a honeyed female voice speaking the strapline: 'This is not just food, this is M&S food.' According to Rael, M stands for 'manifestations' and S for 'the beautiful one.'

Understanding Rael's definitions of letters can give more information about the deeper levels of any word meaning. The vibrations of the vowel sounds enter at the breath level (spirit) and then through the physical level (matter) and then flow (movement) through the body. F, for example, stands for faith; O (oh) is for innocence and constant ascending spirituality; R is for abundance; and D is for touch. Every time the car manufacturer's name is uttered, these are some of the messages being delivered. An alternative ancient attribution of meaning to initials would interpret Ford thus: F stands for fire, O for the sun or the perfect One, R for a shepherd's crook and D for the brilliant.[19]

As a side issue, an article in *National Geographic* magazine pointed out that the current preference for the choice of baby names leans towards those with: ' . . . Vowels airing out the consonants rather than the harder sounding appellations like Gertrude, an 1890s hit.'[20]

Sound does not need to be heard through our ears in order to affect us. The vibration of the sound in the air can affect the vibrations that exist within our own bodies. This is particularly apparent in live music; with drums and violins, for example, we can sense how they resonate with different areas of our bodies. There are specially designed music pieces that claim to harmonise different fields of energy within us (the chakras) and it is advised that the use of earphones will render the music ineffective as it will not reach the relevant area.

This means that, when we hear the sound of the name of a brand, it can, at some point, be resonating with the energy of our body. Different parts of us will pick up the different vibrations of particular vowels and consonants. Some branches of complementary medicine work with sound to rebalance personal health. A spoken logo word could be said to shift our balance towards the brand. If the sound of the logo resonates with even a small part of us, then we will want the product in our lives; it will go some way towards making us feel 'whole.'

Attention to these small details in a logo can go some way to ensuring the continuing health of the brand.

CHAPTER TEN

Symbolising a future

'Since early antiquity people have oriented themselves by natural signs: sailors navigated by constellations, the Magi followed a star. When these proved insufficient, we invented others, some of which are culturally specific. Invented signs were added to the natural ones.'

GEORGES JEAN, SIGNS, *SYMBOLS AND CIPHERS*

Giving the name a face

Symbols give us something to remember; they put a face on a brand after we have been introduced to the name. Not all logos have a separate symbol; some rely entirely on the name. But even in these cases the way in which the name is written, the typeface and the shape it makes, will create an abstract shape that we will remember and recognise whether we can read the letters of the name of not. Illiterate people in poor countries recognise Coca-Cola, in whatever language it is written. Boots the Chemist's logo is a triangular-shaped name in an oval—we don't need to read the name to recognise the presence of an outlet on the high street. If we catch a glimpse of a FedEx truck driving by, we will immediately note the logo by the unique shape formed by the cap initials flanked by lower-case letters.

When a company chooses a symbol, they will look for subjects that resonate with their core values and attract their ideal customer. Research might play a major part in choosing the right symbol; alternatively, the choice could be more personal.

Linux founder Linus Torvalds did not want the ferocious eagles, sharks or foxes that were being considered for his company's symbol; instead, he wanted the converse—a penguin, because penguins are cute and cuddly. Torvalds explained, on a web posting after the launch: 'All the other logos were too boring. I wasn't looking for the Linux corporate image, I was looking for something fun and sympathetic to associate with Linux. A slightly fat penguin that sits down after having a great meal fit the bill perfectly.'[1]

Symbols add character and personality to the brand name; they give us something to judge, to recall and to love. We will create our own opinions and feelings towards them, even if the company that commissions and markets the design has prompted these in the first place.

But symbols can trigger deeper responses within us. Bypassing our subconscious, the subject matter, the shape, size and placement, even its position in relationship to the logo word, can evoke existing sensitivities. Ancient symbols that resonate with our psyche may be deliberately or unwittingly selected and placed by the designer. Animals, plants, birds and shapes will be chosen for their inherent attributes, whether they are aggressive, friendly, cuddly, stable, aspiring and so on. The brand will tap into this ready-made, existing powerful element. With the support of sophisticated delivery systems, we will be subjected to the sight of them until they become synonymous with the brand.

The ancient Hebrews, among others, believed that the act of physically articulating a concept, such as God, through writing or speech, could dis-empower the energy. This might explain why symbols are so powerful for organisations, such as Nike and Shell, which use them as their main form of identification.

When I was a child, my mother took me to a show in Melbourne; on our return home she asked me what I remembered as the best bit. I can't remember what the show was, but I remember my answer; it was the neon brand symbol of Skipping Girl vinegar atop one of the buildings on the way home. I can still vividly recall the details of the skipping rope flashing around as if the girl were skipping high in the sky.

Since the beginnings of brands, symbols have been the most recognisable, memorable and powerful identifiers. Whether they are sourced from, or inspired by, the actual product, the natural world, abstract shapes or ancient signs, the symbol is the bit of the brand identification that we notice and recall even when we can't read the words.

Mountains symbolise strength, (peak) performance, immovability, stature, achievement and grandeur. They are highly visible in their environment and a popular choice for companies including Paramount, Invesco, Evian and Toblerone.

Realistic symbols

One of the most common and effective ways to represent a business visually is by using realistic symbols. They provide a range of readily recognisable and memorable subjects, often conveniently imprinted with a predetermined, desirable set of values with which we are already familiar.

Realistic symbols can be attributed with different meanings. Some of these might be ancient; more recent characteristics might be the result of those imprinted by the current brand designers. Each meaning will temper the effect of all the others. Brand managers know the power of symbolism and they cannot afford to have their take on it diluted.

Throughout the ages, animals have been attributed with various powers. We even refer to human characteristics using animal tendencies—strong as a horse, gentle as a lamb or slippery as an eel.

Our relationship with animals is not merely a physical one; it involves our mystical side as well. There have been links between animals or birds and the human psyche ever since humans became conscious. The different powers that animals symbolise include material, spiritual or even cosmic ones. Egyptian gods had animal heads, as does Ganesh the elephant-headed god of the Hindus.

The crocodile, signifying Lacoste and prominently displayed on the clothing, could signify that we are wearing the primal energies of birth, motherhood and initiation. To the ancient Egyptians, crocodiles were associated with fury and ferocity as well as with fertility and power. Being reptiles living in and out of water, they are seen as representing water and land, creators and destroyers, birth and death. As excellent mothers, and living in water (associated with the Great Mother), they are 'the primal mothers in whom all knowledge rests and waits to be born.' In Europe they were associated with the dragon, which was known, among other things, as the keeper of treasure, often of hidden wisdom.[2]

Our attraction to these species is verified by the success of fashion designer Chris Kane's crocodile T-shirts, which have a photograph of a crocodile's head with huge open jaws across the solar plexus. At their launch, 2,000 were sold by Topshop in two days.[3] Are those who bought these subconsciously displaying a powerful aspect of their solar plexus, the area of our energy bodies that is our interface with the outside world?

Kangol gained its kangaroo by popular demand. The Kangol name was made up from *K* (from silk/knitted/knitting), *ang* (from angora) and *ol* (from wool). The brand took off so well that people asking for it, unable to remember the name, asked for the kangaroo brand—so Kangol went with the flow and replaced the original logo of crossed needles with the kangaroo symbol to its branding. US sales doubled that year.[4]

With their ability to live on the ground and in the air, birds are a popular choice to symbolise businesses. Penguin Books was the brainchild of Allen Lane, who realised there was a gap in the market for affordable quality books. He wanted a dignified but flippant name for his company and it was his secretary who is believed to have suggested the penguin.

In 1986, designers Chermayeff and Geismar chose a peacock with its tail fully spread to represent colourfully the expansiveness of the broadcasting network NBC. Barclays Bank and American Airlines share the eagle, which is a symbol of height and of the spiritual principle in general. Interestingly, in the Egyptian hieroglyphic system, the letter 'A', as used by American Airlines, is identified by an eagle that in itself represents the warmth of life and the day and is linked with the sun, the father and nobility. It is also associated with war, and the ability to dominate and destroy baser forces. Because it flies higher than other birds, the eagle is seen as a messenger from heaven, symbolising divine majesty.

According to Ted Andrews, in his book *Animal Speak*, the penguin stands for 'lucid dreaming' and 'astral projection'—the ability to move freely and change your dreams. The peacock is 'resurrection and wise vision'—associated with many myths and traditions. The eagle represents 'illumination of spirit, healing and creation'—bringing new dimensions and heightened responsibilities. Lofty values indeed for companies to aspire to.

Plants too have long been used to represent powerful qualities. Note the traditional use of yarrow stalks for I Ching sticks, a time-honoured tool of divination, and the symbolic lotus blossom, seen in the East as the embodiment of all life.

Apple Computers might have chosen an apple because it is friendly, recognisable and associated with good health. The apple also represents knowledge, immortality and freedom; the bite out of it alludes to the biblical sin. An alternative and even richer reason for the choice is that

Birds, not necessarily limited to the ground, provide a rich source of inspiration for brand designers. Nestlé's birds are safe in their nest, **NBC** is recognised by its colourful peacock and Linux and Penguin books display friendly penguins. Barclays Bank and American Airlines use an eagle, which symbolises divine majesty, the sun, the father, a messenger from heaven, nobility and creation.

the missing bite is a symbol attributed to Alan Turing, who famously unlocked the German Enigma codes during the Second World War and is also acknowledged for laying the foundations for today's computers. Unfortunately, Turing's contribution was not recognised at the time, partly because the classified information could not be revealed, but also because he was homosexual and unaccepted in less tolerant social times. Eventually, he committed suicide by taking a bite from an apple that he had laced with cyanide. The Apple symbol finally publicly acknowledges Turing's immense contribution to the computers that have become part of our lifestyle today.[5]

The apple image is so successful that Apple Computers was charged with violating a 1991 agreement not to enter the music business under the apple name, as agreed with Apple Corps. In the end, both companies are allowed to use the name—but it cost a fortune to get to the point where a common piece of fruit could be used to identify more than one brand. Both Apple Computers and Apple Corps refused permission to reproduce their logos in this book!

When Woolworths, one of Australia's largest retailers, created an apple-shaped logo in 2008, the move largely went unnoticed. But when the company decided it would put the symbol on an array of products, Apple decided to fight Woolworths in Australian court.[6]

People, real and mythical, including Poseidon, Goliath, Eve and Napoleon have all been used in branding. Their traits are obvious and require little, if any, explanation. We get the message!

With the limited number of existing, recognisable characters, however, many brands have developed their own characters over which they have much more control. Fred the Homepride man, Bibendum (who has been in action as the Michelin Man for more than a hundred years) and Bertie Bassett, made from the liquorice allsorts that share his name, are examples of how we are encouraged to identify with and warm to the corporations they represent.

Stars are used on many company images, including Danone and Subaru. Two coffee and fast-food competitors, Pret à Manger and Starbucks, both use stars in their imagery. Perhaps it is one of our favourite symbols—we all want to be a star. We felt rewarded when the teacher placed a star on our school work; we may have been inspired by the Bible stories of the three

At least three companies use a single piece of fruit as their identification. Apple (computers), Apple (records) and Woolworths (Australia) have all been in court to defend their use of the apple. They are so protective of their logos they refused permission to reproduce their apples in this book.

wise men guided by a star, and we were awed when the Hubble telescope provided us with the most fantastic pictures yet of other starry worlds in outer space.

The sun, a powerful and male symbol, was the choice for the financial services company Sun Life. It also represents an English newspaper of the same name. The swastika is an ancient sign representing the sun.

Abstract symbols

As more competitive products and businesses jostle for position in our lives, and as companies grow to unprecedented size, often by acquiring other businesses with their own established and valuable brands and identities, designers are challenged to find imagery that can authentically represent increasingly diverse products and abstract brand values.

Abstract shapes are among the most powerful symbols. Apart from being less specific and therefore more versatile, they impact on our subconscious in a different way. For example, we are less likely to have a preconceived opinion about an abstract shape than we are about a bird, animal or flower—thus providing the corporation and its advertising agency with a clean slate on which to imprint a range of values, to tempt us towards the product.

Seemingly meaningless abstract symbols can be branded with virtually any meaning through exposure in advertising, PR and marketing.

Sometimes, apparently abstract symbols can be endowed with a variety of realistic attributes. Landor Associates' design for Lucent Technologies essentially appears like a brushstroke starting on the left and circling until it meets with the beginning. On the one hand, we can analyse this shape by drawing on the wealth of historical meanings attributed to circles including the sun (light and life), perfection, holiness, God and eternity; on the other hand, Mark Fox, in his article in *Design Annual*, in 1999, stated that for him it represented the mythic ouroboros, an image of a self-consuming serpent. The serpent represents immortal energy and consciousness shedding one generation after another, to be born again. Mark notes that although this connection was probably not made consciously, it may be entirely appropriate for a company born from the restructuring of AT&T.

The power of abstract shapes is not lost in realistic symbols. A seated lion makes a triangular shape; a standing one forms a rectangle. This overall shape as well as those created by its legs, its rounded mane or curved tail, and the spaces they form, all combine to complete a united intention composed by the designers. Every shape will affect our reaction to the image.

Designers are aware of the values of each shape. With the development of sophisticated software and advancements in computer technology, they can easily manipulate colour and distort abstract shapes into multi-dimensional forms. Amec changed its symbol from a structural-looking triangular form to a soft blob. The Total fuel symbol became a tangle of swooshes. Sony and Ericsson combined to form a decorated orb. BT moved from a realistic figure to a sphere of coloured discs. Nike uses a stylised tick shape, Budweiser an off-centre bow, and Levi an inverted elongated shield.

All these familiar logos and symbols are a mixture of simple shapes, woven into a combination that delivers a deliberate corporate message.

As we delve further into the history of shapes and forms, we can begin to see how ancient symbols are able to hold energy imprints, which can resonate with our psyche at deep levels to elicit responses from well beyond our conscious brain. We can inherit these responses from our ancestors.

Ancient symbols

'Any object or symbol, used for one specific purpose, for a very long period of time, soon becomes a reservoir of energy and thus a source of power for those who know how to tap into it'

KALA AND KETZ PAJEON, *THE TALISMAN MAGICK WORKBOOK*

Ancient symbols include both abstract and realistic designs. Historically, they were seen as sacred devices and attributed with powers to affect us at many levels. Used thousands of years ago by our ancestors, they were developed to bridge the gap between the conscious and subconscious. Recognising their power to convey messages simply, quickly and effectively, older civilisations used symbols extensively in religion, art, myths and rituals.

Jung, in studying this aspect, concluded that symbolism plays an important part in the psychic processes that influence every aspect of human thought and endeavour.

Of course, these ancient symbols became even more effective through consistent use, reinforcing their meaning through the constant repetition of their display in the appropriate context. This process is precisely the same as the one used in modern corporate imagery today, when it is promoted through television and other high-profile displays.

Angeles Arrien, an anthropologist, educator, author and corporate consultant, discovered, after seven years of research, that five basic shapes appear in the art of all cultures. These are the circle, the cross, the triangle, the square and the spiral. She outlines details of the significance of these in her book *Signs of Life*.[7]

Essentially, the circle symbolises wholeness; the cross represents relationships; the triangle stands for goals and dreams; the square indicates stability, and the spiral means growth. Moreover, people in different cultures give similar meanings to these shapes. Arrien believes that these five shapes are external symbols of internal psychic states and has developed the 'Preferential Shapes Test' using the symbols as tools to enable those taking the test to assist transformation in their current life situations. We are drawn to certain symbols above others and our choice tells something intrinsic about us. The logos we are drawn to will tell us something about us and their shapes can be chosen to appeal to the desired target audience.

A study at Rice University, Houston USA found that interdependent cultures, such as those found in Asian countries including India and China, prefer rounded shapes as they represent harmony, which is consistent with an interdependent view of the world. Researcher Vikas Mittal said; 'Those countries tend to have a higher percentage of rounded logos compared with individualistic countries, and logos and product shapes that are rounded are more acceptable and embraced in those cultures.' Western cultures, on the other hand, tend to have a more independent or individualistic culture and the study showed that changing a logo to a round shape was negatively perceived.[8]

Square
Stability

Triangle
Goals & Dreams

Circle
Wholeness

Spiral
Growth

Cross
Relationships

Five basic shapes appear in the art of all cultures and many logos.

The Swiss psychologist Carl Jung stated that the circle is the archetypal symbol for the totality of the psyche. Examples of companies using a circle include Mobil, Audi, BMW and Starbucks.

The square, used by Orange and the BBC, symbolises permanence, strength and security. A spokesperson for the design group responsible for the new Hotpoint image, comprising a square with a dot in the top centre, stated that: 'The square represents strength and reliability.'

An oval or egg shape, is like a compressed circle. Used by Ford, Pfizer and Boots the Chemist, it symbolises abundance, creativity, fertility, increase, and new beginnings.

As one of the oldest symbols in the world, the cross can stand for eternal life and divine protection. Swiss Air uses a cross to identify its airline. Perhaps the most famous representation is the Red Cross organisation. When the lower vertical line is extended, we have the Christian cross that has influenced many of us for more than 2,000 years.

The equilateral triangle on its base, as used by NatWest Bank, is a fire symbol, a male and solar sign representing divinity, life, the heart, ascent, prosperity, harmony, stability and permanence, like a pyramid. Reversed, it is a water symbol, female and lunar. Standing on a point it looks much more unstable, ready to topple over. Highway signs are triangular, warning us of danger ahead when on their base, or signalling us to give way when on the apex. The triangle is also the sign for God in some major religions.

Simple lines trigger varying responses depending on their style. According to Gestalt psychology, human attention is primarily attracted by vertical and horizontal movements. Adrian Frutiger, author of *Signs and Symbols*,[9] defines these differences as the horizontal representing things that *are*, and the vertical representing things that *happen* (rain, lightning, etc). We are vertical and we move on static horizontal surfaces such as land and floors. Because of this perceived variation, we react differently to each of these lines. Two of the most well-known symbols, the Christian cross and the swastika, combine horizontal and vertical lines. When lines are angled, they look less stable, with potential energy, as in italic type. Lines are used as an underline to give logotypes emphasis, such as in the Tesco design.

The arrow is one of the earliest signs to be used by humans and is associated with hunting and injury, life and death. Adrian Frutiger says

Interdependent cultures, such as those found in Asian countries, prefer rounded shapes as they represent harmony, which is consistent with an interdependent view of the world. Western cultures, on the other hand, tend to have a more independent or individualistic culture and prefer squares and researchers found that changing a logo to a round shape was negatively perceived.
The circle is the archetypal symbol for the totality of the psyche. Examples of companies using a circle include Mobil, Audi, GEC, BMW and Starbucks.
The square, used by Orange, GAP, Lego and the BBC, symbolises permanence, strength and security.

that, because of this, it awakens feelings of aggression and anxiety. Of course, it is also directional. The Royal Bank of Scotland uses four arrows pointing into the centre, in a configuration that also represents the St Andrew's Cross of Scotland.

The diamond shape is a further adaptation of the square and elicits a completely different, more disquieting response in the viewer. Because of its ability to attract our attention, a diamond is used for traffic signs in some parts of the world. Renault and Agfa also use the diamond shape.

The oblong, unlike the equal-sided square from which it is adapted, can evoke different responses depending on whether it is upright or landscape, in the same way as vertical and horizontal lines have different effects.

All these shapes are commonly incorporated into logos. They can be arranged in an infinite range of forms, simply by joining, overlapping or duplicating them—making them solid, dimensional or outlined. Every variation has a different impact, however subtle, on our being.

The future is bright; the future is a colour

'Colour is the place where our brain and the universe meet.'

PAUL KLEE

At the basic level, colour is what we see when light rays are reflected off an object. What we perceive as a blue flower has absorbed all the other colours except blue. Each colour has its own wavelength and rate of vibration. Red has the slowest vibration and longest wavelength, then orange, yellow, green, blue, indigo and finally violet.

Colour is one of the most recognisable parts of a logo. Once the brand has associated a colour with the product, they become inextricably linked. Who would consider changing Cadbury's purple or Coke's red?

According to research by patent and trademark attorneys Withers & Rogers, colour is the strongest visual element of a brand. They found that the AA has the highest colour recall of any brand and 64% of respondents rated colour more important to a brand than a slogan, typeface or logo shape. The yellow and black of the AA logo was recognised by 98% of

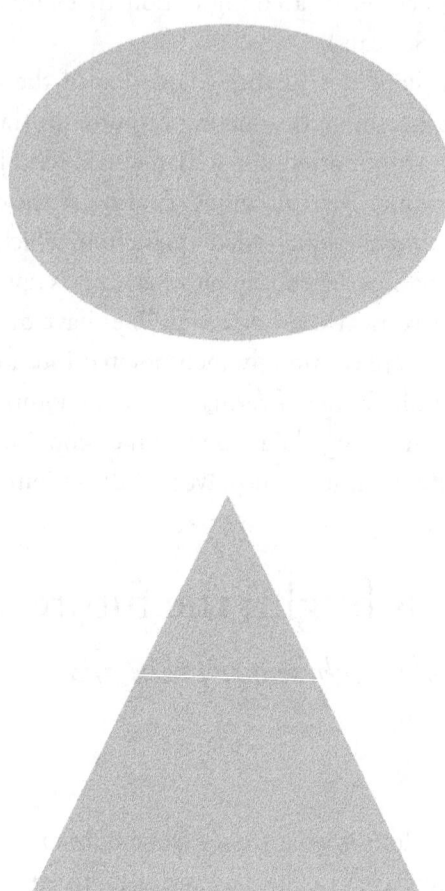

An oval or egg shape, as used by Ford, Pfizer and Boots the Chemist, symbolises abundance, creativity, fertility, increase, and new beginnings.
The equilateral triangle on its base, as used by NatWest Bank, is a fire symbol, a male and solar sign representing divinity, life, prosperity, harmony, stability and permanence. Reversed, it is a water symbol, female and lunar. Nabisco and Qantas use right angled red triangles.

respondents, EasyJet's distinctive orange colour by 93%, and Cadbury's purple and BP's green by 88%.[10]

We even refer to Gauloises blue, and Marlboro or pillar box (Post Office) red. Oxford University has a colour associated with it known as Oxford blue (identified in print as Pantone 282).

If one brand has secured a colour in a particular field it can be difficult, even illegal, for another brand to use the same colour. Chocolate giant Cadbury is fiercely protective of its signature colour and has trademarked it in more than 20 countries. In Australia, it has been locked in a legal dispute for more than five years with the Australian confectioner Darrell Lea over its rights to use the colour.[11] It is the dream of brand managers to firmly associate their brand with a particular colour. If they could claim that field of colour energy for their own, every time we see the colour, wherever that might be, our thoughts would be attracted towards their brand and we would help feed its success.

Tiffany's blue was chosen when the stores opened in the nineteenth century because it was already familiar to wealthy, well-educated customers. Used by Jean-Marc Nattier, a famous painter, who pioneered its use in his portraits of female members of the royal court at Versailles in the 1700s, this blue had pre-existing values that were attractive to the elite. It was registered as a federal trademark in the USA in 2000.[12]

The colour pink has now become synonymous with breast cancer charities. Initially identified with a pink ribbon, in times of peak fundraising, this has extended to anything pink from sparkling wine to sugar-coated doughnuts.

The importance of colour in branding becomes obvious when we see it referred to as a primary identification in the corporate image. Orange (telecommunications), Purple (finance), the Big Yellow Box Self Storage Company and the Red Cross are all examples of brands that use simple imagery and rely strongly on colour.

Our ability to respond to and recognise the colour of a logo was apparent in an advertisement for Superbrands seen on a bus in London in April 2008. The display simply comprised blocks of colour, which immediately prompted a recognition of some of our most popular brands.[13] Squares of purple, red, black with cream, and yellow with green, labelled

We will see the same shape differently depending on the layout but we will still register the shape and all that goes with it.

simply with the words 'the chocolate', 'the soft drink', 'the pint' and 'the fuel', succinctly identified Cadbury, Coca-Cola, Guinness and BP.

While some of our responses to colour have been learned through exposure to the accompanying brand, others are inherent or cultural. Green, for example, used by BP, Holiday Inn and National, relates to nature and money. Perhaps because of these strong related associations, it is one of the less used logo colours. Blue is avoided by fast food retailers because food does not grow blue in the natural world and we don't have an inherited appetite response. Dieticians even suggest eating off a blue plate or putting blue lights in a refrigerator to put us off eating. McDonalds, KFC and Burger King do not package their food in blue. Blue, however, is the most popular colour for logos and is used by over 50 per cent of FTSE 100 companies.[14] It is a popular choice for financial institutions and pharmaceuticals because it inspires trust and stability; it is used by IBM, Pfizer, Invesco, Boots and Ford, to name just a few. Red is used to attract attention and is the second most popular brand colour in the FTSE 100 logos. Signifying good luck in Eastern countries, it is used to attract attention, as in HSBC and Marlboro. Fast-food businesses are often identified by their use of red and yellow. The yellow 'M' in McDonalds makes us feel optimistic.

Research can tell us what colours are recognisably acceptable in certain sectors and the most suitable for a specific product. It can also calculate our responses depending on where we live, what hidden associations we might have with colours, and what drives us to choose a brand in one colour over another. While this might be an excellent starting point for any designer; not all brands can appear the same and colour is one of the key ways in which competitors differentiate themselves. Avis is red, Hertz is yellow and National is green.

There is a risk of disassociating a brand from its core activity, but changing from the accepted colour norm can pay high dividends for the company brave enough to take a stand.

We have strong beliefs about colour, and our perceptions of a product can be changed simply by varying the colour of the outer packaging. In research, washing detergent was packaged in three containers: one yellow, one blue, and one a mix of the two colours. The results showed that for the majority of people, the powder in the mixed-colour pack was just right;

the stuff in the yellow being too harsh, and in the blue too mild, despite the fact that the contents were all identical.[15]

Hundreds of people were asked to choose the sweetest lemon and lime flavoured drink from samples coloured in various degrees of intensity. Believing that the stronger the colour, the sweeter the drink (the opposite of the reality), most people got it wrong.[16]

The colour of pills can actually change our physical response. When participants were given either a blue or a pink pill, the former colour acted as a sedative and the latter as a stimulant. Nexium, a heartburn drug from AstraZeneca, has built on this and now patients ask their doctor for the purple pill.[17]

Simply using our eyes to gain information on a brand can mislead us; the message the brand people want us to get is not necessarily our truth.

And colour does not have to be seen in order for us to feel its effect.

The logo colour meeting our colour

'. . . *There is a connection between our physical eye and the third eye of the psyche; a connection between the skin and the aura; between the glandular system and the circulation of unseen energies. The symbol of that connection is colour.*'

ANNIE WILSON AND LILLA BEK, *WHAT COLOUR ARE YOU?*

Theo Gimble, in *Healing Through Colour*, says: 'As a form of energy, colour is active at all levels of our being—mental, emotional, physical and spiritual.'

The skin sees in Technicolor. The position of a colour on our bodies, its hue, the shape it forms and how much it covers us can have different effects on our wellbeing.

Each of our bodies' seven main energy centres, known as our chakras, has a colour associated with it and can respond to the colours around us. The first chakra, known as the root chakra, is situated at the base of the spine and its colour is red.

The second, the sacral chakra, just below the navel, is orange. The third, the solar plexus chakra, is above the navel and is yellow. The fourth, the heart chakra, is green. The fifth, the throat chakra, is blue. The sixth chakra, situated in the centre of the forehead, is indigo. At the crown of the head, the uppermost chakra is violet (or white in some systems).

Our red centre is associated with our sexual energy, our basic raw energy, and our attachment to the earth. It is the second most popular colour choice for logos; Red Bull, Vodafone, Virgin, Coca-Cola and KFC are a few brands that use it. Hertz might consider itself number one, but its yellow gives way to the Avis red. Avis still tops the car rental league.[18]

Author and intuitive Carolyn Myss[19] calls the red energy centre the tribal power chakra. Perhaps the popularity of red logos reflects the need to belong to the tribe that the logo identifies. The fear and insecurity felt within this chakra is echoed when we do not feel as if we are supported by fellow tribal members. As the foundation of our emotional and mental health, these fears and insecurities can be soothed by the brands we trust.

The second energy centre shares its colour, orange, with the telecommunications company of the same name, and is understood to govern self-confidence and creativity.

Yellow, the colour of the third chakra, is concerned with our personal power, with Hertz ('number one') using this colour.

Red, yellow and orange stimulate our digestive system. The logos of fast-food companies, including McDonalds, KFC, Pizza Hut and Burger King abound with these colours. They want to motivate us to eat!

Green resonates with our heart energy; it is concerned with love, compassion and universal goodwill, as well as emotions. It is used by environmental and charitable organisations such as Oxfam who want to appeal to our compassion and caring. Starbucks and BP include it in their logo, as they surely want us to believe that they care.

Our blue throat chakra is the seat of our self-expression and communication. Skype and IBM firmly lay claim to this attribute. It is also the centre of our trust, faith and knowledge. We can begin to understand why it is the most popular colour for logos, and a favourite for financial institutions and pharmaceutical manufacturers including Barclays Bank, Invesco, Boots and Pfizer.

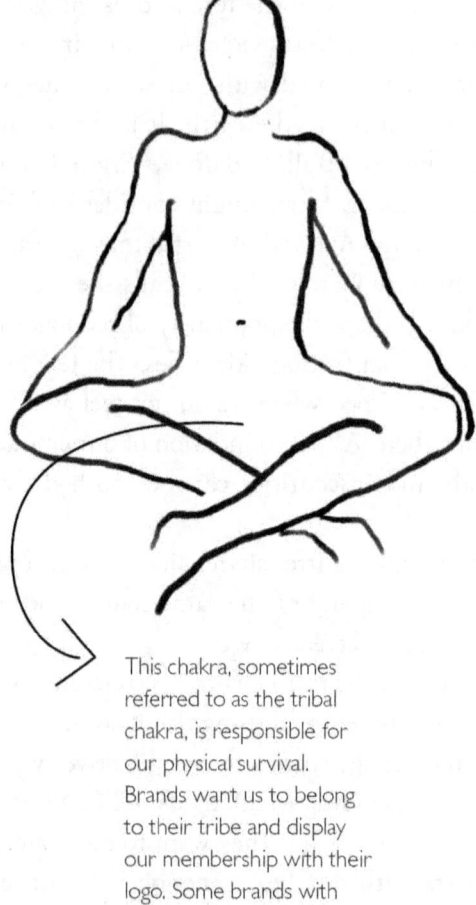

This chakra, sometimes referred to as the tribal chakra, is responsible for our physical survival. Brands want us to belong to their tribe and display our membership with their logo. Some brands with red logos include Vodafone, Kellogg's, Marlboro, Virgin, KFC, NatWest, Avis, Texaco, Budweiser, Coca-Cola, Mitsubishi, Safeway, Qantas and Levis.

The base chakra red is the second most popular colour for logos.

Our sixth chakra is attributed with the colour indigo, which is not used on many logos. This chakra, also known as the third eye chakra, is associated with clarity, insight, clairvoyance and intuition. Perhaps brands do not want us to have our own intuitive insights about their business, or maybe it is just a difficult colour to print.

The seventh chakra, at the crown of our head, is white (some say violet). It is concerned with higher spiritual matters, faith and humanitarian values. Cadburys, Silk Cut and Hallmark, as well as a plethora of logos related to healing, use violet. While white is apparent in pharmaceuticals' graphics, for example, it is not a primary logo colour because it needs another colour alongside to enable it to be seen.

Every colour has the ability to interact with our own energy colours to affect us physically, mentally and energetically, consciously and unconsciously.

History of colour use

Designers and researchers might have honed their talents and abilities to ensure they use colour to the full effect, but they are utilising skills that extend into ancient history. Throughout the ages, colour has been used to effect change in us. From the royal purple robes of ancient Greece to the red colour of the carpet rolled out for dignitaries, colour is specially chosen to enhance occasions, products and services. Ancient societies went to a great deal of effort to acquire and produce colours for their use. In parts of Zambia, India and Europe, archaeological sites dated to between 200,000 and 300,000 years ago have been found to contain vast quantities of imported pigment—haematite, limonite, manganese dioxide and other substances.[20]

According to studies carried out by anthropologists, words describing colour are acquired by cultures in a strict sequence. All languages have terms for black and white; if there are three terms for colour then the third is red; if four, it is green or yellow; if five, it is both. The sixth and seventh terms for colour are blue and brown and only if the language has eight or more terms does it have words for purple, pink, orange and grey.[21] It is interesting that HSBC, focusing a recent advertising campaign around

The throat chakra is responsible for communication; our voice in the world. Brands have their own tone of voice and their success depends on us speaking the same language. Blue also makes us feels calm and instils feeling of trust. Brands with blue logos include IBM, American Express, ADT, Boots, Pfizer, Barclays Bank, Skype, AT&T, Ford and Twitter.

Blue, our throat chakra colour, is the most popular colour for logos.

language differences to promote itself as an international bank, uses the colours red, white and black.

Ancient civilisations practised colour therapy. Hippocrates recommended the use of sunbaths in ancient Greece; the Egyptians used coloured oils and applied coloured pastes made from ground crystals to afflicted parts of bodies, as well as creating temples of colour for healing. The ancient Chinese would treat epileptic patients by laying them on violet surrounded with beams of the same colour; those with scarlet fever were surrounded by red, with red light beams directed on them; those with disorders of the colon were painted yellow, which was also projected to ease cramps.[22] Traditionally, sick people were taken to lie in the pools of light created by the sun shining through the stained glass windows in churches.

Colour therapy is practised extensively today.

Colour and our health

While branding experts use research and design techniques to shift our perceptions and pull on our emotions, the ability of colour alone to cause profound changes in our state of being is apparent in its effective use in healing.

Colours for healing can be applied using gemstones, fabric, coloured oils or colour-saturated water, potentised by exposing water to sunlight through coloured glass, and even visualised and directed accordingly. We are affected by colour and this effect is so profound that we don't even have to see the colour in order to be transformed by it. This fact was verified by the noted neuropsychologist Kurt Goldstein; in his modern classic *The Organism*, he noted that stimulation of the skin by different colours leads to different effects. He stated: 'it is probably not a false statement to say that a specific colour stimulation is accompanied by a specific response pattern of the entire organism.'

Theo Gimbel, in his book *Healing Through Colour*, confirms that while sounds, like mantras (those repeated often, such as a person's name), can affect us profoundly, colour has an even deeper impact on humans. As a much higher vibration than sound, he believes it has a stronger effect.

Our third eye chakra
gives us clarity, insight
and intuition

Hats with logos on the front are very popular.

Gimbel agrees that we do not have to *see* colour for it to affect us. People can be treated with colour from a distance; it is possible to use colour by sending it effectively via thought projection. Ghadhali, a Hindu scientist who worked in the USA in the 1930s, believed that colours are potent chemical entities that operate as vibrations of high frequency, which we can draw in to balance our aura and keep healthy.[23]

Corporate colourist Angela Wright,[24] recognised as a world expert on the unconscious effect of colour, states that: 'Colour has a profound effect on human behaviour and it is better understood now than at any time in history'. She claims: 'Colour is energy and the fact that it has a physical effect on us has been proved time and again in experiments—most notably when blind people were asked to identify colours with their fingertips and were all able to do so easily.' Since it has been observed that the cells in our body respond to colour—and with the skin being the largest organ—it becomes apparent just how much we can be influenced by the colour of our surroundings. On her website, Angela suggests the choice of a brand colour palette: 'First, identify the brand's characteristics, values, aspirations; decide on the most appropriate colour group to communicate the brand personality, and the desired messages, most powerfully and thereafter, make sure that every hue, shade, tone or tint used in any brand communication is drawn from that colour group.' She believes that, among other actions, colour can increase a brand's popularity and increase sales. Colours can keep brands healthy too.

Swiss psychotherapist Professor Max Lüscher developed the Lüscher colour test for assessing a patient's psychological and physiological characteristics based on the colours they like or dislike. He used four colours—red, blue, yellow and green, which stood respectively for self-confidence, contentment, freedom and self-respect. The test was based on the theory that colours stimulate different parts of the autonomic nervous system, affecting the metabolic rate and glandular secretions. Studies in the 1950s showed that yellow and red light raised blood pressure, while blue light tended to lower it.

Some colour therapists advise on what colours to wear, to eat, or use in home decorating. They may also include advice on the times to wear colours—for example, before going to bed or before a potentially stressful meeting—and on which parts of the body. Logo designers too will decide on the most effective position for a logo on an article of clothing.

A very precise method of colour application for health is achieved by shining coloured beams of light onto acupuncture points using a specially designed tool.[25] In a review in *Kindred Spirit* magazine on the technique of iridology (where diagnosis of imbalances in the body are made by looking at differentiations in the iris of the human eye, which correlate to individual organs), recent experiments were outlined where thin beams of light were directed at specific sites in the iris. These were subsequently found to stimulate the body's organs relating to that site.

The colour therapy company Aurosoma has developed a system that enables the diagnosis and redressing of imbalances in people through the use of colour. Based on the principle that we are innately aware of what we need for our optimum health, the client is presented with a range of bottles—each filled with two liquids, kept separate by their differing densities. From the bottles chosen, an analysis of the imbalance can be ascertained and the coloured liquid can then be physically applied to specific areas on the body to help restore optimum health. Could we choose a particular logo colour to display for our own wellbeing?

I have witnessed at first hand how people can change when they have been through a colour choice exercise, where trained specialists categorise individuals with their ideal colour scheme. Often this bears little resemblance to the clients' previously favoured colours, and when they start to wear the selected colours, the change can be profound. In the main, it is only the colour of their clothes that has varied.

Dr Valerie Hunt states that sometimes we don't like the colours that we need in order for us to heal and that a therapist might have to establish different ways of approaching clients so that they will accept the needed frequencies. She has noted in her research that people with cancer, for example, don't seem to be attracted to red, but she has found that their bio energy fields need energies in the red frequencies in order for them to heal. And it must be the right shade of red.[26] Not everyone will like the carefully chosen brand colour, but somehow the designers and branding experts must persuade them to accept it into their own energy field for the good of the brand.

Andrew Elliot, Professor of Psychology at the University of Rochester, USA, says: 'Colours function as a subtle primer, exerting a direct influence on motivation and behaviour without individuals' conscious awareness.' He adds: 'Given that the influence of colour on our behaviour is so prevalent, it's shocking that we aren't more aware of it.'[27]

Different colours affect us differently. Red is associated with excitement and passion, blue with peace and harmony, green with peacefulness and tranquillity, yellow with joy and intelligence, orange with enthusiasm and communication, purple with spirituality and integrity, white with cleanliness and purity, and black with mystery and sophistication. This is a fraction of what we know about these colours. They can be mixed, combined and fine-tuned to project an exact intention onto customers, both existing and potential.

The effectiveness of colour to make a difference to our personal health makes it a formidable tool for the brand experts. Taking one colour—red—as an example, we can get a feeling of the power of colour and the benefits of getting the logo colour right.

Colours can create change—red, for example

The colour red stimulates energy and has therefore provoked a lot of research. Research shows that wearing red gives sportspeople a better chance of winning. Evolutionary anthropologists Russell Hill and Robert Barton of Durham University, UK, noted that in certain sports in the 2004 Olympics, competitors were randomly assigned a red or a blue kit. When they analysed the results, they found that competitors in red won the majority of bouts. Barton says: 'Skill and strength may be the main factors—if you're rubbish, a red shirt won't stop you from losing, but when fights were relatively symmetrical, colour tipped the balance.'[28]

Since 1947, English football teams wearing red shirts have won more games than would normally be expected. Analysis verified this. 'A matched-pairs analysis of red and non-red wearing teams in eight English cities shows significantly better performance of red teams over a 55-year period.'[29] This might help explain how Liverpool, Manchester United and Arsenal have won 38 out of 63 league titles between them since the Second World War. Red shirts are now associated with long-term team success in English football.

It might be that part of the success is due to the referee favouring the red team. Sports psychologists at the University of Münster, Germany, showed 42 video clips of games to experienced referees. They then showed the same games with the clothing colours digitally swapped. In each case, the red competitors were awarded more points.[30]

Andrew Elliot has demonstrated that even a brief glimpse of red can change human behaviour. Volunteers were assigned a number in an experimental IQ test. Those who had their numbers written in red, rather than black, scored consistently lower on the tests. Elliot has noted evidence of 'avoidance behaviour' caused by seeing red for a brief time and believes that: 'These results show that at a very basic level, your body is pre-wired to move away from red.' He attributes this, as well as the success of wearing it to win at sport, to the link with 'red for danger.'[31]

Elliot further observed that men rated women photographed on a red background more attractive than those on a white background. 'Red is clearly context-specific. In achievement situations, red means danger, which leads to avoidance, but in romance situations red means sexual availability or romance, and that leads to approach behaviour.'[32]

Physiologically, rather than being related to culture or memory, red light has been shown to stimulate the autonomic nervous system, evoking more tension, excitement, and hostility than, for example the colour blue. Moreover, red light seems to produce anger and anxiety in infants and the mentally ill. Tests at Yale University indicated that the colour red tended to affect detrimentally such mental activities as problem-solving, decision-making, and social conversation.[33]

The effect of red is not limited to humans. Male mandrills use red coloration on the face, rump and genitalia to communicate their fighting ability to other males. Those displaying paler red will normally stand down before fighting.[34]

Tests have shown that chickens wearing red-tinted contact lenses behave differently from birds that don't. The chickens are calmer, less prone to pecking and cannibalism and their mortality rate is lower. They also tend to eat less feed while producing, on average, the same number and size of eggs as other chickens.[35]

According to Lindstrom, author of *Brand Sense*, Santa Claus traditionally wore green until Coca-Cola began to promote him in the 1950s. Today he wears the colour of Coke.[36]

The subtleties and value of fine-tuning

Because of the potent capacity of different colours to influence moods and feelings in us, designers need to be skilled in the language of tints, shades and hues. Subtle variations in colour reproduction can influence our perception. Even the descriptive colours of red give us clues to the exact shade and its impact. Blood, scarlet, maroon, magenta, vermilion, flame, fire engine, claret, russet, ruby and brick all tell us the subtle characteristics of the described red colour.

Virgin, Coke and Vodafone catch our attention with their familiar bright red. But a little burgundy added to a red logo makes it looks expensive and the price of the product can be raised because we believe it. Alfa Romeo and Ferrari owners know the specific red that identifies their car.

When we add a little white we get pink, which has a totally different set of values and effects. Pink has been associated with baby girls and, in the main, with the feminine.

Alexander Schauss, director of the Institute for Biosocial Research in Tacoma, Washington, reported that aggressive, hostile and anxiety-ridden behaviour could be suppressed in minutes by exposure to a specific shade of pink. By painting prison walls pink, stress, violence and self-harm in inmates were reduced.[37]

At a county jail in Texas, the sheriff took this pink effect a stage further. As well as being surrounded by pink walls and sheets, inmates were supplied with pink jumpsuits and pink slippers. The sheriff of Mason County told the Associated Press that inmates, 'don't want to wear them.' He confirmed that the reoffending rate was down by 70 per cent, possibly due to a combination of the calming effect and the threat of further embarrassment.[38]

Designers understand minute differentiations in colour, and combine experience, logic, research findings and preferences to fine-tune colours for logotypes. Small tweaks to shades and hues of a brand colour can make dramatic changes in our perception of a particular company or product.

A little more red in a blue colour will shift it towards a warm purple; more black will darken it and make it more sombre, yellow will turn it towards a turquoise; each of these subtleties will prompt a different response in us.

Each colour emits a different and scientifically measurable frequency. Although there are tens of thousands of specified colours in the internationally recognised Pantone colour standard used by the design and print industry, every colour could be credited with individual qualities and deliver a unique and specific response to the viewer—however subtle. We could, theoretically, rechart the entire reference book according to our emotional and physiological reactions, and select brand colours accordingly.

Brand designers never underestimate the effect of colour on our decision-taking processes. Using computer technology they have an infinite range of colours from which to choose, and they can spend weeks fine-tuning a shade so that it will hit us in just the right spot. To ensure it keeps tickling that same spot to continually reinforce the logo impact, specially trained design managers will ensure that it is reproduced faithfully every time.

Printing colours

Every colour we see in a magazine or poster is created from the combination of a few special printing colours. The most commonly used colours, in the four-colour halftone process, are cyan (blue), magenta (red), yellow and black. A combination of different-sized dots of these colours makes up all the shades we normally see in printed material.

Cyan is a turquoise colour regarded as sacred by the Egyptians, native American Indians and the Tibetans. Turquoise itself is believed to rejuvenate cell structures and aid immunity.

A dark shade of pink, magenta is attributed with knowledge, co-operation stimulation, affection, force, love and wisdom, as well as being a colour of high spirituality and individuality. Yellow, as described above, stimulates our appetite and energy. Black is all colours, totally absorbed, representing, in Western culture, death and oneness.

Colour and power

The American Faber Birren (1900-1988), author of about 25 books on colour, was employed by both industry and government to increase production, improve efficiency, and enhance worker safety and welfare by manipulating interior colour and light. In his book *Color Psychology and Color Therapy*, he states: ' . . . as this book strives to show, the influence of color is by no means limited to the psychological realm; its direct biological and physiological effects are rapidly becoming more evident as new research data accumulate.'[39]

When we combine this information with the power of a logo, we have a formidable tool to effect change on behalf of the brand.

Focused colour will naturally have a focused effect. So, while the colour of our general surroundings—such as wearing particular colours or painting rooms in certain shades—may influence the overall state of our mind and body, the colour of the logo can be specifically fine-tuned and controlled, then consistently applied and delivered worldwide via products and the media. Like the beam of coloured light on a tiny acupuncture point, a logo can specifically target and deliver a concentrated focus of colour that is intended to, and can, affect us in a specific way whether we see it or wear it.

When we take the above into account, and consider the attention spent on detailing and delivering the corporate colours precisely, we can begin to see how a brand colour can affect us, whether it is projected from a cinema or TV screen onto our retina, worn directly over a potentially sensitive point on our body, or absorbed by our aura as we walk into a branded store. With the power to deliver selected brand colours to individuals and the four corners of the world, brands can display an aspect to their future that encourages participation. Rather like laying out a red carpet before us, we want to walk on it whether we are invited or not.

CHAPTER ELEVEN

Making the corporate dream real

'To charge with meaning an abstract (visual) sign, detached from any concrete reality, is a process as powerful as that which led to the invention of writing.'

JEAN ABÉLANET, SIGNES SANS PAROLES (WORDLESS SIGNS)

The value of the logo

Immense effort and enormous budgets are spent in establishing and maintaining a brand. Without a logo, including a name, colour and graphics, we would not be able to recognise the brand and express a full opinion about it. It is the logo that we fall in love with. The logo makes a brand unique; it makes it stand out from its competitors and it delivers the brand promise. The logo is how we make sense of a company.

Without a logo, a high street bank is simply another bank; a packet of digestive biscuits appears much the same as the next packet on the supermarket shelf, and a hamburger is just fast food. This lack of identification affects our purchasing choice.

There is substantial evidence that removing branding from cigarette packaging would contribute to a reduction in smoking and help change the social context in which smoking is judged. Cigarettes are known as 'badge' products—smokers buy the brand that will reinforce the characteristics they want to project. This is reinforced each time they pull out the pack of cigarettes in front of their friends. Consumer theory and research has demonstrated that these 'incidental brand encounters' powerfully affect buying patterns in ways in which the consumer is not fully aware. The plain packs were seen as less attractive; the smokers of the packs were seen as less stylish and sociable, and the cigarettes were thought to be less satisfying and of a lower quality. Without doubt, removing branding from cigarette packs would affect buying patterns. Professor Mike Daube, President of the Public Health Association of Australia, remarked: 'The tobacco industry has responded to this move more ferociously to anything in tobacco control in 20 years and I think that sends out a signal, if the tobacco industry is so worried about it, then we've got to be on the right track.'[1] Recognition of the logo became apparent in the success of the brand. When changes to some brands of cigarette packaging were noted and queried by researchers, the latter were told that the company was 'playing with the logo because we can't do any advertising any more.'

The identifying logo can become more important than the product alone, in much the same way as a signature on a painting dramatically increases the value of the art. Salvador Dalí discovered he could earn money in advance by signing blank sheets of paper for future editions. By signing one sheet every two seconds with the help of a colleague, he could generate $72,000 an hour. (Unfortunately, some of the 350,000 sheets fell into the wrong hands and there are now many Dalí fakes with genuine signatures.)[2]

Choosing the brand future

Logos are tools of manifestation. Companies secure the future they desire by choosing their name, symbols and colour and combining these in a unique piece of design that they share with the world. Names are carefully selected on their meaning, or the lack of it. They can have an inherent value, such as General Motors or Pink Elephant, or be abstract, with a clean slate, such as Verizon and Pfizer. Clichés abound in the world of symbols; mountain peaks, whether realistic (Invesco) or symbolic (Nat West's triangle), eagles, acorns, dolphins and many, many others conjure up pre-existing aspirations. The skill of the designer lies in detailing these in a unique way or finding another suitable device to represent the brand values. 'Calling in' the power of an eagle, a mountain or a flower was thought to imbue the caller with the same powers. Companies make their own choice of what 'powers' to call in. Even abstract symbols are attributed with their own effective values.

Colours are evaluated according to the area of business, competitors and our reaction, then fine-tuned to display a unique visual message.

Deliberately designed and consciously controlled, a logo is able to take us to new dimensions, to connect with a reality that has been specially created to entrance us. Once this connection has been established, we are open to having our minds changed. We will see and relate to a brand differently.

Encapsulating a host of promises, a logo secures a part of our mindset and ringfences a territory for a brand in our psyche. If the designers and brand managers are successful, we will become set in the ways of the brand and continue to pursue the security of the familiar. We will reject unwelcome competitors, remain loyal to the brand, and even pass our preferences on to our offspring. Constantly and consistently delivered, a logo prompts our memory of the product and imprints the values over and over again so we continue to choose it, we feel good, and we don't know why.

An excerpt from one specialist company's website more than hints at the efficacy of this process. 'Welcome to our Psychographic Profile website. This process was formulated to measure the emotional drivers your business wants to communicate to its target market and shows you the best colour, shape and font to subconsciously communicate these intended messages. This is fantastic information to have when designing any branding or marketing material.'[3]

How does a logo do this?

Our brains are amazingly plastic. Every time we have a thought, for example, about standing up or waving our arm, or have feelings about a person, a colour or an event, a series of neurotransmitters, chemical messengers that enable our brain cells to communicate, stimulate a specific response in our brain. As we think the same thoughts over and over again, millions of new connections are created and strengthened so that these thoughts flow more and more easily. This is good news for the musicians, tradespeople and students who need to remember specific ways of repeating and building on existing information, but it can lead to us becoming habitually set in certain ways. The brand marketers, through advertising and marketing, stimulate our brain cells to fire in a particular way. Prompted again and again with a simple glance at the logo, this connection is strengthened and the memory soon becomes entrenched in our minds. We don't even have to remember the advertisements and the underlying intention; our brains are perfectly capable of recalling them subconsciously when prompted. Eventually our purchasing becomes a habit, we have significantly rewired our brain and, what is more, since our thoughts affect our genes, we can pass on this memory to our children! Our relationship to the logo will also be deepened with stories that are invented to support the brand.

The storytellers

'The empires of the future are empires of mind.'
WINSTON CHURCHILL

In the days before advertising, even before the written word, it was the storytellers who told specially formulated tales to move people in a particular way. Mikela Tarlow and Philip Tarlow state in their book *Digital Aboriginal* that we are seeing the return of the storytellers. We have been bombarded with so much information that the information era is now making way for the experience economy, so that the participant must be involved. As we move from the world of information to the world of imagination, corporate tales have immense appeal.

Seth Godin, author of numerous marketing books including *Permission Marketing*, and Marc Gobé, author of *Emotional Branding*, agree that the trends of brands telling complex authentic stories has just started and it is the future of branding.

Of course, the opponents to branding can also use stories including the mouse in the cola bottle, chicken nuggets filled with a cream that turned out to be an abscess, and the soft drink turning people bright orange. These may have origins based in reality, or be totally fabricated, but we are still attracted to them, whether we find them appealing or shocking.

We warm to logos with history; they are familiar to us. Their quirky beginnings serve to endear us. The Lloyds Bank black horse happened to exist on a sign outside a building where the bank first traded. Boots the Chemist endorses its products with the founder's signature. Jesse Boot built the Boots company from a small herbal store, and the company still acknowledges his vision to push boundaries and seek new solutions, claiming that this same spirit powers their business today.[4] It is unlikely that current research findings would include recommendations to name a chemist Boots, or even a food company Bird's Eye. Even the stories behind their naming, as well as their familiar historic value, endear them to us. Without these branding tales, would we feel so warmly about the company?

Those without the benefit of history weave their own stories to create depth, meaning and memories for the future. Through these we become endeared to the brands. They help to build and strengthen the energy around the logo as they secure our relationship via inner revelations.

Tales about the design origin of corporate symbols abound. When Imation was formed, the new corporate symbol, a hand holding a wand creating a flow of stars, was known as the 'hand of imagination'; it is believed to have been inspired by Arthur C Clarke's observation that technology is becoming more and more like magic. When the Japanese company Sanrio created Hello Kitty in 1974, they claimed that the character was born in London weighing three apples and was the daughter of an airline pilot and a concert pianist. She now has an official website, a blog and has appeared on thousands of products.[5]

The brand experts are skilled in creating stories with happy endings and they have a wealth of techniques to ensure the logo is firmly linked to the publicity that displays them. And it works. We hate it when our beloved logos are changed.

Changing the dream

'That nothing is static or fixed, that all is fleeting and impermanent, is the first mark of existence.'

PEMA CHODRON

Having spent millions getting our neurons firing to the same tune as the brands' values, brand managers hold tightly onto the goodwill invested in the logo. A logo change is not taken lightly. The value of its link to the company's activities is such these days that logos are handed down from generation to generation of CEOs, like a precious inheritance and sold on their merit. Logos are only changed to signify a new brand structure or ethos, or to align the brand with (or even create) new fashion trends in the outside world in order to stay ahead of the game.

Changing the logo is an extremely effective way of signalling and creating change in an organisation. It is probably the most cost-effective as well. A company may retain the same products, people, building and business strategies, but displaying a new logotype will send out a strong message that it is a very different business.

While huge sums of money are spent on the branding and design processes to raise, maintain and spread the 'goodwill energy' of the logo, there may be times outside the control of the company when undesired events occur to its detriment. These may be political, health, economical and fashion issues, but the logotype carries the brunt as it is usually displayed alongside the offending publicity; it can lose its 'glow'.

If, for example, the company has been receiving bad press, it may change its business practice and announce this adjustment via a new visual image. William Press, a large engineering company, was the subject of a dawn raid in London by the Inland Revenue some years ago. Although no evidence was found that suggested malpractice, the resulting bad publicity prompted a fundamental change in its corporate logo. With a simple design change, it was able to shed its tarnished image and present a new face to the outside world.

The change can be driven by a voluntary event, such as Diageo being formed out of the merger of Guinness plc and Grand Metropolitan plc, or self-initiated, as when Abbey National decided to shorten their name to

Abbey (and then again to indicate their new ownership as part of Grupo Santander). CGNU changed to Aviva to signify the combination of brands that included Norwich Union and RAC breakdown recovery. Aviva is a Jewish name referring to spring, representing new beginnings, new shoots and growth.

New management will often view a logo change as a medium through which to tell the outside world about the changes they plan and to make their stamp on the company in a highly visible manner. In other words: *control the logo and you control the company.*

A name change for a product, where the product remains the same after the design update—such as Jif to Cif, Opal Fruits to Starburst, Kentucky Fried Chicken to KFC, and Immac to Veet—presents a different challenge. It is usually accompanied by massive consumer advertising brimming with reassurance that it really is the same beloved product after the change.

Unilever upgraded its familiar U image in 2004 to represent its new theme of 'vitality' and to coincide with the 75-year anniversary of the company. The new logo is made up of 25 icons relating to the company's products, customers and environment. It is identified with the Unilever name, written in a signature style that, according to Lee Coomber, creative director of creative agency Wolff Olins: 'Conveys a sense of flexibility, friendliness, creativity and modernity.' He also states: 'It is about taking off the suit and showing Unilever's true colours.' Niall Fitzgerald, chairman of Unilever, says: 'The new symbol is a powerful expression of our vitality mission . . . . Our new brand will help us confidently identify ourselves in every aspect of our business.' This is a long way from Unilever's beginnings, when, in 1885, William Hesketh Lever was the first person to stamp Sunlight soap with a brand name and wrap it before selling it to the public.[6]

Rebranding needs to be company-led, not just an artistic device to signify insignificant or non-existent change. If a change symbolised by a new logo is not manifested on the ground, then the integrity of the brand will suffer along with the company's credibility. The public will spot the hype. Paul Durman quotes several examples that illustrate how rebranding can fail—and can even be detrimental to a company. He feels that the list of Britain's biggest companies is: ' . . . in a state of flux as they continually combine and divide their assets in unfamiliar new patterns.' He quotes British Gas as disappearing into Centrica, Lattice and BG Group, stating: 'Most big companies end up opting for vaguely futuristic neologisms—Aventis, Visteon, Agilent, Verizon, Agere,' and refers to the 'demise' of Midland Bank, Hong Kong and Shanghai Bank and the Bank of the Middle East when HSBC was adopted as the global name.[7]

A friend recently bought a Fiat and was compelled to ask a group of us what we thought the logo for this car brand was. The answers varied, but none was right. She felt vilified since she had felt quite uneasy buying a car from a company that, in her words, looked all over the place and could not even get its act together to decide on a consistent logo. It appears, from Fiat's website, that the logo has been changed twice in her lifetime, once from four blue rhombuses (1968-1999) to a blue disc with a laurel wreath, and then to a red shield in a silver square in 2006.

Whatever the reasoning behind the decision to change an existing corporate or brand image, it is the single most powerful tool with which to communicate change to the outside world—as well as within the organisation itself. It is immediately recognisable, transcends language and (in the main) can be controlled.

A new design, however, requires careful management and strategic business planning to back up the new claims projected by the 'new, improved' image. Publicly stating a new set of values, displayed on a subjective piece of design, opens the doors to public opinion. The logo provides the medium to communicate change, but it also enables the outside world to participate in the conversation.

This can prove embarrassing for high-profile companies, as in the case of BP when it launched its sunflower (known as Helios) image in an attempt to signify its commitment to human rights and environmental leadership. The branded image was held up in an attempt at cynicism when the company failed to meet these expectations—such as when they were accused of collaborating with China to help consolidate its violent occupation of Tibet.[8] The obviously 'environmentally conscious-looking' sunflower logotype provides a strong visual tool to journalists, who can display it alongside headlines such as 'Exposed: BP, its pipeline, and an environmental time bomb'[9] referring to shoddy workmanship on part of a 1,000-mile pipeline from the Caspian Sea to the Mediterranean port of Ceyhan in Turkey and 'Oil spill nears the beaches of Florida.'[10]

The danger of this is that the logo can begin to take on associations other than the desired brand values—in effect this can become an uncontrolled rebranding process.

The swastika is probably the best-known example of a symbol that has had its meaning changed. The swastika shape has been found all over the word including Japan, Ireland and in some American Indian tribes. In Chinese, the shape is referred to as *wan*; in Old English as *fulfot*; the Irish know it as Brigit's Cross, and in Germany it is *hakenkreuz* or 'hooked cross'. Originally a symbol of life and happiness in Eastern religions, as well as the sun and power (and one of the oldest symbols known), its meaning changed dramatically after the Nazi party adopted it. Subsequently, the swastika became identified with the holocaust and Hitlerism, virtually the opposite of those values with which it was originally attributed.

We react differently to this symbol now.

Logos hold brands accountable

Like the key on a map, a logo enables us to recognise and understand that which it identifies. If we change the key, we will interpret the map differently. For example, maps made it easy for European states to carve up Africa and other 'heathen' lands, and to lay claim to land and other resources. They used the map as an intellectual tool for legitimising territorial conquest, economic exploitation and cultural imperialism—lending weight to the saying that the pen is mightier than the sword.[11] Although it seems far-fetched to draw a piece of land on paper, call it a name and claim it, this is precisely what has happened in the past—and it is similar to branding, where a logo claims values and stakes out the brand territory.

If we change the logo, we will interpret the brand accordingly. We will not recognise the familiar territory of the brand and our familiar link to the values and promises will be severed. If McDonald's changed its name and symbol overnight, would we still feel the same about their burgers? Would they even taste the same? I think not.

Although the press often reflects a cynical attitude to the hype generated by costly new corporate imagery, research has shown that, in part at least, it works. Since any petroleum company must plunder the Earth's finite natural resources in order to survive, by visually stating a more caring stance and responsible attitude, BP's green sunflower image could actually have put pressure on the company to make fundamental changes in their attitudes to human resources and environmental concerns. An international study on corporate citizenship and social responsibility, published by communications research group Echo, placed BP at the top of the tree. BP even beat the Co-operative Bank in its level of political correctness.[12]

Brands must be seen to be responding to consumer demands, even if they appear to have created them in the first place. Supermarkets cleared genetically modified (GM) foods from their shelves because a survey of their customers pointed out that they did not want them. It was nothing to do with the supermarkets' corporate ethics or even pressure from environmental groups. As a result, Monsanto's stocks dived. PepsiCo did stop trading with Burma—not because of the regime's appalling human rights record, but because the company believed that the damage to its reputation would outweigh any financial gain.[13]

Brands can make firms accountable to consumers by putting pressure on the companies to live up to their intended promises.

Signalling a dream change

The logotype is how companies share their vision with us. Every business starts with a dream, an idea, and the only way in which this can be shared is by bringing it into physical, commercial reality. We buy into the company's dream world through the purchase of brands, with their accompanying promises, via the logo.

Paul Virilio, in his book *The Information Bomb*, articulates this process in the ability of movies to transform us: 'The cinema was in fact a **new energy**, capable of carrying your gaze to other places even if you yourself did not move.' Like the tree in Enid Blyton's *The Magic Faraway Tree*, where the children in the story climb a magic tree to reach strange and wonderful lands at the top, the logo is the means by which we reach other desired places, the promised land at the top of the tree. These places may be states of mind existing only in our imaginations, but by purchasing and displaying the logotype we too can share in the brand dream.

We may hate the logotype, find the ads silly and hate the company's moral values, but the logotype will reach us anyway. Ultimately, our reactions to it can make or break the company it represents.

The diagram above illustrates how the logo filters our response to a product. Linking the visions and aspirations (the unformed world) of a company with the physical products (the formed world) it enables everyone to share the dream. Physicist David Bohm refers to these two worlds as the *visible* and *invisible universe*. These inner and outer worlds are described in the *Tabula Smaragdina*, a cryptic text used by European alchemists, as the threefold principle of the analogy between the inner and outer worlds: '(i) the common source of both worlds (ii) the influence of the psychic upon the physical; (iii) the influence of the physical world on the spiritual.'[14]

Intention and attention

'If you dream it, you can do it.'

WALT DISNEY

According to quantum physics, we create our world through our intention and the attention we pay to that intention. Lynne McTaggart, author of *The Intention Experiment*, sponsored experiments to test whether, as she believes, 'human thoughts and intentions are an actual physical "something" with the astonishing power to change our world.'

At one of Lynne's conferences in March 2007, I participated in two experiments. The first was conducted by one of the speakers, Konstantin Korotkov, Professor of St Petersburg State University of Information. Korotkov has developed a machine that measures energy, and he connected it to water in the glass that he had been drinking from previously. He then asked the audience, around 400 of us, to send an intention to raise the energy of the water. We were able to see the results on the screen and after a few minutes we noted a distinct rise on the graph that continued throughout the session.

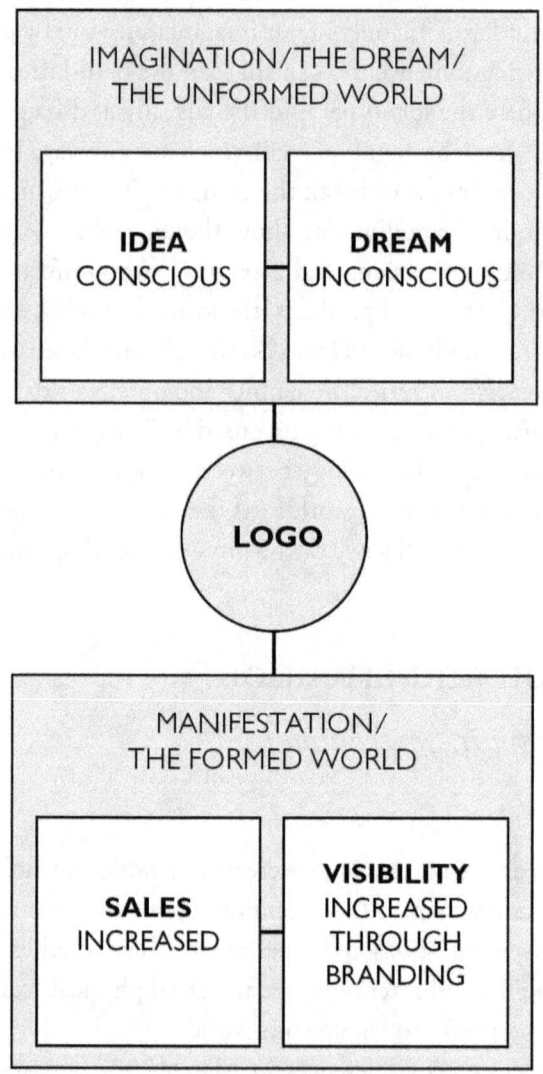

A logo design links the visions and aspirations of a company with its physical products; it enables everyone to share the dream and participate in the success of the brand.

The second experiment was timed with a link to a laboratory in Arizona. A webcam enabled us to see two leaves positioned there. One leaf was chosen as a focus and we were asked to use our intention to make it glow. Light-sensitive cameras on the chosen leaf would enable readings that could be analysed. We were informed that the chosen leaf glowed so brightly that it was visible to the naked eye. In Lynne's words, from her ensuing E-News Report: 'Yes, our thoughts—and only our thoughts—altered a leaf that was 5,000 miles away.'

Lynne concludes one of her chapters with a chilling thought, based on her collected evidence on the effects of our mind: 'Once constructed, a thought is lit forever.' All the intense creative thinking that goes into a logotype design, the thoughts around its current and future objectives as well as related design opinions, are around us forever. And every time we see the logo, we will think of the product and help build the energy for others to tune into.

This theory—that we create our world through our thoughts, the intention behind them and the attention we pay to them—gathers momentum with the compelling evidence portrayed by physicists on popular DVDs, and in books including *The Secret* and *What the Bleep*. If only a fraction of what these experts say is true, then we can only begin to imagine the power of a logo with its ability to transmit a powerful intention, to benefit a brand, backed by an investment of millions of dollars on marketing.

In her book *The Evidence for the Sixth Sense*, Hazel Courteney introduces William H Tiller, PhD, author of *Conscious Acts of Creation* and *Science and Human Transformation*, as one of the world's leading physicists on the structure of consciousness and matter. Hazel asked Professor Tiller whether or not it is possible that, if enough people believed something would happen, then it would manifest in reality.

He said: 'Right now this whole subject remains an open question . . . it could be either/and/or people's actual thoughts and physical actions, or it could be their subconscious thoughts actually creating what they think about most, or a combination of both . . . but from all our experiments of placing an intention in a box, which in time creates a specific reality, we can surmise that if enough people are thinking something, even at a subconscious level, then this too could be imprinting the invisible lattice structure mentioned previously, which in turn can imprint itself on the "terrorists" minds when they suddenly have an idea of attacking a certain place.

'You could even include the media in this equation—after all, we are constantly bombarded by more negative than positive news. This is sustained and therefore I would theorize that it adds to the "lattice", which "conditions" our world space.

Edgar Cayce, perhaps the world's major psychic of the last century, warned us about this kind of thing—that thoughts are things and, if strongly focused on, can participate in their materialism into physical reality.'

Like Aboriginal songlines, logos create a trail of energy for the brand; if we think it we link it.

Deepak Chopra believes that there are only two kinds of thoughts we can have: memories and imaginings, and everything that starts in the universe starts with intention. This intention always arises in the universal mind but localises in the individual mind; having localised, it becomes physical reality. He quotes the example of the increase of a person's white blood cells in a test tube when the donor of the cells looks for a scalpel, with the sole intention of cutting her hand and states: 'Whatever you turn your attention to becomes energised,' and: 'In fact, physical reality would not exist if it were not for intent.' He summarises: 'You could say that attention activates the energy field and intention activates the information field, which causes transformation.'

'In every tradition, mantras involve chanting to create special vibrations, sounds of the universe that create something from nothingness, that move energy from the unmanifest to the manifest.'

He goes on to say, in his book *Synchro Destiny*: 'The Sutra is a mantra that has meaning . . . It becomes a sutra when there is an intention coded in the sound,' and: 'The messages in a sutra are simple and complex at the same time.' Deepak quotes the sutra *'aham brahmasmi'*, which stands for 'the core of my being is the ultimate reality, the root and ground of the universe, the source of all that exists.' To say that in full, it might take all day to explain the concept to someone, but when it is chanted, it needs no lengthy explanation. The words, encoded with the complex meaning, can be completely understood simply when we put our attention to them. He says: 'You don't have to understand the meaning of the sutras in order for them to work.'

We don't need to understand the logo name for it to work its effect upon us. When we repeat a brand name it becomes imprinted in the morphic field and begins to become commonplace—to become the norm. Deepak confirms the additional value of using something, such as a word or image, that has been used many times previously as there is a 'memory' of it in existence. He says: 'Every time a wave-particle collapses as a particular wave pattern, it increases the likelihood that it will collapse as that same pattern of wave again in the future. Sutras are actually intentions that increase the statistical likelihood of the collapse of a wave function along predictable probability amplitudes. This means that the more a sutra is used, the greater the likelihood that its original intention will be fulfilled.'

Denise Linn, author of *Sacred Space*, believes that those symbols that have remained constant through the ages have a power of their own. She cites the circle, a symbol representing wholeness and completion, and believes that every time someone draws a circle, this energises the energy of 'circle' that exists on a different plane of energy. By drawing a circle in ceremony and ritual, you are calling in the power of the shape as well as accessing the power of the collective consciousness.

It follows that the more a logo is spoken, or seen, the greater the likelihood that *its* original intention will be fulfilled. Older logos will take on more power and meaning through the ages.

The truth is out there—but whose?

Truth is within us; it takes no rise
From outward things whate'er you may believe.
There is an inmost centre in us all
Where truth abides in fullness; and around,
Wall upon wall, the gross flesh hems it in
This perfect, clear perception—which is truth

ROBERT BROWNING, *PARACELSUS*

Om Mani Padme Hum Buddhist mantra to inspire us to compassion

So Hum Sanskrit mantra, I am that I am to inspire us to consciousness

Om shanti shanti shanti Buddhist mantra to inspire us to reach peace

I radiate prosperity Affirmation by Will Bowen *A Complaint-Free World*

I open my heart to love Affirmation by Louise L. Hay

The power of all of us eBay

Impossible is nothing Adidas

Think different Apple computers

Because I'm worth it L'Oreal

Choose freedom Toshiba

The power of dreams Honda

Have it your way Burger King

For the Journey Lloyds TSB

For life Volvo

Rethink possible AT&T

Get the feeling Toyota

Just do it Nike

It's the real thing Coca Cola

I'm lovin' it! McDonald's

A mantra is a sound (syllable, word, or group of words) that is
considered capable of creating transformation.
An affirmation is a declaration that something is true and often used
to programme the subconscious mind to bring about positive change.
A tagline is a group of words that is considered capable of creating an
emotional connection with the essence of the brand
The intention behind each of these is to enable a particular shift in
our mindset. The more each is used the more effective they become.

If our thoughts can affect our reality and therefore our life, it stands to reason that those who control our thoughts affect our lives.

Since our thoughts lie outside our minds in the universal field, in the so-called collective, what is the nature of the ownership of thought? Whose thoughts are we picking up? Are they our own thoughts, or those that others have created and posted in the letterbox of the quantum field, in the hope that they will be collected and delivered? And to whom?

Symbols, as we have seen, are effective tools for bypassing our consciousness. Those who create logo designs deliver carefully combined words and images, effectively imbued with packets of *intention*. The recognition of this skill is blatantly apparent in the amount of money that can be exchanged for brands, and the costs and time spent in protecting the logotype. Working through our emotions, brands attempt to control our thinking by creating new realities, different ways of being and doing, in order that we 'buy' into their way and purchase more or believe their 'truth'. This type of process happens all the time—whether it is a politician, corporation, terrorist or even our own children and mothers who are manipulating us to their way of thinking. Most of us probably don't know when, or even how, we are doing it, or having it done to us.

In the quantum field of no beginning or end, time or space, how do we decide on, create and protect our personal boundaries? If it is possible to connect with everything via the field and consciously affect change, even within another human being, then what stops everyone from doing this all the time?

The truth is that this is probably happening right now and the logo is the perfect medium for delivering and coordinating the message. But we are beginning to become aware of the hype.

The brand wobble

Modern branding techniques are a sophisticated process and a complex juggling act; our relationship with the brand is changing. Increasingly we encourage, even demand, a two-way communication where our values and desires are recognised. We will wear the logo and advertise the brand for free as long as this two-way relationship thrives and survives. As companies set themselves up as our friends and the caretakers of our emotions, albeit to sell us more products, people are beginning to respond to this and demand more of them. We expect them to become charitable; to be responsible for the education of our children, our health and the health of our planet. Companies have been accused of being both spiritually empty and of trying to fill the space left by the decline of organised religion. These attributes have been popularised by dissatisfied consumers and authors such as Eric Schlosser in *Fast Food Nation*, Robert Frank's *Luxury Fever*, François Duffar's *The World is Not for Sale* and Naomi Klein's *No Logo*.

Corporations donate millions to charities. They financially support schools and universities in return for sole product placement, and they make health and sustainability claims about the products and their business practices. Paradoxically, brands are accused of all sorts of negative aspects, such as destroying our health, our environment and our children. (Naomi Klein's book *No Logo* articulates this in more depth.) In response, companies focus attention on the good they do, through charitable contributions or by developing an ethical standpoint. Often they will embrace an advertising style or public relations exercise, which has little to do with the physical reality of the product although it is based on a life-enhancement promise.

But can a chocolate bar sell 'chunks of happiness' (Cadbury), or soap (Dove) bring out your 'real inner beauty'? Does a painkiller (Nurofen) really 'understand your pain'?

This attachment and extension of qualities is so successful, and such is our desire to identify with them, that even when consumers have no choice, as in the government sector, the Home Office, the National Health Service and the Inland Revenue have all undergone major branding exercises. This enables them to use the techniques established by corporations where brands signify a degree of reliability and quality as well as the capacity to project confidence and professional efficiency via a visual device, the logo. But even they are not immune from the ripples of dissatisfaction around brands.

According to one UK daily newspaper: 'Home Office ministers have spent nearly £900,000 on logos for failing policy initiatives and quangos.' Under the heading '£870,000 bill for the logos that are a sure sign of failure', the article outlines several cases where vast amounts have been spent on design. One example cited was the £200,000 spent by the Criminal Records Bureau, which, at the same time, was criticised as being 'more interested in presentation than sorting out its shambolic handling of immigration, the justice system and prisons.'[15]

Some brands that target children have made an effort to redeem themselves. McDonald's decided to stop producing educational material for the under-13s. Paul Ennals, the chief executive of the National Children's Bureau, commented in the bureau's publication *Children Now*: 'I am very pleased. I hope that some of the other multinationals will follow suit. Businesses need to realise that there are responsibilities beyond their profit motives.' In the same article was the information that in 2006 Coca-Cola had decided to remove branding from 4,000 vending machines across the UK. Emma Wigzell, head of citizenship at Coca-Cola, GB stated: 'There is a heightened sense of duty of care, particularly relating to young people and the school environment.'[16]

If we are not strong enough to cut the labels off our children's clothes or remove logos from our lives, then we might be able to rely on the government to do this for us if we live in Australia. The government has announced plans, from July 2012, to force cigarette manufacturers to remove all branding colours and logos from cigarette packs. It is believed that this move will be a highly effective strategy to reduce the incidence of smoking.[17]

There is also evidence that we are falling out of love with the world of celebrities. An article headed 'Zeta-Jones axed as "celeb fatigue" hits ads' reports that consumers are becoming increasingly resistant to celebrity marketing. Despite its initial success, due in part to the novelty factor, one advertising executive is quoted as saying: 'It's become so ubiquitous it's one big bore.' Jonah Bloom, editor of *Advertising Age*, states: 'People don't hold these icons in such regard any more.'[18]

Brands invite us to feel that they care for our 'unique requirements' and respect our individuality. But at the end of the day, in order to survive, they need to appeal to us *en masse*, requiring as many of us as possible, in their chosen market, to buy their products.

What does it all mean?

'The purpose of life is happiness.'

THE DALAI LAMA

Symbols are powerful portals to our subconscious. They connect with our inner psyche and they affect us at some level—otherwise companies would not spend billions designing and promoting their own unique versions.

Logotypes help us, as well as the companies they represent, to shift into a particular way of being in the three-dimensional world of our physical lives. Branding experts create a future that is expressed in our present, creating an energetic pathway for the materialisation of the dream to settle into.

They call in the spirit of the company through a symbol (the logo), and proceed to energise it for effect through a series of rituals (the branding). Typically shamans use stones, crystals and other natural objects. Just as a shaman may search for a special stone or stick, which he utilises in a series of ritualistic processes and imbues with sacred intent, we in the Western world create a logotype, with a ritualised branding programme and strict guidelines for implementation.

The layers of intention added to a logo through these rituals and usage will gradually build up its power. Both shamans and brand experts work with imagery to effect change. Whether the symbol in question is a tribal painting, a corporate logo or a Reiki symbol, if enough people believe in it then it will—in the realm of quantum physics—become a self-fulfilling reality.

Wittingly or unwittingly, corporations and branding experts have put into practice ancient and powerful procedures that have been known to work for thousands of years; they have developed an effective tool for profound change.

If we should doubt the ability of a symbolic device to affect our wellbeing, recall the bone-pointing curse that has been used by Australian Aborigines. The person seeking revenge would take a kangaroo bone and carve it to a point at one end. A hole was made in the other end, through which a strand of the proposed victim's hair would be threaded. Usually performed in public, the bone would be pointed at the victim, who would more often than not die within days.[19]

Our modern logos are honed and pointed at us to create a profound effect. We won't die, but their intention to change our future is powerful. By being aware of this power, its effect and its objective, we are able to make informed choices about the logos we invite into our lives.

'Never imagine yourself not to be otherwise than what it might appear to others that what you were or might have been was not otherwise than what you had been would have appeared to them to be otherwise.'

THE DUCHESS, *ALICE'S ADVENTURES IN WONDERLAND*, LEWIS CARROLL

Bibliography

Andrews, Ted (2009) *Animal Speak,* Dragonhawk

Argüelles, José (1987) *The Mayan Factor,* Bear & Co

Arrien, Angeles (1998) *Signs of Life,* Tarcher

Birren, Faber (1978) *Color Psychology and Color Therapy,* Citadel

Bohm, Dr David (1993) *Wholeness and the Implicate Order,* Ark Paperbacks

Boorman, Neil (2008) *Bonfire of the Brands,* Canongate

Brennan, Barbara Ann (1990) *Hands of Light,* Bantam Books

Chopra, Deepak (2003) *Synchro Destiny,* Rider

Cirlot, JE (1990) *A Dictionary of Symbols,* Routledge

Courteney, Hazel (2005) *The Evidence for the Sixth Sense,* CICO

Crow, David (2003) *Visible Signs An Introduction to Semiotics,* AVA Publishing

Currivan, Jude (2005) *The Wave,* John Hunt Books

Dalichow, Eileen and Booth, Mike (1997) *Aura Soma,* Hay House

Elkington, David (2001) *In the Name of the Gods,* Green Man Press

Emoto, Masaru (2004) *The Hidden Messages in Water,* Beyond Words

Fletcher, Alan (2001) *The Art of Looking Sideways,* Phaidon

Fontana, David (1997) *The Secret Language of Symbols,* Piatkus

Frutiger, Adrian (1989) *Signs and Symbols,* Ebury

Gerber, Richard (1998) *Vibrational Medicine,* Bear & Co

Gimbel, Theo (2000) *The Book of Colour Healing,* Gaia Books

Gimbel, Theo (1987) *Healing Through Colour,* CW Daniel

Gladwell, Malcolm (2001) *The Tipping Point,* Abacus

Gobe, Marc (2001) *Emotional Branding,* Allworth Press

Godin, Seth (2007) *Permission Marketing,* Pocket Books

Goleman, Daniel (1999) *Emotional Intelligence,* Bloomsbury

Guénon, René (2004) *Symbols of Sacred Science,* Sophia Perennis

Gullen-Whur, Margaret (1984) *What your Handwriting Reveals,*
The Aquarian Press

Haig, Matt (2005) *Brand Failures*, Kogan Page

Harman, William and Rheingold, Howard (1984) *Higher Creativity,* Tarcher Puttman

Hatfield, Elaine, Cacioppo, John and Rapson, Richard L, (1994) *Emotional Contagion,* Cambridge University Press

Hawkins, David R (2002) *Power Vs. Force,* Hay House

Hunt, Dr Valerie (1995) *Infinite Mind: The Science of Human Vibrations,* Malibu

Jean, Georges (1999) *Signs, Symbols and Ciphers, Decoding the message,* Thames and Hudson

King, Francis (1975) *The Western Tradition of Magic,* Thames & Hudson

Klein, Naomi (2001) *No Logo,* Flamingo

Leadbeater, CW (1973) *The Chakras,* Quest books

Lewin, Roger and Regine, Birute (2000) *The Soul at Work,* Simon and Schuster

Lindstrom, Martin (2005) *Brand Sense,* Free Press

Linn, Denise (2005) *Sacred Space,* Rider

McMoneagle, (1997) *Mind Trek,* Joseph Hampton Roads

McTaggart, Lynne (2003) *The Field,* Harper

Mohr, Barbël (2001) *Cosmic Ordering Service,* Hampton Roads

Mollerup, Per (1999) *Marks of Excellence,* Phaidon

Morehouse, David (2000) *Psychic Warrior,* Clairview

Myss, Caroline PhD (1997) *Anatomy of the Spirit,* Bantam

Olins, Wally (1989) *Corporate Identity,* Thames & Hudson

Pearce, Stewart (2007) *The Alchemy of Voice,* Hodder Mobius

Playfair, Guy Lyon and Hill, Scott, (1978) *The Cycles of Heaven*, Souvenir Press

Pumphrey, Angela (Ed) (2003) *Cool BrandLeaders,* Superbrands

Ries and Ries (1998) *The 22 Immutable Laws of the Brand.* Harper Collins

Renfrew, Colin and Morley, Iain (Ed), (2009) *Becoming Human: Innovation in Prehistoric Material and Spiritual Culture,* Cambridge University Press

Ronson, Jon (2009) *The Men Who Stare at Goats,* Picador

Sheldrake, Rupert (1997) *A New Science of Life*, Paladin

Sheldrake, Rupert (2004) *The Sense of Being Stared at,* Arrow

Somé, Malidoma Patrice (1995) *Of Water and the Spirit*, Penguin

Stockton, Eugene (1996) *The Aboriginal Gift,* Millenium

Talbot, Michael (1991) *The Holographic Universe,* Grafton

Tarlow, Mikela and Tarlow, Philip (2002) *Digital Aboriginal*, Piatkus Books

van Praagh, James (2003) *Heaven and Earth*, Rider

Villoldo, Alberto (2001) *Shaman Healer Sage,* Bantam

Virilio, Paul (2005) *The Information Bomb,* Verso Books

Tresidder, Jack (2000) *Symbols and their Meanings,* Duncan Baird

Whacker, Watts and Taylor, Jim (2000) *The Visionary's Handbook*, Capstone

Zukav, Gary (1991) *The Dancing Wu Li Masters,* Rider

Logo & Websites

AA
http://www.theaa.com/

Adidas
http://shop.adidas.co.uk/

AEG
http://www.aeg.co.uk/

Agfa
http://www.agfa.com/en/co/index.jsp

Alfa Romeo
http://www.alfaromeo.com/com/—/
home

Altria
http://www.altria.com/en/cms/Home/
default.aspx

AOL
http://www.aol.com

Apple Corps
http://applerecords.com

Apple Inc
http://www.apple.com/

American Airlines
http://www.aa.com/

American Express
http://www.americanexpress.com

Andrex
http://www.andrexpuppy.co.uk/

Armani
http://www.emporioarmani.com

Amec
http://www.amec.com/

Associate British Foods
http://www.abf.co.uk/

AT&T
http://www.att.com

Audi
http://www.audi.co.uk/

Avis
http://www.avis.co.uk

Aviva
http://www.aviva.com/

Avon
http://avon.com

Bacardi
http://www.bacardi.com/

Barclays
http://www.barclays.co.uk

Barbie
http://www.barbie.com/

BBC
http://www.bbc.co.uk/

Ben& Jerry's
http://www.benjerry.com/

BG Group
http://www.bg-group.com

Birds Eye
http://www.birdseye.co.uk/

Birds
http://www.birdscustard.co.uk

Bisto
http://www.premierfoods.co.uk/

BMW
http://www.bmw.com/

Boots the Chemist
http://www.boots.com/

BP
http://www.bp.com/

Braun
http://www.braun.com

British Airways
http://www.britishairways.com

British Gas
http://www.britishgas.info/

BT
http://www.bt.com/

Budweiser
http://www.budweiser.com

Burberry
http://www.burberry.com

Burger King
http://www.bk.com/

IBM
http://www.ibm.com

Cadburys
http://www.cadbury.co.uk

Calvin Klein
http://www.calvinkleininc.com

Centrica
http://www.centrica.com/

Chanel
http://www.chanel.com

Cheesestrings
http://www.cheestrings.co.uk/

Chloé
http://www.chloe.com

Cif
http://www.unilever.co.uk/brands/
homecarebrands/cif.aspx

Citroën
http://www.citroen.com/

Clairol
http://www.clairol.com/

Coca-Cola
http://www.coca-cola.com

Colgate
http://www.colgate.com

Compare The Market
http://www.comparethemarket.com
(Compare The Meerkat http://www.
comparethemeerkat.com/)

Co-operative Bank
http://www.co-operativebank.co.uk

Criminal
http://www.criminalclothing.com/

Currys
http://www.currys.co.uk

Danone
http://www.danone.com

Darrell Lea
http://www.dlea.com.au/

Diageo
http://www.diageo.com

Disney
http://www.disney.com

Domino
pizza http://www.dominos.com/

Dove
http://www.dove.com/

Dr Pepper
http://www.drpepper.com/

Dulux
http://www.dulux.com

Dunkin' Donuts
http://www.dunkindonuts.com

Du Pont
http://www2.dupont.com

Easy Jet
http://www.easyjet.com/

E! Entertainment
http://uk.eonline.com

Evian
http://www.evian.com/

Ericsson
http://www.ericsson.com

Exxon
http://www.exxonmobil.com

Facebook
http://www.facebook.com

Fat Face
http://www.fatface.com

FedEx
http://fedex.com

Ferrari
http://www.ferrari.com/

Fiat
http://www.fiat.com

Flora
http://www.florahearts.co.uk

Ford
http://www.ford.com/

Fortnum and Mason
http://www.fortnumandmason.com/

French Connection (FCUK)
http://www.frenchconnection.com

GAP
http://www.gap.com/

Gauloises
http://www.imperial-tobacco.com/
index.asp?page=399

GE
http://www.ge.com

General Motors
http://www.gm.com/

Gillette
http://www.gillette.com

Grey Goose vodka
http://www.greygoose.com/

Santander
http://www.santander.co.uk

Gucci
http://www.gucci.com

Guinness
http://www.guinness.com/

Halifax
http://www.halifax.co.uk

Hallmark
http://www.hallmark.com

Heinekin
http://www.heineken.com

Heinz
http://www.heinz.com/

Hello Kitty
http://www.hellokittyonline.com/

Hermès
http://uk.hermes.com

Herta
http://www.hertafrankfurters.co.uk/

Hertz
http://www.hertz.com/

Holiday Inn
http://www.holidayinn.com

Hilton
http://www1.hilton.com

Home Office
http://www.homeoffice.gov.uk

Homepride
http://www.homepride.co.uk/

Hoover
http://hoover.com/

Hotpoint
http://www.hotpoint.co.uk

HSBC
http://www.hsbc.com

Hush Puppies
http://www.hushpuppies.com

IBM
http://www.ibm.com

Ikea
http://www.ikea.com/

Invesco
http://www.invescoperpetual.co.uk

Jacksons of Piccadilly
http://www.jacksonsofpiccadilly.co.uk/

Jaguar
http://www.jaguar.com

Jamie Oliver
http://www.jamieoliver.com/

Kangol
http://www.kangol.com

Kraft
http://www.kraftfoodscompany.com

Kellogg's
http://www2.kelloggs.com/

KFC
http://www.kfc.com/

Kingsmill
http://www.kingsmillbread.com/

Kit Kat
http://www.kitkat.com/

Lacoste
http://www.lacoste.com/

Lancôme
http://www.lancome.co.uk

LEGO
http://www.lego.com

Levi
http://eu.levi.com

Lexus
http://www.lexus.com/

Linda McCartney
http://www.lindamccartneyfoods.
co.uk/

Linux
http://www.linux.com

Little Chef
http://littlechef.co.uk/

Lloyd's of London
http://www.lloyds.com/

Lloyds Banking Group
http://www.lloydsbankinggroup.com/

Lloyds TSB
http://www.lloydstsb.com/

Louis Vuitton
http://www.louisvuitton.com/

Lucent Technologies
http://www.goodlogo.com/
download/lucent_technologies_logo_
vector_2406

Lufthansa
http://www.lufthansa.com

Lux
http://www.unilever.co.uk/brands/
personalcarebrands/lux.aspx

Lynx
http://www.lynxeffect.com

Marks & Spencer
http://www.marksandspencer.com/

Marlboro
https://www.marlboro.com

Marmite
http://www.marmite.com/

McDonald's
http://www.mcdonalds.com

Microsoft
http://www.microsoft.com

Michelin
http://www.michelin.co.uk

Mitsubishi
http://www.mitsubishi-motors.com/

Mobil
http://www.mobil.com

Monsanto
http://www.monsanto.co.uk/

NASA
http://www.nasa.gov/

National
https://www.nationalcar.com/

National Children's Bureau
http://www.ncb.org.uk/

National Health Service
http://www.nhs.uk

Nat West
http://www.natwest.com

NBC
http://www.nbc.com/

Newcastle brown ale
http://newcastlebrown.com/

Nestlé
http://www.nestle.com

Nickelodeon
http://www.nick.com

Nike
http://www.nike.com

Norwich Union
http://www.aviva.com

Nurofen
http://www.nurofen.co.uk

O books
http://www.o-books.com/

O2
http://shop.o2.co.uk

Olympics 2012
http://www.london2012.com/

Omo
http://www.omo.com/

Orange
http://shop.orange.co.uk

Oxfam
http://www.oxfam.org.uk

Pearson
http://www.pearson.com/

Pepsi
http://www.pepsi.com/

Penguin
http://www.penguin.com/

Persil
http://www.persil.com/

Pfizer
http://www.pfizer.com/home/

PG Tips
http://www.pgtips.co.uk/

Philip Morris
http://www.pmi.com

Pink Elephant
http://www.pinkelephantparking.com/

Pizza Hut
http://www.pizzahut.co.uk

Polaroid
http://www.polaroid.com

Ponds
http://www.pondsinstitute.co.uk/

Perrier
http://www.perrier.com/

Playboy
http://www.playboy.com

Poison Angel
http://www.poisonangel.co.uk/

Primark
http://www.primark.co.uk/

Pret à Manger
http://www.pret.com/

Proctor and Gamble
http://www.pg.com

Puma
http://www.puma.com/

Quaker Oats
http://www.quakeroats.com

RAC
http://www.rac.co.uk/

Ralph Lauren
http://www.ralphlauren.com

Red Bull
http://www.redbull.com

Red Cross
http://www.redcross.org.uk

Reebok
http://www.reebok.com

Renault
http://www.renault.com

Rolls-Royce
http://www.rolls-royce.com/

Royal Bank of Scotland
http://www.rbs.co.uk/

Santander
http://www.santander.co.uk

Sega
http://www.sega.com

Shell
http://www.shell.com

Silk Cut
http://www.gallaher-group.com/
brands/overview

Skipping Girl vinegar
http://www.nattrust.com.au/trust_
register/search_the_register/skipping_
girl_vinegar_sign

Skype
http://www.skype.com
Sony (see Ericsson)
http://www.sony.com/

Starburst
http://starburst.com/

Starbucks
http://www.starbucks.com/

Stolichnaya
http://www.stoli.com/us-ca/

Subaru
http://www.subaru-global.com/

Sun Life Financial
http://www.sunlifedirect.co.uk

Surf
http://www.surf.co.uk/

Swiss Air
http://www.swiss.com

Tag Heuer
http://www.tagheuer.com/

Target
http://www.target.com/

Tesco
http://www.tesco.com/

TGI Friday's
http://www.tgifridays.com

Tiffany
http://www.tgifridays.com

3M
http://www.3m.com/

Total
http://www.total.com

Toyota
http://www.toyota.com/

Tupperware
http://www.tupperwarebrands.com/

Twinings
http://www.twinings.co.uk/

Unilever
http://www.unilever.co.uk/

United Airlines
http://www.united.com/

Veet
http://www.veet.co.uk/

Verizon
http://www22.verizon.com

Virgin
http://www.virgin.com/

Visa
http://www.visa.co.uk

Visteon
http://www.visteon.com

Vodafone
http://www.vodafone.com

Volkswagen
http://www.volkswagen.com

Volvic
http://www.volvic.co.uk/

Walmart
http://walmartstores.com/

Woolworths (Australia)
http://www.woolworths.com.au

Wrigley
http://www.wrigley.com

Zegna
http://store.zegna.com

Glossary

Acupuncture
Ultra-fine sterile needles are inserted into specific acupuncture points on the body to re-establish the free flow of qi (life energy), trigger the body's natural healing response and restore balance.

Aura
The field of energy that surrounds and permeates our physical body.

Brand
A name, design, symbol, or any other feature that identifies one seller's goods or services from another's.

Chakra
The name is derived from the Sanskrit word for wheel and refers to the energy centres that regulate our body's energy and its interaction with the outside world

Die stamping
Also known as engraving it is a prestigious printing process that results in a three dimensional affect over the design.

Dowsing
A type of divination used to locate objects such as water or find answers to questions by noting the resulting movement of a forked stick, or rods, held over the area or the swing of a pendulum.

Embossing
Raising an area, usually on paper or card, to display a particular design.

Feng shui
An ancient Chinese system of analysing and influencing the interaction between people, buildings and the environment, intended to promote a prosperous and healthy life.

Flower remedies
Diluted infusions of flowers used to relieve emotional, mental and spiritual imbalances.

Foil block
A printing process that includes the application of a pigment, often metallic, usually onto paper or card.

Geomancy
A method of divination that interprets patterns such as those formed on the ground by throwing dirt or special dice, the topography of the land or the selection of beans.

Homeopathy
A system for the treatment of disease by dosing the patient with highly diluted minute doses of substances with the aim of triggering the body's natural system of healing.

Kirlian photography
A form of photogram named after Semyon Kirlian who discovered in 1939 that energy flow could be recorded on film.

Logo (logotype)
A specially designed mark, identifying a brand, usually comprising a name in a specially drawn typestyle with a colour and sometimes an accompanying symbol.

Mantra
A word or phrase repeated for a specific effect such as to aid meditation or spiritual transformation.

Meridians
Invisible channels throughout the body, connecting acupuncture points, through which qi (life energy) circulates.

Morphic field
A term introduced by Rupert Sheldrake, which refers to a field of energy with its own structure and pattern as well as its own memory.

NLP (Neurolinguistic Programming)
NLP is the practice of understanding how people organise their thinking, feeling, language and behaviour to produce results and utilising this for personal development and for success in business.

Placebo
Any medical treatment that has no specific action on the body; its effect is well documented.

Psi
Parapsychological or psychic phenomena.

Psychokinesis
The ability to move objects using the mind alone.

Radionics
A method of sending precisely defined healing energy to people, animals or plants, no matter where they are in the world by using something personal to them such as hair or a signature.

Reflexology
A system of massage applied to specific areas of the feet to affect healing in the whole body.

Reiki
Originating in Japan Reiki is a healing practice that is built around the use of life force energy and includes the use of symbols.

Tattwas
Geometric symbols representing the five universal energies, which aid clairvoyance.

Thermography
A type of printing that uses heat to raise lettering or images on paper or board.

Trademark
A distinctive mark, a symbol or words, legally representing an individual, business, product or service or any other legal entity.

Typeface
A particular design of type.

Typography
The designed layout, style and appearance of type.

Yantra
A symbol designed to balance or focus the mind as an aid to meditation.

Zero Point
The lowest possible energy that a system can possess, which remains when all other energy is removed.

Appendix

Introduction

1. Cusick, William J. (2009) *All customers are irrational: Understanding what they think, what they feel, and what keeps them coming back,* New York: Amacon

2. Somé, Malidome Patrice, (1999) *The healing wisdom of Africa,* Tarcher (reprint ed.)

3. Connor, Steve (2007) 'Subliminal messages do reach your brain—but you don't know it', *The Independent,* 9 March [Online] Available: http://www.independent.co.uk/news/science/subliminal-messages-do-reach-your-brain—but-you-wont-know-it-439456.html [20 Feb 2011]

4. Brasel, S.Adam and Gips, James (2008). 'Breaking through fast-forwarding: Brand information and visual attention', *Journal of Marketing,* *v*ol. 72 (November), p31-48

5. Heath, R.G., Nairn, A.C. & Bottomley, P. (2009) How effective is creativity? Emotive content in TV advertising does not increase attention, *Journal of Advertising Research.* Vol. 49 Issue 4: 450-463

6. Chartrand, T. L. (2005). The role of conscious awareness in consumer behavior. *Journal of Consumer Psychology,* 15, p203-210

7. Fitzsimons, Grainne M., Chartrand, Tanya L. and Fitzsimons, Gavan J. (2008) 'Automatic effects of brand exposure on motivated behavior: How Apple makes you "think different"' *Journal of Consumer Research,* 35, June, p21-35, [Online], Available: http://faculty.fuqua.duke.edu/~gavan/bio/GJF_articles/apple_ibm_jcr_08.pdf [5 July 2011]

8. 'Familiarity increases liking', *Science Daily* [Online] Available, http://www.sciencedaily.com/articles/e/exposure_effect.htm [8 Mar 2011].
    Full copy of article [Online] http://en.wikipedia.org/wiki/Exposure_effect

Chapter 1

1. McClure, Samuel M. et al. (2004) 'Neurol correlates of behavioral preferences for culturally familiar drinks', *Neuron,* vol.44, issue 2, 14 October, p.379-387.
   In Bioedonline Ross Tomlin, in his article 'Neuroscience breaks down soft drink "battle" inside brain' reported from the above research that 'A study involving 67 people showed no preference for either Coca-Cola (Coke®) or Pepsi® when the drinks were administered anonymously. However, when told what they were drinking, roughly three-fourths preferred Coke'. [Online] Available, http://www.bioedonline.org/from-the-labs/article. cfm?art=283 [8 Mar 2011]
2. Frutiger, Adrian (1998) *Signs and Symbols,* London: Ebury Press
3. Kress-Rogers, Erika (Ed.) (1996) *Handbook of biosensors and electronic noses: medicine, food, and the environment,* CRC Press.
4. Grandin, Temple and Deesing, Mark J. (1998) *'Genetics and the behavior of domestic animals',* (Chapter one), San Diego: Academic Press, [Online], Available: http://www.grandin.com/references/genetics.html [8 Mar 2011]
5. 'The Ghost in Your Genes: The scientists who believe your genes are shaped in part by your ancestors' life experiences', *Horizon* on BBC television, [Online],
   Available: http://www.bbc.co.uk/sn/tvradio/programmes/horizon/ ghostgenes.shtml [8 Mar 2011]
6. Ibid
7. Sheldrake, Rupert (1997) 'Part I: Mind, Memory, and Archetype: Morphic Resonance and the Collective Unconscious', *Psychological Perspective,* [Online], Available: http://www.sheldrake.org/Articles&Papers/papers/ morphic/morphic1_abs.html [5 July 2011]
8. DeRusha, Jason (2007) 'How many brands do young children recognise?' Campaign for a commercial free childhood, 14 May, [Online], Available: http://www.commercialfreechildhood.org/news/brandschildren. htm [11 Mar 2011]
9. A blog posted on 25 August 2008 [Online], Available: (http://rateyourmusic.com/board_message/message_id_ is_1632173) [11 Mar 2011]

10. Dilts, Robert (1977), 'Eye movements', *Encyclopedia of systemic NLP and NLP new coding,* [Online], Available: http://nlpuniversitypress.com/ [11 Mar 2011]

11. Pabst, Maria A. et al. (2009) 'The tattoos of the Tyrolean iceman: a light microscopical ultrastructural and element analytical study', *Journal of Archaeological Science,* vol. 36, Issue 10, October, p2335-23412. 'Angelina Jolie Tattoos', *International Business Times,* 21 Oct 2009, [Online], Available: http://www.ibtimes.com/contents/20091021/angelina-jolie-tattoos-pictures.htm [28 Feb 2011]

13. Moeun Chhean Nariddh (1995) 'Magic art of bullet-proofing the troops' *Phnom Penh Post,* Issue 4/18, September 8-21, [Online], Available: http://mcnnews.wordpress.com/2007/10/02/magic-art-of-bullet-proofing-the-troops/ [28 Feb 2011]

14. *Speeders,* Dave TV, 21 January 2010

15. Erwin, Miles (2009) 'Kellogg's laser logo will fight against fake flakes', *Metro* 14 October, [Online], Available:http://www.metro.co.uk/weird/751827-kelloggs-laser-logo-will-fight-against-fake-flakes [14 Mar 2011]

16. *Business Wire* (5 Jan 2009) 'Angry Whopper sandwich adds fierce new kick to the menu at Burger King restaurants', [Online], Available: http://www.businesswire.com/news/home/20090105005267/en/Angry-WHOPPER%C2%AE-Sandwich-Adds-Fierce-Kick-Menu, [14 Mar 2011]

17. Springett, Ulli (2001) *Symbol therapy: Use your inner wisdom to solve your physical and emotional problems, London:* Piatkus Books

18. Eickermann, Frank (2001) 'Energy feng shui', *Kindred Spirit,* Issue 56, Autumn

19. Laszlo, Ervin (2005) 'The convergence of science and spirituality', *Syntropy,* 3, p. 69-84, [Online], Available: www.sintropia.it/english/2005-eng-3-2.pdf [13 Mar 2011]

20. www.saisanjeevini.org

21. *Kick Ass Miracles* Dave TV, October 2009

Chapter 2

1. Stanley, Milgram (1963) 'Behavioral study of obedience', *Journal of Abnormal and Social Psychology vol.67(4), Oct., p.371-378,* [Online], Available:http://www.psychwiki.com/wiki/Milgram,_S._(1963)._ Behavioral_study_of_obedience._Journal_of_Abnormal_%26_Social_ Psychology,_67(4),_371-378. [14 Mar 2011]
2. László, E. (2007) *Science and the Akashic Field: An integral theory of everything,* Rochester, VT: Inner Traditions
3. http://www.kyriacou.com/ [Accessed 18 July 2011]
4. *Daily Telegraph,* 19 March 1999
5. Jean, Georges (1999) *Signs, symbols and ciphers, Decoding the message,* Thames and Hudson/New Horizons
6. Renfrew, Colin and Morley, Iain (Ed.) (2009) *'Becoming human: Innovation in prehistoric material and spiritual culture',* Cambridge University Press
7. Jean, Georges (1999) *Signs, symbols and ciphers, Decoding the message,* Thames and Hudson/New Horizons
8. Clarke, Boyd and Crossland, Ron (2002) *The leader's voice,* New York: SelectBooks
9. Linn, Denise (2005) *Sacred space,* Rider & Co
10. Argüelles, José (1987) *The Mayan factor,* Santa Fe: Bear & Co.
11. Somé, Malidoma Patrice (1995) *Of water and the spirit: Ritual, magic and initiation in the life of an African shaman,* New York: Penguin
12. Mitchell, Edgar D & Williams, Dwight (1996) *The way of the explorer— An Apollo astronaut's journey through the material and mystical worlds,* G.P. Putnam and Sons
13. Mininni, Ted 'Nothing says brand like the package' *Brandchannel,* [Online], Available: www.brandchannel.com/papers_review.asp?sp_id=435 [14 Mar 2011]
14. Bhattacharya, Shaoni (2003) 'Humans trained to hunger like Pavlov's dogs', New Scientist, [Online], Available: http://www.newscientist.com/article/dn4083-humans-trained-to-hunger-like-pavlovs-dogs.html [14 Mar 2011]

15. Renfrew, Colin and Morley, Iain (Ed.) (2009) *'Becoming human: Innovation in prehistoric material and spiritual culture'*, Cambridge University Press

16. Jung, Carl. (1928). "On psychic energy" (subsection C: Entropy), in *On the nature of the psyche* (1960). Princeton University Press

17. Cirlot, J.E. (2003) *A dictionary of symbols* (2nd edition), Dover Publications Inc.

18. Guénon, René (2004) *Symbols of sacred science* (2nd edition), New York: Sophia Perennis

19. Hope, Jane (1997) *The secret language of the soul*, (1st ed edition), San Francisco: Chronicle Books

20. *Design Annual*, 1999

21. *The Daily Mail*, 31 March 2006

22. *Metro* newspaper, London, 9 June 2006

Chapter 3

1. Dr Valerie Hunt is a research scientist, author, lecturer and Professor Emeritus of Physiological Science at the University of California, Los Angeles.

2. www.barbarabrennan.com

3. Brennan, Barbara Ann (1988) *Hands of light: Guide to healing through the human energy field,* Paperback ed., Bantam Books

4. Karagulla, Shafica and Kunz, Dora van Gelder (1989) *The chakras and the human energy fields,* Wheaton: The Theosophical Publishing House

5. *The Global Consciousness Project* researches and analyses this phenomenon, [Online], Available: http://noosphere.princeton.edu [14 Mar 2011]

6. *London Evening Standard*, 28 February 2007

7. Boorman, Neil (2007) *Bonfire of the brands,* Edinburgh: Canongate Books

8. Cova, B and Cova, V (2002). Tribal marketing: the tribalisation of society and its impact on the conduct of marketing, *European Journal of Marketing, 36 (5/6), 595-619*

9. McTaggart, Lynne *The Field: the quest for the secret force of the universe,* 2003 New Ed. Edition, Element Books

10. *The Sunday Times,* 9 August 2009

11. Professor, Deputy Director of St Petersburg Research Institute of Physical Culture korotkov.org/
12. *The Sunday Times*, 20 November 2005
13. Merrifield, Jeff, (1998) *Damanhur, the real dream*, London: Harper Collins
14. www.adenergy.com.au/ [Online] [Accessed 18 July 2011]
15. *The Daily Telegraph*, 19 March 1999

Chapter 4

1. *Seven Ages of Britain,* BBC television, written and presented by David Dimbleby, February 2010
2. *Material World* BBC Radio Four, September 2006 (This experiment was based on a study undertaken by Carol Nemeroff and Paul Rozin in the US, who were interested in psychological contagion. In their study they used Hitler's jumper.)
3. *The Sunday Times*, 27 February 2005
4. *Body Language Secrets*, 2010 Carbon Media Production for Sky Television, [Online], Available http://blogs.skyplayer.sky.com/featuredtv/Post:8d2cdf6d-29b9-4e9d-9b55-30c8366806ce [15 Mar 2011]
5. *Kindred Spirit*, May/June 2008, 'Bowled Over!'
6. Dr Hawkins is an internationally renowned psychiatrist, physician, researcher, and pioneer in the fields of consciousness research and spirituality. in his book Power Vs Force. He describes the technique of muscle testing whereby the person being tested stands up with their arm extended and is asked to resist the pressure when the tester presses gently downward on the outstretched hand. The person being tested is subjected to different stimuli, such as foodstuffs but it can be virtually anything, and the strength of the resistance is noted. A weak response indicates that the matter being tested will weaken the person being tested.
7. *The Sunday Times*, 23 January 2005
8. Fukuyama, Francis (1992) *The end of history and the last man*, London: Hamish Hamilton
9. Brands lecture, 2001
10. Haig, Matt (2003) *Brand failures: The truth about the 100 biggest branding mistakes of all time,* London: Kogan Page

11. Ries, Al and Ries, Laura (1999) *The 22 immutable laws of branding*, London: HarperCollins
12. http://brandpower.com [Accessed 18 July 2011]
13. Quart, Alissa (2003) *Branded: The buying and selling of teenagers*, Cambridge MA: Perseus Publishing
14. Swoboda, Frank (1998) 'Pepsi prank fizzles at school's Coke Day' *Washington Post*, 26 March, Thursday Final Edition
15. Walsh, Kate and Dowling, Kevin (2010) 'Children paid to plug junk food on Facebook and Bebo' *The Sunday Times,* 14 February
16. McCutcheon, L.E., Maltby, J., Houran, J and Ashe, D.D. (2004) *Celebrity worshippers: Inside the minds of stargazers*, PublishAmerica
17. Harlow, John (2003) 'Blinded by the Stars' *The Sunday Times*, 17 August News Focus
18. *The Sunday Times Magazine*, 23 September 2007
19. Ephraim Hardcastle's column in the *Daily Mail*, 22 May 2007
20. 'History will be made on 20 January 2009', http://www.benjerry.co.uk/yespecan/?mtk=557, [Online], Available: [15 Mar 2011]
21. Hyde, Marina (2010) 'London's olympic rings start losing their halo effect' *The Guardian*, 26 August [Online], Available: http://www.guardian.co.uk/sport/blog/2010/aug/26/ioc-london-2012-olympic-games [15 Mar 2011]
22. Waterfield, Bruno (2008) 'EU court to rule on use of 'Adidas stripes' ', *The Telegraph*, World News 10 April
23. As 21.

Chapter 5

1. *Daily Mail* 12 August 2009 'How thinking of yesterday can make you happy today'
   Wiseman, Richard (2009) *'59 seconds: Think a little, change a lot'*, London: Macmillan
2. Bloom, William (2001) *The endorphin effect: A breakthrough strategy for holistic health and spiritual wellbeing*, London: Piatkus Books
3. *The Sunday Times*, 29 May, 2005
4. *Daily Mail,* 28 September, 2004

5. *'Is black the new British racing green?'* (2004) Metro (Home article), London, 20 September, [Online], Available: http://www.metro.co.uk/searc h?q=jaguar+green&ob=createdDate%2CDESC&page=2 [15 Mar 2011]

6. McCraty, R., (2004) *The energetic heart: Bioelectromagnetic interactions within and between people.* Chapter published in: *Clinical applications of bioelectromagnetic medicine,* edited by P. J. Rosch and M. S. Markov. New York: Marcel Dekker, 2004: 541-562. Available as ebooklet through www. heartmath.org

7. Lame Deer, John (Fire) and Erdoes, Richard (1972) *Lame deer, seeker of visions,* New York: Simon and Schuster. Revised edition (1994) Pocket Books

8. Weisnewski, Mary (2006) 'Bypass the brain and go straight to the heart: Connecting with emotion builds a brand and keeps it vital', [Online], Available: www.brandchannel.com/papers_review.asp?sp_id=1232 [18 July 2011]

9. Bradford, Laura R (2008) 'Emotion, dilution and the trademark consumer', *Berkeley Technology Law Journal,* 1227

10. Uleman, James S., and Bargh, John A.(ed.) (1989) *Unintended thought,* New York: The Guilford Press

11. Kane, Siegrun D. (1991) *Trademark law: A practitioner's guide,* 2 ed., New York: Practising Law Institute

12. Mishawaka Rubber & Woolen Mfg. Co. v. S. S. Kresge Co. Supreme Court of the United States, 1942, 316 U.S. 203

13. Schechter, F.I. (1927) 'The rational basis for trademark protection', 40 *Harvard Law Review* 813

14. Hawkins, David R. (2002) *Power vs. force,* Hay House

15. *Daily Mail,* 9 January 2007

16. 'Jamie's pots are panned by critics', *Daily Mail,* 20 February, 2007, [Online],
Available: http://www.dailymail.co.uk/tvshowbiz/article-437161/Jamies-pots-panned-critics.html [15 Mar 2011]

17. 'Money bags', *The Sunday Times,* 2 September 2007

18. *The Sunday Times,* 27 August 2006

19. *MX News,* Melbourne 9 April 2008

20. Lindstrom, Martin (2005) *Brand sense: Build powerful brands though touch, taste, smell, sight, and sound,* New York: Free Press

21. Ibid

22. 'Who's wearing the trousers?' *The Economist* (8 September 2001)

23. 'Eweida v British Airways plc [2010] [Online],
    Available: http://www.bailii.org/ew/cases/EWCA/Civ/2010/80.html [15 Mar 2011]

24. Gledhill, Ruth (2005) 'Hindus reclaim their symbol of life', *The Times*, 19 January

25. *Women's Hour* BBC Radio 4, 22 March 2006

26. *Metro* London, 21 June 2007 (Norwich Union usually offer to 'quote you happy')

27. Chartrand, T. L. (2005). The role of conscious awareness in consumer behavior. *Journal of Consumer Psychology*, 15, p203-210

28. Gladwell, Malcolm (2001) *The tipping point: How little things can make a big difference*, Abacus.

29. Horgan, John (1999) *The undiscovered mind: How the human brain defies replication, medication, and explanation*, New York: The Free Press

30. Ibid.

31. 'Banner ads work—even if you don't notice them at all', *ScienceDaily* (11 May 2007)
    University of Chicago Press Journals. *ScienceDaily*. Retrieved April 1, 2010, from http://www.sciencedaily.com/releases/2007/05/070510123709.htm

32. 'I'm sticking with my brand: Loyal customers perceive competitor ads differently' *ScienceDaily* (21 November 2008) University of Chicago Press Journals. Retrieved 1April 2010, from http://www.sciencedaily.com/releases/2008/11/081117121231.htm

33. Somé, Malidoma Patrice (1995) *Of water and the spirit: Ritual, magic and initiation in the life of an African shaman*, New York: Penguin

34. Arbib, Michael (2004) 'Beyond the mirror system: From monkey-like action recognition to Human Language: An evolutionary framework for neurolinguistics, behavioral and brain sciences.' (Revision completed Feb 1, 2004), *Computer Science Department, Neuroscience Program, and USC Brain Project*, University of Southern California, Los Angeles. [Online], Available:http://www3.isrl.illinois.edu/~junwang4/langev/localcopy/pdf/arbib04BBSmonkeylikeAction.pdf [17 Jul 2011]

35. Motluk, Alison (2001) 'Read my mind', *New Scientist,* vol 169 issue 2275 p.22, 27 Jan.[Online] Available:http://inst.eecs.berkeley.edu/~cs182/sp07/readings/ns/article.html [17 July 2011]

36. Merzenich, Michael (2008) 'About brain plasticity' 16 April [Online], Available:http://merzenich.positscience.com/?page_id=143 [17 July 2011]. Michael Merzenich is Professor Emeritus, University of California at San Francisco and Chief Scientific Officer, Posit Science

Chapter 6

1. Zukav, Gary (1991) *The dancing Wu Li masters: An overview of the new physics* (New ed.), London: Rider Books

2. Solomey, Nickolas (1997) *The elusive neutrino: a subatomic detective story,* W.H.Freeman & Company. Reviewed by Stephen Battersby (1998) 'The great elusionist' *Nature* 391, p858 (26 February)

3. Nadeau, Robert and Kafatos, Menas (1999) *The non-local Universe: The new physics and matters of the mind,* Oxford: Oxford University Press

4. Talbot, Michael (1991) *The holographic Universe,* Grafton

5. http://www.whatthebleep.com/ [Accessed 18 July 2011]

6. Sheldrake, Rupert (1987) 'Society, spirit & ritual: Morphic resonance and the collective unconscious, Part II', *Psychological Perspectives,* 18(2) Fall 1987, p320-331

7. Sheldrake, Rupert (1997) 'Mind, memory, and archetype: Morphic resonance and the collective unconscious, Part I', *Psychological Perspectives,* 18(1) Spring 1987, p9-25

8. Sheldrake, Rupert (2009) *A new science of life: The hypothesis of formative causation,* 3 ed., London: Icon Books

9. Talbot, Michael (1991) *The holographic Universe,* Grafton

10. Director of the Human Energy Systems Laboratory and Professor of Psychology, Medicine, Neurology, Psychiatry and Surgery at the University of Arizona

11. *The Sunday Times,* 13 February 2005

12. Talbot, Michael (1991) *The Holographic Universe,* Grafton

13. Wikipedia

14. McTaggart, Lynne *The Field: the quest for the secret force of the universe,* 2003 New ed. Element Books

15. McTaggart, Lynne (2008) *The intention experiment: Using your thoughts to change your life and the World*, Paperback ed. New York: Free Press

16. Klopfer, B. (1957) Psychological variables in human cancer, *Journal of Projective Techniques*, 21 (337-39), cited in Walsh, Roger N. (1990) *The Spirit of Shamanism*, Los Angeles: Tarcher

17. Rauscher, Elizabeth A. and Targ, Russell (2006) *Investigation of a complex space-time metric to describe precognition of the future*, [Online], Available: http://adsabs.harvard.edu/abs/2006AIPC..863..121R [16 Feb 2011]

18. McTaggart, Lynne *The Field: the quest for the secret force of the universe*, 2003 New ed. Element Books

19. Researcher, writer and educator in areas of inclusive, integrated psychology; transpersonal and spiritual studies. Currently Professor and Dissertation Director within the Global Doctoral Program of the Institute of Transpersonal Psychology in Palo Alto

20. Scientist, anthropologist, President and CEO, Institute of Noetic Sciences

21. McTaggart, Lynne *The Field: the quest for the secret force of the universe*, 2003 New ed. Element Books

22. McTaggart, Lynne (2008) *The intention experiment: Using your thoughts to change your life and the world*, Paperback ed. New York: Free Press

23. http://noosphere.princeton.edu

24. Reeves, Jay (2008) The Associated Press, 5 May

25. *The Sunday Times Magazine*, 27 August 2006

Chapter 7

1. Phillips, Helen (2005) 'Creativity special: Looking for inspiration' *New Scientist*, issue 2523, 29 October

2. *The Sunday Times*, 20 April 2008 www.postsecret.com

3. Phillips, Helen (2005) 'Creativity special: Looking for inspiration' *New Scientist*, issue 2523, 29 October

4. *Design Week*, 15 January 2004

5. 'It's the image men we answer to', *The Sunday Times*, 6 January 1991

6. 'Meet Umpqua, the bank that became No1 by thinking like Starbucks' *Design Council Magazine*, Issue 1, Winter 2006

7. Ragas, Mathew W. and Bueno, Bolivar J. (2002) *The power of cult branding: How 9 magnetic brands turned customers into loyal followers (and yours can, too!),* New York: Crown Business.

8. Foster, Mark (2007) 'Tribal marker unearthed by archaeologists' *The Northern Echo,* 11 October

9. Wong, Kate (2002) *Ancient engravings push back origin of abstract thought* [Online], Available: http://www.scientificamerican.com/article.cfm?id=ancient-engravings-push-b [16 February 2011]

10. Wong, Kate (2010) *Engraved ostrich eggshell fragments reveal 60,000-year-old graphic design tradition* [Online],
    Available: http://www.scientificamerican.com/blog/post.cfm?id=engraved-ostrich-eggshell-fragments-2010-03-01 [16 February 2011]

11. http://brandchannel.com [Accessed 18 July 2011]

12. 'Testimony that the world would be poorer without it' *Design Council Magazine,* Issue 1, Winter 2006

13. Fox, Mark (1999) 'Logos=God: Observations on logo design and sacred cows at the century's close' *Communication Arts Design Annual 40,* p4

14. *Sunday Times Magazine,* 21 August 2005

15. Fletcher, Alan (2001) *The art of looking sideways,* London: Phaidon

16. Rand, Paul (1991) *Logos, flags, and escutcheon,*[Online],
    Available: http://www.graphicdesignforum.com/articles/logos_rand.htm [16 February 2011]

17. *Design Council Magazine,* Issue 1, Winter 2006

18. Startz, Stephanie (2009) *Nickelodeon's brand cohesion grows up,* [Online]
    Available: http://www.brandchannel.com/home/post/2009/09/29/Nickelodeons-Brand-Cohesion-Grows-Up.aspx#continue [16 February 2011]

19. Dobie, Monica (2008) 'Beautiful art eases pain', University World News, issue 0047, 5 Oct., [Online],
    Available: http://www.universityworldnews.com/article.php?story=20081002145858911 [17 Feb 2011]

20. 'In pain? Take one masterpiece, three times a day' *New Scientist,* issue 2674 (18 September 2008)

Chapter 8

1. Haig, Matt (2003) *Brand failures:The truth about the 100 biggest branding mistakes of all time,* London: Kogan Page
2. Schlosser, Julie (2005) 'Scanning for dollars', *Fortune Magazine,* vol. 151, 1 October
3. 'Testimony that the world would be poorer without it' *Design Council Magazine,* Issue 1, Winter 2006
4. Lindstrom, Martin (2005) *Brand sense: Build powerful brands though touch, taste, smell, sight, and sound,* New York: Free Press
5. Palombo Terzi, Ana Paula (2008) *Branding by the nose in Brazil,* [Online 8 Dec],
   Available: http://brandchannel.com/features_effect.asp?pf_id=453[17 Feb 2011]
6. Service, Robert F (1998) 'Your (light-emitting) logo here', *Science,* vol. 279, no. 5354, 20 February, p. 1135. (DOI:10.1126/science.279.5354.1135b)
7. Lindstrom, Martin (2005) *Brand sense: Build powerful brands though touch, taste, smell, sight, and sound,* New York: Free Press

Chapter 9

1. Levitt, Steven D. and Dubner, Stephen J. (2005) *Freakonomics: A rogue economist explores the hidden side of everything,* London: Harper Perennial, rev. ed. 2009
2. Parkinson TV show, episode: 4 November 2006
3. *London Evening Standard,* 18 October 2006
4. Sauer, Abe (2010) *Brand of crazy,* Brandchannel 19 April [Online] Available: http://www.brandchannel.com/home/post/2010/04/19/Gucci-v-Guess-Gee-Whiz.aspx [18 Feb 2011]
5. Ciani, Keith D. and Sheldon, Kennon M. (2010) 'A versus F: The effects of implicit letter priming on cognitive performance', *British Journal of Educational Psychology* [Electronic], vol. 80, March, issue 1, p99-119. Article first published online: 24 DEC 2010 DOI:10.1348/000709909X466479.
   Available: http://onlinelibrary.wiley.com/doi/10.1348/000709909X466479/full [18 Feb 2011]

6. Nelson, Leif (2007) 'What's in a name? Initials linked to success, study shows', *Association for Psychological Science,* [Electronic], News release 14 November.
    Available: http://www.psychologicalscience.org/media/releases/2007/nelson.cfm [18 Feb 2011]

7. Anseel, Frederik and Duyck, Wouter (2008) 'Unconscious applicants: A systematic test of the name-letter effect', *Psychological Science,* 26 October, vol.19, p1059-1061 [Online] doi:10.1111/j.1467-9280.2008.02199.x

8. Rohrer, Finlo (2007) 'Helvetica at 50' *BBC News Magazine* [Online] Available: http://news.bbc.co.uk/1/hi/magazine/6638423.stm [18 Feb 2011]

9. Dirix, Chantal E. H., Nijhuis, Jan G., Jongsma, Henk W. and Hornstra, Gerard (2009) Aspects of fetal learning and memory. *Child Development,* vol 80, issue 4, pp1251-1258 July/August.
    [Online] Article first published online: 15 July 2009, DOI:10.1111/j.1467-8624.2009.01329.x

10. Grossmann, Tobias et al. (2010) 'The developmental origins of voice processing in the human brain', *Neuron;* DOI:10.1016/j.neuron.2010.03.001

11. Whitwell, Giselle E. (Column editor), 'The importance of prenatal sound and music'
    Birth Psychology, [Online],
    Available: http://www.birthpsychology.com/lifebefore/soundindex.html [18 Feb 2011]

12. Wolf, Maryanne (2008) *Proust and the squid: the story and science of the reading brain,* Reprint ed., New York: Harper Perennial

13. Chopra, Deepak (2005) *Synchrodestiny: Harnessing the infinite power of coincidence to create miracles,* Ryder & Co.

14. Pearce, Stewart and Stacey, Sarah (2005) *The alchemy of voice: Transform and enrich your life using the power of your voice,* Hodder Mobius

15. Errede, Steven (2005-2010) 'Pre-historic music and art in palæolithic caves', Department of Physics, The University of Illinois, [Online], Available:http://online.physics.uiuc.edu/courses/phys193/Lecture_Notes/Acoustics_of_Palaeolithic_Caves/Acoustics_of_Palaeolithic_Caves.pdf [18 Feb 2011]

16. Blackburn, Zacciah www.thecenteroflight.net

17. John Reid in an interview with Laura Lee http://www.lauralee.com/index. cgi?asx=121504.asx
18. Brown, Juanita and Isaacs, David and the World Cafe Community *(2005) Shaping our futures through conversations that matter,* San Francisco: Berrett-Koehler Publishers
19. Bayley, Harold (2006) *The lost language of Symbolism,* Dover Books
20. Roth, Siobhan (2007) *National Geographic* magazine, January

Chapter 10

1. Pumphrey, Angela (ed.) (2004) *Cool brand leaders: An insight into Britain's coolest brands 2004,* Superbrands Ltd
2. Andrews, Ted (2004) *Animal speak,* Llewellyn Publications
3. *The Sunday Times,* 4 October 2009
4. McNeill, Sarah (2001) 'Kangol hip hoppin', Brandchannel, [Online] 5 March 2001,
   Available: http://www.brandchannel.com/features_profile.asp?pr_id=6 [20 Feb 2011]
5. 'Alan Turing' (2005), The Times [Electronic] 25 Jan,
   Available: http://www.timesonline.co.uk/tol/driving/article414765.ece [20 Feb 2011]
6. http://www.dailyfinance.com/2009/10/05/apple-battles-woolworths-over-new-logo/ [Accessed 18 July 2011]
7. Arrien, Angeles (1998) *Signs of life: The five universal shapes and how to use them,* New York: Tarcher/Penguin
8. Stark, Jessica (2011) 'Rice University research shows Starbucks' logo redesign could prove beneficial to company', 1 July, [Online],
   Available: http://www.media.rice.edu/media/NewsBot. asp?MODE=VIEW&ID=15216 [18 July 2011]
9. Frutiger, Adrian (1998) *Signs and symbols,* London: Ebury Press
10. Fitzgerald, Miranda (2009) 'The AA logo tops ranking of brands by colour recall' *Marketing Magazine,* [Electronic] 10 March,
    Available: http://www.marketingmagazine.co.uk/news/888532/AA-logo-tops-ranking-brands-colour-recall [20 Feb 2011]
11. Ibid

12. Bradford, Laura R. (2008), 'Emotion, dilution, and the trademark consumer', *Berkeley Technology Law Journal*.

13. Superbrands commissions independent research to identify leading brands. See www.superbrands.com for more details.

14. 'Top 100 companies mistake brand for bland', *Creative Match*, [Online], Available: http://www.creativematch.com/viewnews/?92270 [20 Feb 2011]

15. Mortensen, Kurt (2006) 'Color sells', *Ezine articles*, 31 May, [Online], Available: http://ezinearticles.com/?Color-Sells&id=209714 [20 Feb 2011]

16. Roth, H.A. (1988), 'Psychological Relationships Between Perceived Sweetness and Colour in Lemon-and-Lime Flavoured Drinks', *Journal of Food Science*, 53:1116-1119

17. http://www.purplepill.com/ [Accessed 18 July 2011].

18. Avis Recognized as Top Car Rental Brand for Customer Loyalty for 11th Consecutive Year http://www.avis.com/car-rental/content/display.ac;jsessionid=Z1xDMZ1Jfy vsfnLM7hthJ2Vy6BLKNWBpB0WT6p78w2MJhQ2x8vvf!242667057?co ntentId=press-release-US_en-018 [Accessed 20 Feb 2011]

19. Myss, Caroline (1997) *Anatomy of the Spirit*, Bantam Books

20. Renfrew, Colin and Morley, Iain (ed.) (2009) *Becoming human: Innovation in prehistoric material and spiritual culture*, Cambridge University Press

21. Berlin, Brent and Kay, Paul (1991) *'Basic color terms: their universality and evolution'* (1st paperback ed.) University of California Press

22. *Aura-Soma* is a formal body of knowledge organized around a teachable and accredited system of colour healing.

23. Gimbel, Theo (1987) *Healing through colour*, C W Daniel Co Ltd

24. Angela Wright, author, psychologist http://www.colour-affects.co.uk [Accessed: 20 Feb 2011]

25. www.colorpuncture.com [Accessed: 20 Feb 2011]

26. http://www.netmar.com/~maat/archive/nov1/vh.htm interview between Dr Valerie Hunt and Susan Barber

27. Elliot, Andrew J., Maier, Markus A., Moller, Arlen C., Friedman, Ron and Meinhardt, Jörg. (2007) 'Color and psychological functioning: The effect of red on performance attainment.' *Journal of Experimental Psychology: General*, vol. 136(1), Feb, p.154-168.

28. Elkan, Daniel (2009) 'Winners wear red: How colour twists your mind' *New* Scientist issue 2723, 28 August, [Online],

Available: http://www.newscientist.com/article/mg20327232.400-winners-wear-red-how-colour-twists-your-mind.html?full=true[20 Feb 2011]

29. Attrill, Martin J., Gresty, Karen A., Hill, Russell A. and Barton, Robert A. (2008) 'Red shirt colour is associated with long-term team success in English football', *Journal of Sports Sciences*, vol. 26, Issue 6, April, pages 577-582

30. Hagemann, N., Strauss, B., and Leißing, Jan (2008) 'When the referee sees red . . .', Psychological Science, vol 19, issue 8, p 769-771,[Online], Available: http://pss.sagepub.com/content/19/8/769.extract [20 Feb 2011]

31. Elliot, Andrew J., Maier, Markus A., Moller, Arlen C., Friedman, Ron. and Meinhardt, Jörg (2007) 'Color and psychological functioning: The effect of red on performance attainment', *Journal of Experimental Psychology: General,* vol 136(1), Feb, 154-168

32. Elliot, Andrew J., Niesta, Daniela (2008) 'Romantic red: Red enhances men's attraction to women', *Journal of Personality and Social Psychology,* vol 95(5), Nov, p1150-1164

33. Deborah T. Sharpe (1981) *The Psychology of Color and Design,* Totowa, New Jersey: Littlefield, Adams & Co. (cited by Vodvarka, Frank 'Aspects of Color', Associate Professor of Fine Arts, Loyola University Chicago, [Online], Available: http://www.midwest-facilitators.net/downloads/mfn_19991025_frank_vodvarka.pdf [20 Feb 2011]

34. Setchell, Joanna M. and Wickings, E. Jean (2005) 'Dominance, status signals and coloration in male mandrills (Mandrillus sphinx)', *Ethology,* vol. 111, issue 1, p25-50, January. [Online] Article first published online: 13 Jan. 2005, DOI: 10.1111/j.1439-0310.2004.01054.x

35. Posner, Bruce G. (1989) 'Seeing red' *Inc. magazine,* [Online] 1 May, 1989 Available: http://www.inc.com/magazine/19890501/5636.html [20 Feb 2011]

36. Lindstrom, Martin (2005) *Brand sense: Build powerful brands though touch, taste, smell, sight, and sound,* New York: Free Press

37. Schauss, Alexander G. (1979) 'Tranquilizing effect of color reduces aggressive behavior and potential violence', *Journal of Orthomolecular Psychiatry, vol. 8, p218-220,* [Online],

Available: http://www.orthomolecular.org/library/jom/1979/pdf/1979-v08n04-p218.pdf [20 Feb 2011]

38. Glaister, Dan (2006) 'Pink prison makes Texan inmates blush' *The Guardian*, [Online] 11 October, Available: http://www.guardian.co.uk/world/2006/oct/11/usa.danglaister [20 Feb 2011]

39. Birren, Faber (1978) *Color psychology and color therapy,* Citadel (6th printing ed.) (Attributed to Sharpe, *The Psychology of Color and Design*)

Chapter 11

1. Plain packaging of tobacco products: a review of the evidence, Prepared by Quit Victoria, Cancer Council Victoria, May 2011

2. Fletcher, Alan (2001) *The art of looking sideways,* London: Phaidon

3. Home page of http://www.psychographicprofile.com/ [Viewed 20 Feb 2011]

4. http://www.boots-uk.com/About_Boots/Boots_Heritage.aspx

5. Williams, Gareth (2000) *Branded,* London: Victoria & Albert Museum

6. http://www.unilever.com.au/aboutus/ourhistory/History-Australasia.aspx

7. *The Sunday Times,* 27 May 2001

8. Millar, Stuart and Macalister, Terry (2001) 'Tibetan pipeline row dents BP's new image', *The Guardian*, UK News, 19 April, [Online], Available: http://www.guardian.co.uk/uk/2001/apr/19/world.oil?INTCMP=SRCH [18 July 2011]

9. Thornton, Philip (2004) 'Exposed: BP, its pipeline, and an environmental timebomb' *The Independent*, 6 June, p.1

10. Gardner, David (2010) 'Oil spill nears the beaches of Florida, and the leak may not be plugged before Christmas', *Daily Mail* 3 June. [Online], Available: http://www.dailymail.co.uk/news/worldnews/article-1283544/BP-oil-spill-nears-Florida-leak-plugged-Christmas.html [20 Feb 2011]

11. Jean, Georges (1999) *Signs, symbols and ciphers, Decoding the message,* Thames and Hudson/New Horizons

12. *The Guardian*, 19 April 2001

13. *The Sunday Times,* John Humphrys, 29 April 2001

14. Cirlot, J.E. (1983) *A dictionary of symbols,* Routledge, (new ed. of 2)

15. Slack, James (2007) '£870,000 bill for the logos that are a sure sign of failure' *Daily Mail,* 3 January.

16. *The Times,* Public Agenda section, 25 January 2005

17. 'Plain cigarette packs in Australia', *The Lancet,* vol. 375, issue 9726, p1580, 8 May.2010 [Online] doi:10.1016/S0140-6736(10)60684-8

18. *The Sunday Times,* World News section, 1 October 2006,

19. Basedow, Herbert (1925) *The Australian Aboriginal,* Adelaide: P.W. Preece (cited in Hahn, Patrick D. 'Scared to death: Self-willed death, or the bone-pointing syndrome' *Biology Online,*
Available: http://www.biology-online.org/articles/scared_death.html [19 July 2011]

A first-hand account of this ritual is given by Dr. Herbert Basedow, (1881-1933), anthropologist, geologist, explorer and medical practitioner, in his book The Australian Aboriginal, published in 1925:

'A man who discovers that he is being boned by an enemy is, indeed, a pitiable sight. He stands aghast, with his eyes staring at the treacherous pointer, and with his hands lifted as though to ward off the lethal medium, which he imagines is pouring into his body. His cheeks blanch and his eyes become glassy, and the expression on his face becomes horribly distorted . . . He attempts to shriek, but usually the sound chokes in his throat, and all one might see is froth at his mouth. His body begins to tremble and the muscles twist involuntarily. He sways backwards and falls to the ground, and for a short time appears to be in a swoon; but soon after he begins to writhe as if in mortal agony, and covering his face with his hands, begin (sic) to moan. After a while he becomes more composed and crawls to his wurley (hut). From this time onwards he sickens and frets, refusing to eat, and keeping aloof from the daily affairs of the tribe. Unless help is forthcoming in the shape of a counter-charm, administered by the hands of the "Nangarri," or medicine-man, his death is only a matter of a comparatively short time. If the coming of the medicine-man is opportune, he might be saved.'

Although widely practiced and bafflingly effective, bone pointing is not murder by Australian Law.

Index

Y

Z

www.ingramcontent.com/pod-product-compliance
Lightning Source LLC
Chambersburg PA
CBHW071358170526
45165CB00001B/100